NEW NUCLEAR NATIONS

NEW NUCLEAR NATIONS

Consequences for U.S. Policy

EDITED BY

ROBERT D. BLACKWILL

AND

ALBERT CARNESALE

COUNCIL ON FOREIGN RELATIONS PRESS

NEW YORK

COUNCIL ON FOREIGN RELATIONS BOOKS

The Council on Foreign Relations, Inc., is a nonprofit and nonpartisan organization devoted to promoting improved understanding of international affairs through the free exchange of ideas. The Council does not take any position on questions of foreign policy and has no affiliation with, and receives no funding from, the United States government.

From time to time, books and monographs written by members of the Council's research staff or visiting fellows, or commissioned by the Council, or written by an independent author with critical review contributed by a Council study or working group are published with the designation "Council on Foreign Relations Book." Any book or monograph bearing that designation is, in the judgment of the Committee on Studies of the Council's Board of Directors, a responsible treatment of a significant international topic worthy of presentation to the public. All statements of fact and expressions of opinion contained in Council books are, however, the sole responsibility of the author.

If you would like more information on Council publications, please write the Council on Foreign Relations, 58 East 68th Street, New York, NY 10021, or call the Publications Office at (212)734-0400.

Library of Congress Cataloging-in-Publication Data

New nuclear nations : consequences for U.S. policy / edited by Robert D. Blackwill and Albert Carnesale.
    p. cm.
    Includes bibliographical references and index.
    ISBN 0–87609–153–2
    1. Nuclear nonproliferation. 2. United States—Foreign relations—1989–
3. Security, International.
    I. Blackwill, Robert D. II. Carnesale, Albert.
JX1974.73.N44 1993
327.1'74—dc20   93–27807
                                                       CIP

95   96   97   EB   10   9   8   7   6   5   4

Cover Design: Michael Storrings

CONTENTS

Preface   vii

Part I   The New Nuclear Era

1. Introduction: Understanding the Problem
   Robert D. Blackwill and Albert Carnesale   3
2. New Nuclear Threats to U.S. Security
   Lewis A. Dunn   20

Part II   U.S. Diplomatic Efforts for Coping With New Nuclear Nations

3. Arms Control for New Nuclear Nations
   Paul Doty and Steven Flank   53
4. Diplomatic Measures
   Joseph S. Nye, Jr.   77
5. Assistance to Newly Proliferating Nations
   Steven E. Miller   97

Part III   U.S. Military Means for Coping With New Nuclear Nations

6. Implications for U.S. Military Strategy
   Michèle A. Flournoy   135
7. Offensive Military Options
   Philip Zelikow   162

8. Defenses Against New Nuclear Threats
   Albert Carnesale   196
9. The Role of Intelligence
   Robert D. Blackwill and Ashton B. Carter   216

Part IV   Conclusions and Recommendations

10. Conclusions and Recommendations
   Robert D. Blackwill and Albert Carnesale   253

Contributors   261
Index   265

PREFACE

This book grew out of a series of discussions we began about two years ago. The collapse of the Warsaw Pact and the disintegration of the Soviet Union, by then plainly visible on the horizon, forced us to reexamine the sources of threats to U.S. national security. Subsequent revelations about the scope and magnitude of Iraq's nuclear weapons program convinced us that neither we, nor, to our knowledge, others in the national security community, had thought nearly enough about the implications for U.S. security of the potential emergence in this decade of new nuclear weapons states. A cursory search of the literature confirmed this. What exists instead is a vast and familiar reservoir of books and articles on the sources and evils of nuclear proliferation, and on ways to prevent it.

While preventing nuclear proliferation is a worthy goal, Saddam Hussein did not share that objective. Despite Iraq's obligations under the Nuclear Nonproliferation Treaty, he was determined to produce deliverable nuclear weapons. What if he had not been stopped? If confronted with a new nuclear threat (by Iraq or another nation) in the 1990s and beyond, what would the United States do? What would influence its actions in the international arena? What policy options would be available to the president? What should the United States be doing to prepare for such contingencies? Existing scholarship provides few answers to these questions—questions that we believe will be central to American national security objectives in the coming years.

With encouragement and support from the Carnegie Corporation of New York, we recruited a group of colleagues to explore these issues. Bi-weekly seminars were held at Harvard University's John F.

Kennedy School of Government, in which participants discussed, debated, argued, and occasionally cursed over draft after draft of each chapter. This volume is the result of that effort.

We profited throughout from help given by individuals who shared with us the conviction that work on this subject was needed. David Hamburg and Frederic Mosher of the Carnegie Corporation of New York facilitated the financial assistance to support the endeavor and, as always, were valuable colleagues and friends. Michèle Flournoy, who served both as a substantive collaborator and as administrative director of the project, made the seminars run productively and efficiently. Teresa Johnson edited the entire manuscript and caused all of us to appear to be better writers than we are. Finally, we are deeply indebted to our fellow contributors to the volume who struggled along with us to analyze a problem that proved to be exceedingly difficult.

Robert D. Blackwill
Albert Carnesale
Cambridge, Massachusetts
September 1993

PART I

The New Nuclear Era

CHAPTER ONE

Introduction:
Understanding the Problem

ROBERT D. BLACKWILL and ALBERT CARNESALE

This is not another of the many commendable books on the merits of a vigorous American policy to promote nuclear non-proliferation, an objective we heartily endorse. Rather, this volume does something markedly different. It examines the consequences for U.S. policy of the emergence in the 1990s of new nuclear weapons states.[1] The substance and policy conclusions of this book rest on a future in which nations with newly acquired nuclear weapons threaten U.S. interests, thus confronting Washington policymakers with a variety of alternative responses, many of them seriously unpleasant.

Conclusive evidence concerning Iraq's mammoth effort to acquire nuclear weapons makes it plain that the following chapters are, unfortunately, not the stuff of a far-distant eventuality. Indeed, according to Robert Gates, former director of Central Intelligence, Iraq was within a year of successfully weaponizing its vast nuclear program when the Gulf War began. For many Americans who witnessed via television that brief but bloody conflict, and much more for the Americans who actually fought in the mercifully one-sided battle, the prospect of a nuclear-armed Iraq must loom as a nightmare avoided.

What if Saddam Hussein's nuclear program had reached successful weaponization before Iraq invaded Kuwait? What if the Iraqi invasion south had proceeded and the coalition, especially U.S. military forces in and around the Gulf, had been required to deal with the consequences of a likely Iraqi nuclear capability? How would this have affected Saddam Hussein's political and military strategy? What would have been the reaction in the Pentagon, at the White House, in the Congress, and among the American people? How would the Gulf states that allied themselves with the United States have reacted in the face of this momentous increase in the Iraqi threat? What would have been the impact on the other member states of the international coalition so brilliantly put together by the United States?

These questions illuminate some of the profound diplomatic, military, and domestic national security considerations that would arise if the United States were forced to face a nuclear proliferator, either in a customary international environment or in a crisis. This scenario is the essence of this book. The contributors seek to analyze and understand:

- which countries are most likely to go nuclear in the next decade and how they might go about it;

- how U.S. diplomatic and arms control efforts might evolve in this situation;

- what the impact of new nuclear weapons states would be on U.S. military doctrine and on American air, land, and sea operations, including those against a new proliferator;

- what place theater and strategic defenses should play in the U.S. response to this problem;

- whether or not the United States should attempt to provide technical assistance under any circumstances to new nuclear nations; and

- what the role (and limitations) of intelligence would be in penetrating hostile nuclear programs.

The concluding chapter makes specific policy recommendations on how Washington should deal with the eventuality of new nuclear weapons states.

This introduction goes further; it presents a fictional effort to answer the above questions in the context of the allied coalition's 1990–1991 conflict with Iraq. In preparation for the analytical chapters that follow, we envisage the many possible effects that Iraq's possession, or even the possibility of possession, of nuclear weapons would have had on the conduct and outcome of the Gulf War.

Imagine the following. It is dawn at the White House on January 16, 1991. The United Nations ultimatum to Iraq to withdraw from Kuwait ran out at midnight. Coalition forces led by the U.S. military are making ready to go to war in the Gulf. Throughout the day, American combat aircraft in Saudi Arabia and the other Gulf states, and on board carriers in the Persian Gulf and the Red Sea, are armed and fueled for missions to begin at midnight, local time. The president and his chief advisors are psychologically prepared for the conflict to begin. They are convinced that they have done everything possible diplomatically to avoid the conflict; militarily to maximize U.S. success in the field and minimize American losses; and politically at home to equip the American people for both good news and bad from the battlefield. The president and his closest advisors are deeply persuaded, as is the majority of the country after months of sometimes solemn and often excited national and congressional debate, that it is crucial for the long-term interests of the United States and for international peace and security that Iraqi forces be expelled from Kuwait.

At 0500 Washington time, the director of Central Intelligence (DCI) calls on an encrypted line to the president's national security advisor, who has spent the night in his White House office. The DCI stresses that he must see the president immediately, conveys the substance of his information to the national security advisor, and says that he will arrive at the White House from CIA headquarters in Langley, Virginia, in about forty-five minutes. The two agree that the secretary of state, secretary of defense, and chairman of the Joint Chiefs of Staff (JCS) should also attend the briefing. As the national security advisor wakes the president by phone and then walks with his deputy over to the president's private living quarters in the West Wing, the White House Situation Room staff contacts the secretary of state, secretary of defense, the chairman of the JCS, and the White House chief of staff, and informs them of the 0600 session with the president.

The group assembles in the president's private study on the second floor of the White House. As stewards serve coffee and rolls, the DCI briefs: At 0100 Washington time—just five hours ago—the CIA's sole highly placed agent in Baghdad called an emergency meeting to pass to the U.S. embassy two-thirds of a carbon-copy page stamped TOP SECRET. The three paragraphs purport to be an account of a late night January 8, 1991, meeting of Saddam Hussein with his closest advisors in a deep underground bunker on the outskirts of Tikrit, the Iraqi president's home village. It is clear from the fragment that one subject of the gathering was the role of Iraq's nuclear weapons program in the ongoing crisis with the United States and its allies. The Iraqis expressed contempt for Western intelligence capabilities, pride in their own disinformation endeavors, and confidence that Iraq's enemies have no clue that Saddam Hussein's intense efforts have produced four crude nuclear weapons.

The partial page contains no information on the physical characteristics of the Iraqi nuclear devices, their possible delivery systems, their whereabouts, or Saddam Hussein's intentions with respect to their possible role in the current crisis. As the DCI completes his briefing, he is called to a classified phone. He returns to report that Iraqi radio has just announced the apprehension of an "American spy" who, it says, worked as a typist in one of the less sensitive offices of Saddam Hussein's cabinet, and who had under "interrogation" admitted in detail his "treacherous activities" on behalf of the United States. The government bulletin ended by indicating that Saddam Hussein would soon give a speech to the Iraqi nation in which he would reveal the secret that the United States has been so desperately trying to ascertain.

Led by the president, the group quickly agrees that the entire incident in Baghdad, including the single carbon-copy fragment, could be an attempt by Iraq to fool Washington and the coalition into believing that they are facing a nuclear weapons state and therefore should not launch any attack. The deputy national security advisor observes, however, that it is impossible to know whether the typist was in fact a double agent, whether this is an Iraqi ruse, or whether Saddam Hussein actually has four, or even more, nuclear weapons. The DCI stresses that the capture of the Iraqi agent makes it highly unlikely the administration will soon acquire intelligence to confirm or refute Iraq's nuclear capability.

The secretary of state expresses the worry that the coalition, even the UN Security Council, may not hold together in support of an attack on Iraq if the members conclude that an attempt to expel Iraqi forces from Kuwait could lead to nuclear war. The Soviet Union and perhaps even France could reverse their UN votes, and China might shift its former abstentions to a vote against UN-sponsored military action. It is also likely that the United States and those countries that would still join an attack on Iraqi forces should expect an early Security Council resolution calling for an immediate cease-fire in place. One would also expect a new round of frenetic diplomacy to stop the fighting, and, the secretary of state continues, Soviet diplomacy could be revived to this end. With Gorbachev aide Yevgeny Primakov, who is sympathetic to Baghdad, and not Foreign Minister Eduard Shevardnadze, in the lead, Moscow would probably bolster Iraq's position. Similar efforts would probably be undertaken by peripatetic German foreign minister Hans-Dietrich Genscher. There would be demonstrations throughout the world and especially in Western Europe. In the Gulf region itself, it is doubtful that Syria would remain in the coalition, and there would certainly be enormous pressure in the streets of most Arab capitals to call off the effort against Iraq.

The secretary of defense then describes the likely effects of an Iraqi nuclear capability on the military attitudes of U.S. coalition partners. France and perhaps Italy might pull out their troops; the British would probably stay, but only after reviewing the coalition's current military strategy, which would mean a considerable delay in the allied attack. Even more seriously, the Gulf states, beginning with Saudi Arabia, would surely question whether their territories should continue to be springboards for attacks against Iraq, considering their exposure to the threat of an Iraqi retaliatory nuclear strike. And over the long term, these moderate Arab states, and especially Saudi Arabia, would doubtless seek to acquire nuclear weapons of their own to deter Iraq, and to match its power and influence in the region and beyond.

Then there is the Israeli angle. The secretary of defense stresses that if Israel gets even a serious hint that Iraq really has produced nuclear weapons, Jerusalem will face horrendous policy choices. If the Israeli government decides to strike first with its own nuclear arsenal, it would confront a storm of international condemnation with no certainty that it had saved itself from a nuclear attack. But if it waits, Saddam Hussein could fulfill his boast to turn Israel into a bed of cinders.

In short, the secretary of defense concludes, if Saddam Hussein actually controls nuclear weapons, or if the coalition believes that he does, the United States will face a great challenge in persuading others to carry through with the military task of expelling Iraqi forces from Kuwait.

The chairman of the JCS then briefs the group on the implications of a nuclear Iraq for present and planned U.S. force deployments in the Gulf region. The coalition already has targeted Saddam Hussein's known nuclear facilities, but the weapons themselves—if they exist—might well be dispersed and hidden in hardened bunkers far beneath the surface of the earth. It would be incredibly lucky if the United States was able to destroy the weapons in an air attack. They are probably too large to be delivered by ballistic missiles or by artillery systems (the Soviets who worked with Iraq for years on their missile and artillery systems could help answer this crucial question of size), which would mean that U.S. forces would be faced with the possibility of attack by aircraft, by ships at sea, or on the ground. The fact is that the U.S. military has little protection against the effects of a nuclear explosion. We have simply not spent the money to acquire such protection. Our air defenses are superb, but one Iraqi aircraft flying low in a group of two dozen could get through to its target. The target could be U.S. forces near the Kuwait border, one of the coalition's large air bases in Saudi Arabia, the U.S. fleet in the Persian Gulf, or even an Arab city, although that seems much less probable. The president adds that we must consider the possibility that one or more of these weapons, if they exist, might already be outside of Iraq—somewhere in the region, in Europe, or even in the United States.

The chairman emphasizes that he will discuss this matter thoroughly with his JCS colleagues and with the CentCom commander-in-chief and his senior officers. But as a first approximation, his advice is that if the president decides to continue on the present path of expelling Iraq from Kuwait, it may be wise to conduct a much longer air war than originally planned. This would be necessary in any case since more air assets will now have to be devoted to air defense and thus significantly less ordnance will be delivered on target. And, he continues, we may decide to move some of our forward-based aircraft to fields farther in the Saudi rear, which would also diminish the number of attack sorties we are able to generate.

In addition to these technical realities, the chairman postulates that it could well be in our interest to keep our ground forces a good distance away from territory occupied by Saddam Hussein's forces in Kuwait and Iraq, where the nuclear weapons might be located, until a ground war begins. We may also want to move much or all of the fleet out of the Gulf and conduct our air operations against Iraq from farther away, although this, too, will reduce the efficiency of our air assault. And if the other side has nuclear weapons, there might not be a place for amphibious Marine landings. So, the chairman finishes, it seems that our best bet is to bomb Iraq until it agrees to leave Kuwait, and to try to avoid as much as possible putting our air, sea, and ground forces in nuclear harm's way. But, the chairman repeats, he will discuss all this with the Chiefs and the CINCCent before he provides the secretary of defense and the president with an authoritative military view.

Finally, the White House chief of staff reviews the domestic implications of the night's intelligence from Iraq. When this information becomes public, it will reignite the U.S. debate on how to respond to the Iraqi occupation of Kuwait. Many of those in the House of Representatives, and some of the forty-seven senators who voted unsuccessfully a week earlier to delay the use of force while waiting to see if economic sanctions would bring about a change in Iraqi policy, would certainly call for another vote, given the new information. It would be a struggle to avoid a second vote, especially since there would undoubtedly be demonstrations all over the country, a throwback to the "Vietnam syndrome."

Overall, in the chief of staff's judgment, if the president decides to take America into war against Iraq in the new circumstances, he could in the worst case face a negative vote in the House and perhaps in the Senate; a possible constitutional crisis; and perhaps even an impeachment attempt. On the other hand, many Americans would oppose the idea of backing down in the face of Saddam Hussein's aggression or leaving him with a growing nuclear arsenal intact. In any event, the chief of staff concludes, the president would be taking on the toughest domestic battle of his term in office. After another hour of intense discussion, the group breaks up. The president moves to the Oval Office where he is joined by the national security advisor to go over the options. At 0830 the president calls the secretary of defense and instructs him to delay the initiation of the air war against Iraq. He calls in his press secretary and tells him to prepare for a presidential speech to the nation that evening at 2100. In the afternoon, he meets again with his national security team as well as with the leadership of Congress, and calls coalition leaders.

In his speech that night, the president reviews the original reasons for deciding that Iraq's occupation of Kuwait must not stand, and tells the American people that Iraq might possess a small number of nuclear weapons. He says that during the day he has been in touch by telephone or cable with all the leaders of the coalition, informing them of this possibility and seeking their views of how best to proceed. The president then gives the essence of his own judgment on the proper course for the United States:

- the strategic and moral imperatives that led the United States and its allies to commit themselves to forcing Iraq out of Kuwait have not changed;

- it is at present unclear whether Iraq does or does not control one or more nuclear weapons;

- if the answer is no, then nothing has changed;

- if the answer is yes, then Saddam Hussein represents an even greater threat to the region and to global peace and stability than earlier believed;

- every effort will be made to establish whether Iraq possesses nuclear weapons;

- if that turns out to be so, then the coalition and the world community cannot stop at expelling Iraq from Kuwait;

• for the coalition to back down now would only feed Saddam Hussein's appetite for further aggression, which might include nuclear threats or even nuclear use;

• Israel would be especially vulnerable in this regard as the president and the Israeli prime minister had agreed in three telephone conversations in the course of the day;

• for humanity's sake, Iraq must destroy its nuclear capability and its entire nuclear program; and

• should Iraq refuse, it must be made to comply.

The president concludes his speech by asking for the support of the American people and of the Congress.

At midnight local time on January 17, 1991, twenty-four hours after the originally scheduled lift-off, the coalition air war, "Instant Thunder," begins against Iraq.[2] By 0230, Baghdad is being bombed. Complex Air Tasking Orders have been created with the aid of a computerized flight management system. Target sets for the initial and follow-on attacks include air defense radars, missiles, and aircraft; nuclear, chemical, and biological weapons facilities and petrochemical/agrochemical plants; fixed and, wherever possible, mobile SCUD missile batteries (although twelve hours earlier Moscow had informed the United States that Iraqi SCUDs could not carry a nuclear warhead); Su-27 bombers, because of their potential nuclear capability; political and military headquarters including command and control centers and major ministries in Baghdad; bridge, rail, and road systems; and a broad series of industrial targets: the electrical power grid, oil systems, water capacity, fertilizer plants, and the civilian telephone system.

At the outset, F-117A Stealth fighters send GBU-24 laser-guided bombs, fitted with I-2000 warheads, to known or suspected nuclear sites. B-52Gs, based in Diego Garcia in the Indian Ocean, drop less precise 2,000-pound bombs on the facilities. British Tornado GR1s and GR1As assist in the reconnaissance of an attack on the nuclear-related targets. Uranium mining facilities near Al-Kindl and nuclear reprocessing plants at Al-Qaim are hit. Additional laboratories, storage areas, and power plants in Erbil, Bajii,

Tuwaitha, Al-Fallujah, and Salman Pak, believed by U.S. intelligence to be central to the Iraqi nuclear program, are struck by allied aircraft. But inclement weather, uncertain U.S. intelligence data, and efforts by the Iraqis to embed nuclear facilities in civilian industrial complexes as large as twenty square miles leave coalition pilots unsure of their results as they continue sorties from Saudi Arabia and carriers in the Gulf. At daylight, doubts remain about bomb damage estimates. The most sensitive Iraqi deep underground bunkers, including those related to the nuclear program, probably remain unscathed. An eleven-ton U.S. satellite, launched on the space shuttle Atlantis in order to aid reconnaissance, is powerful enough to read the license plates on Iraqi trucks but cannot provide information on these underground complexes. Nor does the coalition have any laser-guided bombs that can penetrate these sites, until, in the course of the war, the 5,000-pound GBU-28 is developed and deployed to the Gulf. It is also difficult for the coalition to ascertain the number of Iraqi aircraft destroyed or disabled in their hardened shelters.

Forty-eight hours into the air war, Saddam Hussein gives his promised speech in Baghdad. It is extraordinarily bellicose but ignores the nuclear issue. Syria, Morocco, and Qatar leave the coalition nonetheless. Egypt is convulsed by riots, but President Mubarak, arresting thousands of radicals, vows to remain a full participating member of the allied cause. Many Palestinians in the occupied territories and elsewhere clamor for prompt Iraqi nuclear use against Israel, evidently overlooking the threat of nuclear fallout over the West Bank. France and Spain announce the immediate withdrawal of their military forces from the Gulf. The Italian prime minister pledges that Italy will remain with its coalition partners to see the Gulf crisis through to a successful end. Britain stands firmly with the United States. Germany wavers amid massive public demonstrations. Japan, without notifying Washington in advance, calls for an end to hostilities and the resumption of negotiations to find a peaceful solution to the crisis. Iran says Iraq's nuclear capability must be destroyed "for the good of the world." At the United Nations, a Security Council resolution drafted by the Soviet Union and India, and supported by a large majority of Third World delegations to the General Assembly, calls for an immediate end to the fighting and resumption of intensive diplomatic efforts to stop the conflict without further bloodshed. The United States and Britain veto the resolution. China votes for it. France abstains.

A political upheaval erupts in Israel. Many call for an immediate Israeli attack on Iraq; implicit but unexpressed because of Israeli censorship is the feeling that Israel's nuclear arsenal should be used to obliterate Iraq. The Israeli cabinet goes into a nonstop twenty-two-hour meeting, punctuated by periodic and mostly distorted leaks to the media about its discussions. In the middle of these deliberations, the U.S. deputy secretary of state arrives in Israel to lend his government's voice to the argument by some in the cabinet for Israeli restraint. A crowd of 4,000 protests in front of the prime minister's office in Jerusalem with signs urging a nuclear attack on Iraq and warning of a "second Holocaust."

When Israel's cabinet meeting concludes, the prime minister announces that any attack on Israel will be met with a devastating response and that only the Israeli government and people will decide the timing and nature of this reaction. He urges the coalition to step up its attack on Iraq with the objective of ending Saddam Hussein's reign and destroying Iraq's nuclear ambitions. Privately, the prime minister tells the U.S. deputy secretary of state that he has barely held his cabinet together in a policy of restraint but that Israel now insists that Saddam Hussein be removed from power and that Iraq's nuclear program and capabilities be eliminated. If the United States and its coalition partners do not accomplish those objectives, then Israel will—"by whatever means necessary." The United States, he says, "can count on this." The deputy secretary promises to convey this message to the president, and returns to Washington.

At home, polls show that 65 percent of the American people support the president's policy. Fifty-three percent of those polled believe that U.S. objectives in the Gulf should now include the removal of Saddam Hussein and the destruction of his nuclear program. The Israeli lobby is busy in the halls of the Capitol. A renewed debate begins in the Congress, but it soon becomes obvious that the leadership there does not wish to reopen the vote to expel Iraq from Kuwait and no new vote on the conduct of the war is taken. Although there are large protest demonstrations throughout the nation led by peace groups and environmentalists, most are non-violent. In all, only thirty-five arrests are made, primarily in San Francisco and New York City. Analysts observe that neither the United Nations, nor the president, nor the Congress has mandated that Saddam Hussein be removed from office, but that such an objective seems the logical policy outcome of the president's speech and the mood of the country. The White House indicates its hope that the Iraqi people will take the matter into their own hands.

The massing of allied ground troops in Saudi Arabia continues. Because of the nuclear issue, no regular military units are deployed closer than forty kilometers to the Kuwait border. In that area only special forces patrol. Occasional Iraqi attempts to penetrate into Saudi territory are easily repulsed by allied aircraft flying from bases deep in the kingdom. The U.S. fleet has largely withdrawn from the Gulf and is now operating in the Red Sea, the Gulf of Oman, and the northern Arabian Sea. Marine amphibious units, under protest, leave their ships and join Army and Marine divisions in Saudi Arabia.

The air war progresses unabated. After the first few weeks, the Iraqi air force has been destroyed on the ground, forced to remain in shelters, or moved into civilian neighborhoods. Other Iraqi air defenses have been neutralized, with the result that allied losses have diminished to less than one aircraft per 2,000 sorties.

By early May, most of Baghdad and Iraq's other major cities have been reduced to rubble. The Iraqi infrastructure lies in ruins. There have been many thousands of civilian casualties. Saddam Hussein, however, has not yet withdrawn his army from Kuwait. The Iraqi president is as defiant as ever. He promises "rivers of blood" if the allies conduct a ground campaign. But he makes no mention of an Iraqi nuclear capability, and allied intelligence, despite the greatest possible effort, is unable to unearth any further information on the subject.

In the United States, pressure grows for an early end to the war so that American troops can come home. Critics increasingly complain about Iraqi civilian deaths. Some strategists worry that if Saddam Hussein does not now have a nuclear weapons capability, further delay in ending his rule will increase the likelihood that he will develop one. Coalition partners fear that in the absence of a ground assault to liberate Kuwait, allied forces will have to remain in the Gulf for years. At a coalition summit in Bermuda on May 9, allied heads of government agree that Saddam Hussein must be driven out of Kuwait. The Saudi representative urges an immediate attack before the upcoming Hajj to begin in June. Although no press statement is issued after the summit, informed press commentary states that a coalition ground attack is imminent.

On May 11, all is ready for the allied assault. That afternoon a letter from Saddam Hussein is delivered to the White House by the embassy of Jordan. Indicating in emotional terms that he is the aggrieved party in the dispute, and saying that the American president would "burn in torment" for his murder of tens of thousands of innocent Iraqi women and children, Saddam Hussein goes on, "The whole world knows that you are preparing to attack the noble Iraqi soldiers who are presently defending from the infidels the holy Arab soil in Iraq's 19th province. Your arrogance leads you to believe that you can mount such a murderous attack without retribution from God. You are wrong. Let there be no misunderstanding here. If you and your servile partners invade, mighty Iraq will respond with nuclear weapons and vanquish your cowardly army. And do not believe that your precious United States will escape the catastrophe. As you read this letter, an Iraqi nuclear device rests securely in our hands in a large American city. Unless you end your fiendish attack on blameless Iraq, unless all so-called coalition military forces withdraw from the Gulf region by June 1, that weapon in America will be detonated. Do not think that this is an empty threat. God is great."

The president immediately gathers together his national security team. They quickly agree that to make public Saddam Hussein's threat could delay the ground attack indefinitely and cause panic in U.S. cities. Nevertheless, the president emphasizes that the American people have a right to know the details and tone of the letter, as do the coalition partners. Unfortunately, however, there is no more evidence today than six months earlier that Iraq actually possesses nuclear weapons. Moreover, it is uncertain whether the colossal air campaign against Iraq's nuclear facilities has destroyed Saddam Hussein's nuclear weapons, or if they in fact exist. And there is no way of knowing if it is true that Iraq has smuggled a nuclear weapon into the United States.

If this is not a bluff, why has Saddam Hussein delayed so long in making this ultimate threat while his country and army have been bombed nearly into oblivion? Perhaps it is a last desperate attempt by the Iraqi leader to avoid the inevitable—the destruction of his armed forces and his removal from power. But if the nuclear danger is real, in the Gulf or even in the United States, the consequences of caving in would be disastrous. If the coalition capitulates now, what would be Saddam Hussein's next blackmail attempt? He would dominate the Middle East (including its oil), put in mortal danger the very existence of Israel, and threaten vital U.S. and Western interests around the globe.

After eighty minutes of discussion and with no dissenting voice, the president and his advisors remain deeply convinced that the coalition must press forward with its attack. Perhaps because of Saddam Hussein's long history of bluster and of bloodcurdling but largely unrealized threats, neither his message to the president nor a repetition of his nuclear warnings in a May 12 radio broadcast from Baghdad reduces the coalition's determination to proceed. The president, through Jordan, responds to Saddam Hussein's letter by promising that if Iraq uses nuclear weapons against coalition forces, Iraq will experience "the full force" of U.S. military might. In cities throughout the Middle East, Europe, and America, law enforcement officials intensify a massive hunt for Iraqi citizens and sympathizers who might be involved in trying to smuggle a nuclear device into the United States. In unofficial U.S. comments to the press, however, many of these officers say that they do not hold out much hope of finding such a weapon unless the culprits make an exceedingly stupid mistake.

At 0400 on May 13, 1991, led by advance elements of the 101st Airborne Division, allied ground forces mount a crushing attack on Iraqi positions. In a stunningly successful left hook, the U.S. Eighteenth Corps cuts off the Iraqi army in Kuwait and southern Iraq, and races toward the Euphrates Valley. The heavy-armored U.S. Seventh Corps and the British First Armored Division begin quickly to destroy the entrapped Iraqi forces. Covering an area 60 miles wide and 120 miles long, the American component of these armored forces includes 59,000 vehicles and 1,600 aircraft. Saddam Hussein's elite Republican Guard, which has been bombed incessantly for months, surrenders or is crushed.

In eastern Kuwait, the First and Second Marine Divisions also jump off at 0400 on May 13. After early light fighting to penetrate Iraqi minefields, trenches, and gun emplacements, they breach Iraqi defenses. The First proceeds northward up the narrow coastal road toward Kuwait City. By late in the day, because of bad terrain, the division is bunched up along a few miles of the road. Marines have taken the Al-Jaber airfield, are approaching the large Al-Burqan oil field, and have destroyed 250 T-55/T-62 and more than 70 T-72 tanks with only six Marine casualties.

By evening, elements of the First at the edge of the Al-Burqan oil field encounter a small convoy of Iraqi military trucks whose personnel quickly indicate they wish to surrender. As the Marines begin to take Iraqi prisoners, a mighty fireball explodes. A primitive fission weapon mounted on the enclosed bed of one of the trucks has detonated. In a billionth of a second, the nuclear device, with a power of devastation greater than the Hiroshima bomb, releases nearly 99 percent of its total energy, most of which goes into radiation. The vaporized materials of the weapon generate a temperature of millions of degrees centigrade. Every flammable object within several kilometers of the detonation ignites. The huge fire storm expands, fed by the oil fields. Approximately 3,000 Marines of the First Division die instantly. As fire, radiation, and blast spread, thousands more Marines and other U.S. military personnel are exposed to nuclear effects that will kill them in hours, months, or years. An enormous cloud of radioactive particles hangs over the site and begins to be carried by the wind westward along allied lines over the Second Marine Division, an Egyptian infantry division, and the U.S. First Armored Cavalry Division.

In Baghdad, Saddam Hussein announces that "God's justice has been visited upon the American invaders" and that Saudi Arabia will be next unless it expels coalition forces. The president receives word of the tragedy within minutes; the rest of the world knows almost as quickly. The mushroom cloud is visible throughout northern Saudi Arabia, Kuwait, and Iraq. After calling for an immediate evacuation of major U.S. cities, the president summons his closest advisors to the Oval Office to consider American responses.

Meanwhile, during the next few hours, Kuwait formally surrenders to Iraq. Saudi Arabia and the Gulf states pull out of the war and indicate they will allow no more coalition military activities against Iraq from their soil. Belgium, Denmark, the Netherlands, Greece, Portugal, Argentina, and New Zealand withdraw from the coalition and push for an immediate cease-fire without preconditions. The Soviet Union and France introduce a cease-fire resolution in an emergency session of the Security Council. A NATO meeting begins in Brussels, but several delegations tell the press that they do not expect any Alliance agreement to emerge from the discussion. The Israeli cabinet goes into urgent deliberation in Jerusalem. The Israeli air force is put on its highest state of alert.

In the United States, the nation is divided concerning the proper course of action. Some support complete U.S. withdrawal from the Gulf and stress that nothing in the Middle East justifies a single additional American death. Others argue that now is the time to end the lunacy and resume peace talks with Baghdad. Environmentalists underscore that the planet is being pushed to the brink; a few scientists of this persuasion warn of nuclear winter. Many men and women of the cloth stress that America should not join Iraq in a moral calamity.

Other Americans have a different view. They say that what is left of the coalition should continue its conventional attack all the way to Baghdad, and beyond if necessary, to destroy the Iraqi army, apprehend Saddam Hussein, and prosecute him and his henchmen for war crimes. Nothing less will solve the Gulf problem, honor the sacrifices of the dead and injured American men and women, and avoid a nuclear escalation that in the long run would cost the United States more than any other nation.

Most of the country seems to believe that the proper response to Saddam Hussein's atrocity is to reply in kind and then some. The majority of demonstrators gathering in front of the White House carry signs imploring the President to "turn Iraq into a nuclear graveyard" as one placard puts it. This is the dominant theme of talk shows across the country and a flood of calls and telegrams to the Congress. With several senators warning that only a comprehensive U.S. nuclear response will ensure that no other "madman" will repeat Saddam Hussein's cataclysmic error, the

White House announces that the president will address the country at 1700, May 13, 1991.

In the speech, which he calls the most consequential of his or any presidency since the Cuban missile crisis, the president describes the Iraqi nuclear attack on U.S. forces in the Gulf and explains the various options before the country. He then tells his fellow citizens what, as commander-in-chief, he has decided to do. . . .

Notes

1. This is an outcome we neither predict nor prefer. It is one, however, that could happen. For that reason, we believe the possibility deserves serious policy scrutiny and prescription.
2. Although most of this chapter is a work of imagination, military details are drawn from Norman Friedman's excellent book, *Desert Victory: The War for Kuwait* (Annapolis, Md.: Naval Institute Press, 1991).

CHAPTER TWO

New Nuclear Threats to U.S. Security

LEWIS A. DUNN

The discovery—after the Gulf War—of the scope, size, and relative sophistication of Iraq's nuclear weapons program jolted political leaders in many countries. This was, however, only the latest and most visible manifestation of a continuing global process; a region-by-region review reveals that nuclear proliferation is under way in many nations and could well accelerate and become more open in the next ten to fifteen years. Different tests can be used of what makes a country a nuclear power. Under the provisions of the 1968 Nonproliferation Treaty, only those countries that had tested a nuclear explosive device by June 1, 1967, can claim international legal status as nuclear weapon states. Alternatively, all advanced industrial countries with sophisticated nuclear power industries might be considered "latent" nuclear weapon states: any one of these countries could, in theory, acquire a nuclear weapon within six to twelve months.[1] At the other extreme, before the collapse of the Soviet Union, only the United States and the USSR ranked as nuclear superpowers, having each deployed upward of 25,000 nuclear weapons.

For our purposes, a nuclear power is a country that possesses the capability to assemble and field a workable nuclear weapon within a matter of hours or at most a couple of days. Important nuclear-force-building choices still have to be made; many diverse outcomes are possible. But having crossed that initial threshold, even a country with only "a single crude bomb" now has access to that same awesome destructive power whose use first shocked the world at Hiroshima.

Nuclear weapons proliferation will pose new security threats and challenges to the United States. American policymakers and defense planners will need to reconcile a series of competing policy priorities; they also will have to strike the right balance between traditional nonproliferation efforts and new initiatives to deal with proliferation's consequences.[2]

NUCLEAR PROLIFERATION IN THE DECADES AHEAD

During the first decades of the nuclear era, several nations joined the United States as acknowledged nuclear weapon states: the Soviet Union (1949), the United Kingdom (1951), France (1960), and China (1964). Since 1964 no country has openly acquired nuclear weapons, but Israel, Pakistan, and India had, by the early 1990s, become unacknowledged nuclear powers. Still other aspiring nuclear powers are standing in the wings, and there may be more than one nuclear-armed successor state to the former Soviet Union.[3]

Toward a Multinuclear Middle East?

An Israeli nuclear monopoly is the defining feature of proliferation in the Middle East.[4] Recent acquisition of chemical weapons and ballistic missiles by many of Israel's neighbors (e.g., pre–Gulf War Iraq, Syria, and Egypt) has only partly changed that equation. This Middle East nuclear status quo, however, is becoming increasingly unstable.

There is little reason to challenge the widely held public assumption that Israel possesses nuclear weapons. The size and characteristics of its nuclear arsenal, however, are more uncertain. Even discounting the most extreme speculation, it appears very probable that Israel's arsenal exceeds a couple of dozen "last resort" nuclear weapons. Israel's Jericho missiles and its advanced aircraft provide possible delivery means.

Over time, the rationale for Israel's nuclear weapons program also appears to have expanded. Perceiving Israel to be militarily insecure and internationally isolated, the Ben-Gurion government took the decision in the mid-1950s to acquire a "last resort" deterrent to a military breakthrough by the armies of its Arab enemies. The purpose was "to threaten Hiroshima to avoid another Holocaust."[5]

By the early 1990s, possession of nuclear weapons—or Israel's "special capability," in the code words sometimes used by Israeli officials—still was seen as insurance against any revival of Arab hopes of destroying Israel.[6] It was also seen as a deterrent to chemical attacks against Israeli military bases and facilities or Israeli cities by Syria, a remilitarized Iraq, or another hostile Arab government. During the Gulf War, the Israeli government apparently debated whether to respond with nuclear weapons if Saddam Hussein attacked Tel Aviv or Haifa with missiles armed with chemical warheads.[7]

Until quite recently, it was widely assumed that Israel's nuclear monopoly would persist for the foreseeable future. Radical countries such as Libya, Syria, or Iraq were presumed to lack the technical skills and organizational capacity to acquire nuclear weapons, and in any case Israeli military action was seen to offer a coercive nonproliferation *deus ex machina*. These assumptions now need to be reassessed in light of revelations about Iraq's nuclear program, the Gulf War bombing of Iraq, and new incentives for proliferation among countries within the Middle East.

The post–Gulf War inspections of Iraq under United Nations Security Council Resolution 687 (which set out the conditions for a cease-fire) revealed that Iraq was pursuing its own mini–Manhattan Project.[8] Development activities were moving steadily ahead in several technologies to enrich uranium to weapon-grade material; in efforts to explore plutonium reprocessing; and in attempts to design, validate, and manufacture a workable nuclear weapon. At least several thousand scientists, engineers, and technicians had been successfully mobilized for this effort. Iraq also proved itself adept at circumventing global export controls, using methods from deception to the outright purchase of complete companies. Public estimates put Iraq within a year or two of acquiring a nuclear device before its Gulf War miscalculation.

While levels of industrialization, technical skills, and organizational abilities vary widely among Arab countries, the Iraq experience is a warning against assuming that such countries are "too technically backward" to acquire nuclear weapons. Moreover, several Arab countries have access to ample financial resources for buying technical talent and inputs. Cooperation among Arab countries, or with more advanced outsiders such as Pakistan, India, and China, would provide still other means to fill technical gaps. Access to materials, technology, components, and possibly personnel from former Soviet nuclear programs would also accelerate the pursuit of nuclear weapons in the Middle East. The first decades of the nuclear age, moreover, amply demonstrate that cooperation in pursuit of nuclear weapons is the norm and not the exception.

Information from the post–Gulf War inspections made it clear that Israel's 1981 attack on Iraq's Osirak nuclear research reactor had short-circuited but not eliminated Iraq's quest for a nuclear capability. Similarly, a decade later, Iraq's duplication, diversification, and concealment of its nuclear infrastructure ensured that some important facilities were not attacked and others were not fully destroyed.[9]

In the future, Israeli military action could probably again disrupt and delay a poorly concealed, easily targeted nuclear weapons program but Israel probably cannot expect to rely on military force to block more sophisticated efforts by Arab countries or Iran to become nuclear powers. Moreover, having learned the lessons both of the Osirak raid and of the Gulf War, other Middle East countries can be expected to place even more emphasis on duplication, diversification, and concealment. Neither U.S. nor Israeli officials can confidently rely on Israeli military action as a solution to dealing with future Arab nuclear weapons programs.[10]

Indeed, there is no reason to believe that Saddam Hussein has lessened his commitment to acquiring nuclear weapons. If the nuclear-related constraints and monitoring imposed by Security Council Resolutions 687 and 715 are lifted, Iraq's nuclear weapons program could again take off. Growing resentment among the elites and officials in many Arab countries over lack of a comparable international effort or concern about Israel's nuclear weapons arsenal makes it likely that consensus for strict controls on Iraq will eventually break down.[11] Such resentment could well be reinforced in turn by recent allegations, repeated in Arab countries, that Israel has several hundred nuclear weapons and has adopted a nuclear-warfighting strategy.[12]

Perhaps equally important, however, is that proliferation incentives are growing throughout the region. U.S. intelligence officials have expressed concern over efforts by Algeria and Syria to build up a nuclear infrastructure, as well as Iran's apparent attempts to put back together the pieces of the Shah's nuclear program.[13] Such concerns have been heightened by declarations of a high-ranking Algerian general, as well as by key ayatollahs in Iran, calling on Muslim countries to match the Israeli bomb.[14] In Egypt, there are signs of reopening the debate over the renunciation of the nuclear option.[15] Egyptians are concerned about the scope and objectives of Israel's nuclear arsenal and resentful of the United States (and others') acquiescence in it; they were also shocked at discovering how close Saddam Hussein had come to acquiring nuclear weapons, and fear Iran's nuclear ambitions.

Progress in the Middle East peace process could help to defuse some of these Arab security concerns. Confidence-building measures could provide Israeli leaders with a way to respond to Egyptian fears, and a political breakthrough on the Golan Heights could lead to constraints on Syria's chemical and missile capabilities, as well as on Israel's nuclear program.[16] But neither Iraq nor Iran, both of which have refused to participate in the peace process, would be greatly affected, nor would longstanding intra-Arab or Arab-Iranian tensions be significantly reduced. Thus, the existing Middle East nuclear status quo could break down in the decade ahead.

Nuclear Restraint or Competition in South Asia?

India and Pakistan now stand on the threshold of open deployments of nuclear weapons, and of increasing competition between each other. Both New Delhi and Islamabad continue to assert their interest in avoiding an arms race, but what will happen in South Asia is at best uncertain.

By the fall of 1990, President Bush could no longer certify, as required by U.S. nonproliferation legislation, that Pakistan did not "possess" a nuclear explosive device. Pakistan's foreign minister publicly admitted as much in February 1992.[17] Similarly, New Delhi has periodically emphasized India's capability to make and deploy nuclear weapons rapidly.[18] Director of Central Intelligence Robert Gates has confirmed that "nuclear weapons could be assembled quickly" by both countries.[19]

In each country, significant parts of the political and military elites oppose open nuclear weapons deployments, but a strong minority disagrees, arguing that such deployments need not result in the type of technically dynamic, politically corrosive, unlimited arms race that defined the U.S.–Soviet nuclear relationship. They argue that acknowledged deployment is a necessary step toward a stable nuclear deterrence relationship, and lack of such openness only increases the dangers of a nuclear clash by making it harder to assess respective capabilities, to remedy the technical weaknesses of their respective nuclear forces, and to learn how to live on a nuclear subcontinent.[20]

Even if deployment were more open, however, regional nuclear arms racing seems almost inevitable. Domestic political pressures in India to exceed Pakistan's efforts would be likely to jump. Worst-case military analysis and scientific pressure on both sides would add momentum for more rapid, more extensive nuclear force building. Especially in India, the availability of large stocks of plutonium would make it easier to pursue a more ambitious nuclear program, once the open-acknowledgment threshold is crossed.

India's nuclear activities cannot be separated from its political security relationships with China and the former Soviet Union. Open nuclear deployments would probably heighten tensions between Beijing and New Delhi. China's military planners could respond with new deployments aimed at deterring New Delhi. Nuclear suspicions between China and India could also accelerate India's program and make it much more difficult to stop at a level of only a handful of nuclear weapons for Pakistan-related contingencies. The collapse of the Soviet Union provides another reason for skepticism about the longer-term prospects for regional restraint since the USSR is no longer the backer for India's nuclear security, nor its source for conventional arms at bargain prices. These changes reinforce other pressures for a more robust nuclear force, both to deter China and as an alternative to diversion of scarce hard currency to conventional arms purchases.

Outside efforts are, however, continuing to cap, if not roll back, both countries' nuclear weapons programs. Washington has proposed a five-country meeting on regional proliferation and security issues, bringing in China and Russia. The governments of India and Pakistan are exploring confidence-building measures.

Even assuming that supporters of nuclear restraint win, both India and Pakistan are already nuclear powers. They have the capability to assemble rapidly a small number of nuclear weapons, to deploy those weapons in a crisis, and to wreak unprecedented damage on each other and on outsiders. In that regard, proliferation already has occurred in South Asia.

Proliferation on the Korean Peninsula: Hope and Caution

Beginning in the early 1980s, concern increased over North Korea's nuclear weapons ambitions. Pyongyang's 1985 accession to the Nonproliferation Treaty (NPT) allayed those concerns only temporarily, until it stalled in meeting its NPT obligation of signing a safeguards agreement for International Atomic Energy Agency (IAEA) inspection of its nuclear facilities. Instead, North Korea made its signing conditional on a U.S. commitment not to use nuclear weapons against it, and on withdrawal of any U.S. nuclear weapons stationed in South Korea. In the meantime, it began building what has now been publicly confirmed to be a plutonium reprocessing facility, leading CIA Director Gates to testify in February 1992 that North Korea could be "a few months to as much as a couple of years" from acquiring a nuclear weapon.[21]

In late 1991 onward, however, there were increasing signs that North Korea might have decided to move back from the nuclear proliferation brink. In mid-December 1991, Pyongyang stated that it would not manufacture, test, possess, acquire, store, deploy, or use nuclear weapons, nor would it enrich uranium or reprocess plutonium.[22] At that time, both Koreas signed a Treaty of Reconciliation and Nonaggression, followed by a "Joint Declaration for a Non-nuclear Korean Peninsula" wherein they agreed to establish a Joint Nuclear Control Commission to work out procedures for bilateral nuclear inspections. Capping these new agreements, Pyongyang finally signed its safeguards agreement with the IAEA on January 30, 1992.[23]

Several considerations may have influenced Pyongyang's decisions. Its economy near collapse, North Korea has been seeking

Japanese economic support in the form of billions of dollars in compensation for Japan's occupation of Korea from 1910 to 1945, as well as direct Japanese investment. But Japan has conditioned its support on North Korea's acceptance of IAEA safeguards and on agreement not to reprocess plutonium. Pyongyang also may have been concerned about possible UN Security Council sanctions, or even an attempt at preemptive military action, like Desert Storm, by Seoul and Washington.[24]

Perhaps equally important was President Bush's September 27, 1991, announcement that the United States would unilaterally withdraw its ground-launched tactical nuclear weapons (later extended to include all nuclear weapons) from South Korea. U.S. flexibility also was evident in a readiness to allow North Korean inspections of U.S. military bases in South Korea if comparable inspections would be allowed in the North. In effect, Pyongyang appeared to have achieved its most important security objective, eliminating what it perceived to be a U.S. nuclear threat from South Korean territory.

North Korea's initial implementation of these new agreements was mixed. As required, it provided the IAEA in May 1992 with a listing of locations subject to safeguards, including three North Korean–built reactors and a long-suspect building at the Yongbyon nuclear complex, declared to be a "radiochemical laboratory."[25] The first IAEA inspection took place in late May and early June 1992. But bilateral inspections, due to begin by June 10, 1992, were delayed and Pyongyang has resisted Seoul's push for challenge inspections of suspect sites.

On March 12, 1993, the North Korean government announced its intention to withdraw from the NPT. This action compounded several other lingering uncertainties about its nuclear intentions. By classifying its reactors in terms of their electric rather than thermal output (which would be up to five to six times greater), North Korea has created some ambiguity about their size and, therefore, about their potential plutonium production capability. There also is uncertainty about the history of the smallest reactor, which began operation in 1986. If it operated continuously, rather than sporadically as Pyongyang claims, it could have produced more spent fuel than it declared, some of which might already have been removed from the reactor. Indeed, the IAEA's request for a special inspection at two sites where waste might be stored from the undeclared reprocessing of spent fuel from that reaction may have triggered Pyongyang's decision to withdraw from the NPT. It seems implausible that North Korea would have built a reprocessing facility without first testing the process. And given the North's general reliance on building underground facilities, there is speculation that its nuclear program has yet to be fully uncovered.[26]

If efforts to roll back North Korea's apparent nuclear weapons program fail, there would be considerable pressure on South Korea and also on Japan to reassess their own non-nuclear status.[27] The likelihood, however, is that both nations would continue to rely on the U.S. nuclear umbrella.

A future unified Korea would raise still more uncertainty about proliferation prospects on the peninsula. Unified, Korea could acquire and deploy nuclear weapons by combining South Korea's nuclear weapons activities of the mid-1970s, its advanced peaceful nuclear infrastructure, and the nuclear inheritance from North Korea's Yongbyon program.[28] Traditional Korean fears of Japan and an escalating U.S. withdrawal from Northeast Asia could increase the incentives for proliferation.

Romancing the Bomb in the Former Soviet Union

The consequences of the collapse and breakup of the Soviet Union jumped to the top of the nonproliferation agenda soon after the August 1991 aborted coup. Although the tactical nuclear weapons of the former Soviet Union have been consolidated in Russia, fears persist that Ukraine, Kazakhstan, or Belarus could block the withdrawal or elimination of former Soviet strategic arsenals on their territories. Post-Soviet economic free-fall has also triggered concerns that proliferation-prone countries could recruit personnel from the former Soviet nuclear program or obtain essential materials, components, and equipment.

Right after the collapse, political leaders and government officials in Ukraine, Kazakhstan, and Belarus reaffirmed their intentions to become nuclear-free territories. They agreed that all of the tactical nuclear weapons of the former Soviet Union would be withdrawn to Russia, a process that was virtually completed by spring 1992.

The situation with regard to the withdrawal or elimination of strategic nuclear weapons, however, remains uncertain. As debate on this issue heated up in early 1992, some officials warned that it could take five to ten or more years to complete the withdrawal of these weapons from their territories. For Kiev and Minsk, this contradicted earlier statements and the December 1991 Minsk agreement which called for completion of withdrawals by the end of 1994. Kazakh president Nursultan Nazarbayev even proposed that Kazakhstan should join the NPT as a nuclear weapons state on the ground that a nuclear weapon was detonated on Kazakh territory before June 1, 1967.[29]

The Protocol to the START Treaty, signed after considerable diplomatic haggling by the United States, Russia, Kazakhstan, Ukraine, and Belarus on May 23, 1992, and the accompanying letters from the leaders of the latter three countries to President Bush, have not fully resolved the nuclear status of these former republics.[30] The START Protocol made Ukraine, Kazakhstan, and Belarus parties to the START Treaty and committed them to adhere to the NPT as non-nuclear weapon states "in the shortest possible time."[31] The three nations also agreed to eliminate all nuclear weapons and all strategic offensive arms from their territories during the seven-year period of reductions in the START agreement, but this commitment was less demanding than the 1994 deadline agreed to earlier by Ukraine and Belarus.

During 1992, Ukrainian reluctance to give up nuclear weapons continued to grow. Moreover, the creation of an independent Ukrainian military in February 1992 is said to have led to the emergence of an alliance of military and former Communist party officials who favor retaining some former Soviet nuclear weapons.[32] By mid-1993, only Belarus had carried out its pledge to ratify the NPT.

At worst, a new form of nuclear ambiguity may be emerging. This would reaffirm yet again the desire and commitment of Kiev and Alma-Ata to be nuclear-free, but it would raise technical problems to stretch out post-START elimination of strategic weapons, and might be used to justify future claims of inability to comply with the original timetable. Final NPT adherence would be delayed. How much the United States should fear such new-style nuclear ambiguity is open to debate. Public opinion in Ukraine, Kazakhstan, and Belarus is still strongly antinuclear.[33] Actual operational control over the strategic missiles and aircraft in these countries apparently still resides as of mid-1993 with the General Staff in Moscow.[34] Even assuming they could successfully seize these systems, the former republics might not be able to overcome technical use-control devices. If so, they would be limited to dismantling the warheads to reuse the nuclear weapons materials in a crude device. Geographical proximity would make it technically very difficult to target Moscow with captured former Soviet ICBMs.

Nonetheless, many Russian officials are persuaded that Kazakhstan and Ukraine will seek to retain some nuclear weapons[35] as they retain deep-seated political and military fears of Russia, fueled by conflicting interests, historical experiences, and Russian rhetoric. Barring a new security structure for these territories, they may hold on to, or seize, former Soviet nuclear warheads. Or a clandestine program might be launched to produce nuclear weapons indigenously. Indeed, if nuclear ambiguity gained internal legitimacy, the institutional, bureaucratic, and political support for retention of some former Soviet strategic weapons could well solidify.

Under the Soviet regime, scientists and technicians in the Soviet weapons complex were barred from unauthorized foreign travel. Foreign trade was a government monopoly, and controls over exports of technology, materials, and equipment were an integral part of centralized Communist control of Soviet economic life.[36] This Soviet export control system no longer exists. By decree, President Yeltsin in early 1992 took over the nuclear-export-related regulations of the former Soviet Union, including the contractual controls on nuclear scientists' foreign travel, but more formal nuclear legislation has yet to be passed. Despite urgings from Russia, moreover, the newly independent republics have refused to adopt the former Soviet regulations as their own. Further, relevant export-control expertise is extremely limited. Even assuming best efforts by the new authorities, some seepage to proliferation problem countries is probably unavoidable.

Access to trained personnel and nuclear-weapons-related exports from the former Soviet Union could make it easier and quicker for a resurgent Iraq, Pakistan, or India to develop more advanced nuclear weapons. Even Israel might benefit. But unless the industrial infrastructure is in place, access to know-how alone would have little impact on a Libyan or Syrian nuclear weapons program; for them, access to equipment, materials, and components diverted from the former Soviet Union would be considerably more useful.

The breakdown of traditional controls in the former Soviet Union may also create for the first time a significant risk that a terrorist or subnational group might acquire nuclear weapons materials.[37]

Two Proliferation Successes—and Some Longer-term Concerns

Two recent and important nonproliferation successes only partly offset this overall trend toward proliferation. In 1991 South Africa joined the NPT, accepted international safeguards on its nuclear facilities, and began the process of rolling back its nuclear weapons program. Two years later, it became the first country to announce that it had built but had then disassembled nuclear weapons.

Proliferation risks have also decreased in Latin America. After uncovering a decade-old secret military program to develop nuclear weapons, Brazil's former president Fernando Collor de Mello in 1990 ordered that it be shut down. In 1991 Brazil and Argentina established a joint Agency for Accounting and Control of Nuclear Materials to put all of the nuclear facilities in each country under IAEA safeguards.[38] This capped a process of nuclear confidence building begun in the mid-1980s.

South Africa and Latin America are the exceptions, however, and more widespread nuclear weapons proliferation in the next decade could have a ripple effect beyond 2000. Open nuclear deployments or initial acquisition by some countries could greatly increase pressures on neighboring countries to reassess their own nuclear weapons status. As noted, North Korean acquisition of nuclear weapons could trigger intense debates in both South Korea and Japan about acquiring matching nuclear capabilities, and a resurgent nuclear-armed Iraq might well lead Turkey to reexamine its non-nuclear posture. Iraqi acquisition of nuclear weapons would prove equally unsettling to Saudi Arabia, whose response could range from seeking an explicit U.S. nuclear guarantee to trying to purchase nuclear warheads for its Chinese-supplied CSS-2 missiles. Elsewhere, a decision by Ukraine to retain nuclear weapons could reopen "the nuclear issue" in several European countries, from Poland to Germany.

Failure to reach agreement on a prolonged extension of the Nuclear Nonproliferation Treaty in 1995 could markedly affect the prospects for more widespread proliferation. One route to such a failure would be a breakdown of START implementation and the nuclear arms control process due to nuclear ambiguity in some of the former Soviet republics. In that event, it could prove very difficult to convince NPT parties to support prolonged extension. As a result, the norm of nonproliferation would be undermined, and more countries might come to believe that pursuit of a nuclear option had become necessary. Furthermore, one or more of the unacknowledged nuclear powers—Israel, Pakistan, and India—could decide to deploy nuclear weapons openly. Other problem countries—Iraq, Iran, Libya, other Middle East states, or North Korea—are technically further from the bomb, but several could reach the nuclear weapons threshold in the decade ahead. A wider proliferation ripple effect could again ensue. Whatever its other characteristics, the post–Cold War world appears increasingly likely to be a world of more rather than fewer nuclear powers.

NEW NUCLEAR FORCES: DEFINING THE POSSIBILITIES

The new nuclear powers confront a series of nuclear-force-building thresholds and choices. Choosing to possess even a single nuclear device would greatly increase a Third World country's capability to wreak destruction on hostile neighboring countries. It would also shift the political and military calculations of both nearby neighbors and more distant outsiders that have ties to that region.

The next most basic choice is whether or not to acknowledge possession of nuclear weapons, which no country has done since

China's 1964 test. (South Africa declared it had produced nuclear weapons, but only after it had destroyed them, according to its claim.) Nonacknowledgment can lessen hostile regional and international reactions, thereby proving politically useful in the initial stages of nuclear force building. It may also make it easier to contain regional nuclear arms racing. But if the top political leadership of a new nuclear power favors expansion of the arsenal (or simply cedes decisions to a group of nuclear and defense bureaucrats), nonacknowledgment might make it easier to augment the force even as it restricts wider technical and professional military input. Lack of this input can hinder development, testing, and exercise of operational procedures that could lessen the risk of a nuclear accident, make crisis management harder, and can possibly heighten the risk of neighbors' miscalculations. In any case, over time, it may be increasingly difficult for new nuclear powers to stick to a policy of nonacknowledgment just to gain the perceived benefits of nuclear weapons; it may be necessary to at least partially "lift the veil."

New nuclear powers can be expected to consider nuclear force survivability to be among their top priorities. How to protect these weapons and delivery systems against possible attack raises still another set of issues. Many different approaches are possible including concealment of the location of nuclear weapons stocks; dispersal of nuclear-capable aircraft in a regional crisis; airborne alerts; or development of unconventional delivery means, for example, smuggling a weapon into an adversary's homeland to avoid offering a conventional military target for a preventive or preemptive strike. Ballistic missiles might be placed in underground shelters or caves, deployed only in preparation for firing. Hardened shelters or mobile missiles might be developed, or even a full nuclear triad of air-launched, sea-launched, and ground-based weapons. The sea-based leg might comprise surface-fired submarine cruise missiles, cruise missiles deployed on surface patrol craft, or eventually sea-launched ballistic missiles.

Economic constraints, technical weaknesses, and political limitations could impede the pursuit of more survivable nuclear forces, as could the trade-offs between peacetime stability and crisis stability, or between crisis stability and military readiness in a crisis. Many new nuclear powers lack the technological depth to contain the risk of accidental detonation. The traditional procedural solutions to survivability and physical security may be seen to entail too high a price, economically and in terms of reduced military readiness in time of crisis. Widespread dispersal of the weapons would lessen the payoffs of attempted preemption (and add to crisis stability), but at the expense of a greater risk of loss of control to domestic opponents in peacetime and of unauthorized use in a crisis.

Diversity of New Nuclear Forces

Different responses to these types of nuclear-force-building choices—as well as to divergent capabilities and threats—are likely to result in considerable diversity among the nuclear forces of the new nuclear powers. As summarized in table 1 on pages 36–37, the range of possible proliferation outcomes may be even more varied than with the first nuclear weapons states.

Virtually all of the new nuclear powers are likely to use either plutonium or highly enriched uranium, but not both. Choices of nuclear materials partly reflect a country's technological infrastructure, which can itself be affected by global export control constraints as well as by past hostile military action. A reluctance to violate safeguards or global norms may play a part, as may a demonstration effect from the successful activities of other problem countries.

Documents uncovered during IAEA inspections after the Gulf War indicate an Iraqi interest in both basic fission and in more advanced nuclear warhead designs. Nuclear powers in the years ahead are also likely to go beyond acquisition of a simple fission device. With the possible exceptions of Israel and India, however, most of them may find it technically very challenging to design, engineer, and manufacture reliable and efficient advanced fission and thermonuclear weapons. (There is continuing public speculation, partly based on Mordechai Vanunu's revelations, that Israel possesses second-generation nuclear weapons.)[39] Decisions not to acknowledge, and therefore not to test, nuclear weapons would make it even more difficult to produce advanced designs without outside assistance.

Wide variations are to be expected in the size of new nuclear forces. By the year 2000, the number of nuclear weapons in the hands of the different potential new nuclear powers could range to well over one hundred warheads. Here, too, as table 1 suggests, Israel and India stand out. For many other new nuclear powers, however, shortages of nuclear weapons materials—barring major unauthorized outflows from the former Soviet Union—could greatly constrain nuclear force building.

Delivery, organization, and doctrine are also likely to vary widely. Most of the new nuclear powers will probably seek to rely on missiles as a preferred means of delivery against nearby neighbors, and virtually all of these countries (India and Pakistan in South Asia; Iran, prewar Iraq, Egypt, Saudi Arabia, and Syria in the Middle East; and North Korea in Asia) already possess or are developing either short- or intermediate-range ballistic missiles. If technical difficulties arise, in miniaturizing nuclear warheads, for example, or making them sufficiently robust, nuclear-capable aircraft also are in their military inventories.[40]

Whether, or perhaps how soon, some of these new nuclear powers might develop intercontinental ballistic missiles capable of threatening more distant adversaries is a matter of considerable controversy. The experience thus far of the few programs aimed at producing longer-range weapons suggests that none are likely to be successful in this decade. Access to foreign space-launch technology or even boosters, however, could speed up acquisition of at least a handful of longer-range systems.[41] Dissemination of missile technology, components, and equipment—or even complete systems—from the former Soviet Union might have a similar accelerating impact. Nonetheless, for this decade, new nuclear powers will probably rely on more unconventional means of delivery (e.g., smuggling across borders) against distant targets.

If Iraq manages to revive its mini–Manhattan Project, the main mission for nuclear weapons would likely be to deter outside political involvement or military intervention in regional confrontations. Deterring nuclear or conventional attack by the threat of counter-city nuclear retaliation may be the ambition of nuclear powers such as Iran facing Iraq, for example, or North Korea confronting a conventionally superior South Korea. Some new nuclear powers may view possession of nuclear weapons as a means to blackmail or coerce weaker non-nuclear neighbors.

Table 1

Potential New Nuclear Forces (Late 1990s–2000+)

	Nuclear Material	Warhead Design	Warhead Numbers	Means of Delivery	Organization	Doctrine(s)
Israel	Pu Heu (?) Adequate Stocks	Advanced Fission Thermonuclear (?)	100+	Missile SRBM IRBM Aircraft	Small, Secret Eventual Separate Command	Deter CW Use Last Resort Deterrent/War Terminator Battlefield Use Deter Outside Involvement
India	Pu Large Stocks	Fission Thermonuclear (?)	100+	Missile SRBM IRBM Aircraft	Small, Secret Eventual Separate Command	Deter Nuclear Use Counter-City Targeting
Pakistan	Heu Pu (?) Limited Stocks	Fission	10+	Aircraft Missile SRBM Unconventional	Small, Secret Eventual Separate Command	Counter-City Deterrent War Terminator via Early Battlefield Use

Country	Material	Weapon Type	Number	Delivery	Arsenal	Purpose/Role
Algeria	Pu (?)	Fission	1 (?)	Aircraft Unconventional	Small, Secret	(?)
Egypt	Pu (?)	Fission	1–3	Missile Aircraft	Small, Secret	Deter Nuclear Use or Coercion Political Positioning
Iran	Heu (?) Pu (?)	Fission	1–3	Aircraft Missile SRBM Unconventional	Small, Secret	Counter-City Deterrent Deterrent of Outside Involvement
Iraq	Heu Very Limited Stocks	Fission	1–3	Aircraft Unconventional	Small, Secret	Deterrent of Outside Involvement Nuclear Coercion
Libya	Heu (Diverted) Pu (Diverted)	Fission	1–3 (?)	Missile Unconventional	Small, Secret	Nuclear Coercion (?) Deter Outside Reprisal
North Korea	Pu Very Limited Stocks	Fission	<10	Aircraft Missile SRBM Unconventional	Small, Secret	Last Resort Deterrent Nuclear Coercion
Syria	Pu (?) Heu (?)	Fission	1 (?)	Missile Unconventional	Small, Secret	Deter Nuclear Use Enhance Political Position

As long as the new nuclear powers remain unacknowledged, nuclear force building will be hidden within the organizational structure of existing military capabilities and plans. No distinctly nuclear command organization is likely to be created. More importantly, because of the need to preserve maximum secrecy, decisions about nuclear force building, deployment, and even planning for use will be taken in private by a very small clique of advisors. Consequently, bureaucratic, parliamentary, institutional, and public checks and balances will be considerably weakened, especially in more democratic societies.

On the Road to "Real" Nuclear Forces

By the turn of the century, Pakistan and India could join Israel on the road to "real" nuclear forces. For these three countries, nuclear proliferation might well entail acknowledged deployments; many rather than few nuclear warheads; explicit attention to safety, security, survivability, and command and control; and increasing integration of nuclear potential into military planning and operations. For other countries, including Iraq, Iran, and possibly Syria, Algeria, or North Korea, their weapons programs would only be beginning to confront the manifold choices and problems of nuclear force building.

NEW THREATS TO AMERICAN SECURITY INTERESTS

Since the 1991 Gulf War, increasing attention has been paid by policymakers, legislators, the military, and the concerned public to the problem of nuclear proliferation. The spread of nuclear weapons to conflict-prone regions would pose an immediate threat to the countries in those regions, as well as to U.S. security interests.

There is a wide range of potential American interests to consider.[42] A traditional American interest in a more politically open, stable, and peaceful world order is perhaps the broadest security-related interest that could be adversely affected in a world of more nuclear weapons powers. This reflects American self-interest as well as American idealism. In addition, the economic well-being of the United States as a great trading nation is tied to that of many other countries, not least those in the oil-rich Middle East.[43]

The security of the United States is also tied to a stable world order. A nuclear conflict among new nuclear powers would shatter more than four decades of nuclear non-use. The consequences as well as the responses of other countries might seriously undermine the implicit global nuclear taboo that has emerged during the past forty years. If nuclear use were not met with a strong international condemnation, perhaps aimed at making the user an "outlaw nation," the likelihood of further use elsewhere could increase. More broadly, extensive nuclear use in a regional conflict could do unprecedented damage to the regional environment.[44]

Concern that nuclear weapons might be used in a conflict among new nuclear powers, moreover, is well founded.[45] Many of the conditions that led to non-use between the superpowers in the Cold War era are lacking in the conflict-prone regions to which nuclear weapons now are spreading. Even assuming that stable deterrent relationships among newly nuclear rivals may eventually emerge—facilitated perhaps by outside assistance—the transition period may be dangerously unstable.[46]

Three political conditions of stable U.S.–Soviet nuclear deterrence were especially important: the limited stakes of the East–West confrontation, with neither Moscow nor Washington committed to the physical destruction of the other side; strong institutional restraints on the use of nuclear weapons; and, eventually, predictability of behavior. By contrast, the stakes of conflict are far higher between Israel and Iraq, Iraq and Iran, India and Pakistan, or the two Koreas. Particularly in dictatorships like Iraq and North Korea, but also in other nations that restrict nuclear decision-making to a small closed circle, institutional restraints are also considerably weaker. Predicting the other side's capabilities and intentions is likely to be considerably tougher, too: nonacknowledgment is an impediment to accurate assessment, while long histories of confrontation and mutual suspicion could heighten the chances of miscalculation and misunderstanding.

For reasons already suggested, some new nuclear powers may find it difficult to meet the technical requirements of stable nuclear deterrence. Resource constraints and an emphasis on crisis readiness, for example, could preclude deployment of accident-resistant nuclear warheads. Concern about loss of control over nuclear weapons to internal rivals might result in peacetime or even crisis deployment patterns that are vulnerable to an opponent's first strike. By contrast, steps to ensure survivability in a crisis, for example, deployment of nuclear weapons on mobile missiles, could heighten the danger of unauthorized use.

Several other features of the U.S.–Soviet political confrontation also contributed to nuclear peace. It was a bipolar standoff, which made it easier for either side to assess relative capabilities and to evaluate possible threats. The lack of common borders provided a psychological buffer to political or military overreaction. The decade that passed between the first Soviet nuclear deployments in the early 1950s and the most intense crisis of the Cold War—the 1962 Cuban missile crisis—permitted both sides time to learn about the other side's intentions, readiness to run risks, and operational procedures, as well as about what steps to take (or avoid) to lessen the risk of an unintended nuclear clash.

These and other unique aspects of the U.S.–Soviet relationship give little basis for confidence in the new nuclear relationships. Even assuming the eventual emergence of stable deterrent relationships among hostile new nuclear powers, the transition is likely to be dangerous and unstable. Throughout, the risk could be high that a low-level conventional crisis or clash could escalate, possibly sparked by a technical mishap.

American security interests could be affected in yet another way. In a world where more nations are nuclear powers, friends and allies of the United States could become victims of nuclear blackmail or even nuclear attack. Historical ties, moral considerations, mutual economic and political benefits, and traditional balance-of-power calculations all help to create an American stake in the outcome of a nuclear confrontation. For example, a resurgent, nuclear-armed Iraq in the late 1990s could seek to blackmail the smaller Gulf countries and Saudi Arabia to gain de facto control over Middle East oil production and pricing policies. This would threaten global economic stability and U.S. economic well-being. Egypt might find its security threatened should Iraq's nuclear weapons program not be checked or should nuclear seepage from the former Soviet Union give Libya access to nuclear weapons. Nuclear threats by North Korea could be aimed at weakening Japan's readiness to permit its territory to be used for the defense of South Korea.

Under some conditions, nuclear weapons might even be used against traditional U.S. friends or allies in Third World regions, perhaps due to escalation from a conventional conflict. Another danger is unauthorized use, such as an attack against Israel by an extremist Arab subnational group that seized a nuclear weapon from Iraq, Syria, or perhaps Iran, or an attack by a Sikh separatist group in India. Even intentional use against a U.S. friend cannot be fully ruled out. Particularly if Saddam Hussein or another radical Arab leader thought that he himself had nothing left to lose, he might strike out against Israel in an attempt to go down in Muslim folklore as a "new Saladin."

Threats to American Forces

In a world of new nuclear powers, the United States would also face increased political constraints on its freedom of action. Shortly after the Gulf War, the Indian army's chief of staff is reported to have stated that one lesson of that war was: "Never fight the U.S. without nuclear weapons."[47] Deterring American military intervention may be an important underlying motivation for acquisition and deployment of nuclear weapons. But a number of very different and partly contradictory judgments can be put forward about how possession of nuclear weapons by a hostile new nuclear power could influence the politics of intervention.

Had Saddam Hussein been known or perhaps only thought to possess a few nuclear weapons, President Bush's strong personal commitment to reverse Iraq's August 2, 1990, invasion of Kuwait might have been strengthened, rather than weakened.[48] From the start, as signaled by his comparisons of Saddam Hussein to Hitler, Bush apparently believed that failure to reverse the invasion would have led to additional aggression.[49] In turn, although the "Authorization for Use of Military Force Against Iraq" passed the Senate in January 1991 by a vote of only 52 to 47, fear and outrage at Iraqi acquisition of nuclear weapons could have strengthened Congress's resolve.

However, the politics of building a regional and global coalition against Saddam Hussein and then maintaining it over many months would have become far more difficult. Already under great pressure to find "an Arab solution," King Fahd might have refused at the start to permit prompt deployment of U.S. forces to Saudi Arabia. Even assuming a Saudi "go-ahead," other neighboring Arab countries would probably have been less ready to confront Iraq. In turn, it is likely that the members of the Security Council would have been more reluctant to authorize use of force. The coalition itself might have broken apart rather than holding together, however tenuously, in the final prewar days.

On the other hand, the fact that the Gulf crisis entailed action to reverse a fait accompli may be important. This required a firmness of will, a level of military force deployments, and a degree of coalition support that might not be necessary in some future nuclear crisis situations. For those lesser contingencies, declaratory statements to back up an ally and symbolic force deployments to pose a credible threat of retaliation on that country's behalf might suffice to deter aggression in the first place. Readiness to take those steps might also be less affected.

The politics of intervention could change again, however, should a hostile new nuclear power be able to threaten the American homeland. The burden of proof needed to support military intervention would almost certainly intensify, but so might pressures for attempted preemptive military action, should a decision be taken to intervene. Neighboring countries' political reluctance to welcome, or even support, U.S. involvement could also increase, owing to fears that the United States would not follow through on its initial commitment. Possibly facing a similar threat to their territories, outsiders beyond the region would also be more likely to resist U.S. coalition building against a hostile new nuclear power.

Assessments vary widely on the extent of the threat posed by a new nuclear power against U.S. forces or military bases overseas. The view that a future nuclear-armed Iraq or Iran would "never dare" to use nuclear weapons against U.S. forces contrasts with the contention that some new nuclear powers could be "undeterrable." Reality is likely to lie somewhere in between.[50] Most leaders of hostile new nuclear nations probably recognize that nuclear use against U.S. forces would almost certainly be met with a devastating, even if not nuclear, counterblow. Nonetheless, under certain conditions, a sufficiently desperate and ruthless leader might use nuclear weapons against U.S. forces overseas.

Use of nuclear weapons against U.S. forces or against a U.S. ally would raise very difficult choices. If a formal treaty relationship exists, as with South Korea, security-related arguments for retaliation would be very strong, although not necessarily with nuclear weapons. If the United States was not to respond, the credibility of U.S. alliances in other regions could sharply decline, indirectly affecting U.S. security interests in yet a different way. U.S. (non-nuclear) retaliation might be essential to restore the presumption against use of nuclear weapons and block such use from becoming a precedent.

At least some hostile new nuclear powers are all but certain to want the capability to threaten the American homeland, in order to undermine American support for a country threatened by a new nuclear power; to create uncertainties about the credibility of such American support; to deter U.S. military involvement; or to deter American military action, whether by punitive raids, attempted nuclear preventive strikes, more extensive countermilitary action in support of conventional forces, or retaliation on behalf of a neighboring country.

At least for the 1990s any new nuclear power that sought to threaten the American homeland would probably need to rely on unconventional means of delivery. However, to increase the perception that a threat exists, these nations would be motivated to acquire even crude, longer-range missile systems. Questions arise over whether a nuclear strike on the American homeland actually would be carried out in the face of likely U.S. retaliation.

Until quite recently, terrorists were usually reluctant to engage in acts of mass murder, and access to nuclear weapons materials was extremely difficult. But both these restraints may be eroding. Until the destruction of Pan Am 103, with nearly 400 deaths, terrorists generally steered clear of acts of large-scale, random violence against civilians. But that, plus the recent bombing of the World Trade Center in New York City, could presage a greater readiness to undertake acts of mass violence. At the same time, the potential supply of nuclear weapons materials that are vulnerable to terrorist theft and diversion could jump in the 1990s. This is due to weakened controls on nuclear weapons materials in the former Soviet Union, future dismantling of U.S. and former Soviet nuclear warheads, and the potential vulnerability of large shipments of plutonium from Western Europe to Japan for use in its civilian nuclear power program. The risk of a nuclear terrorist incident anywhere, including in the United States, could rise considerably.

CONCLUSION: COMPETING POLICY PRIORITIES

Eight countries, apart from Belarus, Kazakhstan, and Ukraine, now possess nuclear weapons or the capability to assemble them quickly, and additional proliferation is highly likely in the decades ahead. As a result, a broader U.S. proliferation strategy is increasingly demanded. Future American efforts must be geared not only to contain the spread of nuclear weapons but also to deal with its regional and global consequences for old and new U.S. security interests.

The design and implementation of a new, more comprehensive strategy will raise many competing policy priorities.[51]

Perhaps the most basic set of competing policy priorities is how much emphasis to place on new measures to deal with proliferation's consequences, as compared with traditional measures to prevent proliferation. Some initiatives to contain proliferation's consequences in one region will make it harder to prevent proliferation elsewhere (see chapter 5 by Steven E. Miller). For example, measures to enhance the technical safety and security of new nuclear forces may directly clash with the obligations of the Nuclear Nonproliferation Treaty, or result in a loss of morale and lessened attention to capping, preventing, or even rolling back proliferation in those regions where that still may be possible.[52]

Some fundamental measures to protect American security interests, however, may reinforce rather than undermine nonproliferation efforts. These include steps to shape new nuclear powers' perceptions of the usability of nuclear weapons and to induce them to accept the decades-old taboo, and more fundamental political initiatives to resolve or alleviate regional confrontations. In addition, there is no reason why American policymakers cannot place a high priority on preventing proliferation in one region while seeking to deal with its threats to American security interests in another.

A second policy decision is whether to isolate new nuclear powers or open a dialogue with them. Efforts to isolate new nuclear powers, for example, by imposing sanctions to punish their acquisition of weapons, can reinforce other countries' disincentives to acquiring them. Refusal to provide assistance to help deploy safer, less accident-prone systems may send the message that proliferation is dangerous. But dialogue aimed at influencing a new nuclear power's capabilities, posture, and thinking about nuclear weapons might be the best means to head off their use in a regional conflict. Such a course, however, is likely to entail closer ties with that country and to run fundamentally counter to an effort to ostracize and "make an example" of it.

In practice, political realities, regional responsibilities, and historical animosities will frequently strike the balance for U.S. policymakers between these two competing priorities. There is little chance, for instance, that the United States would open a dialogue with a future nuclear-armed Iraq, Iran, or North Korea in an attempt to influence its nuclear posture and policy. Other cases are more complex. Fear of alienating Arab countries and of undermining global nonproliferation efforts and institutions has blocked even quiet pursuit of a dialogue on nuclear issues with Israel, though it is long overdue.

A third choice is what balance to strike between efforts to alleviate the technical instabilities of new nuclear forces and to ensure a clear-cut American military edge against new nuclear powers. For instance, several potential measures to enhance command and control would lessen the risk of an unintended nuclear clash but would also make it more difficult to limit damage to U.S. forces by timely, preemptive military action, should that become necessary. Similarly, if new nuclear powers were no longer fearful of a nuclear weapon accident, some might undertake exercises, begin more realistic planning, and take other steps that would enhance their potential threat to U.S. security interests. But here, too, the trade-offs should not be exaggerated. Any such assistance is highly likely to be provided only to friends that could be assumed to support rather than to threaten U.S. regional and global security interests.

As U.S. nuclear and conventional forces are restructured following the collapse of the Soviet threat, how much to plan and posture U.S. forces for contingencies involving new nuclear powers in the Third World, as opposed to more traditional threats, has become a salient issue. In the past, U.S. defense planners have considered nuclear proliferation to be a lesser threat, when it was considered at all. Plans, forces, and operational procedures designed for the "big" Soviet threat were assumed to provide any responses that might become necessary to deal militarily with new nuclear powers. This approach may no longer be valid, both because of the drawdown of Cold War capabilities and because of the likelihood that protecting U.S. interests in nuclear proliferation contingencies will demand some changes at the margin of U.S. military forces.

The United States must also choose how high a priority to give to intelligence and analysis of the efforts by proliferation problem countries to acquire a first nuclear weapon, and how much to what happens afterwards. Little attention is presently paid to the nuclear-force-building efforts of new nuclear powers, but U.S. security interests will call for information about numbers of warheads, deployments and storage sites, warhead designs and vulnerabilities, command and control, safety and security, doctrine, and operational procedures (see chapter 9 by Robert D. Blackwill and Ashton B. Carter on intelligence issues). The Iraq experience, moreover, strongly suggests that the acquisition of this information will also require striking a new balance between technical intelligence gathering and human intelligence in the proliferation arena.

American Leadership—but With Others' Support

Over the past decades, the United States has more often than not taken the lead in winning other countries' support for international nuclear nonproliferation norms, institutions, and agreements. American leadership was essential for establishment of the IAEA, the NPT, the Nuclear Suppliers Group, and, most broadly, on developing a nuclear taboo. American alliances have also been a vital nonproliferation measure. Dealing with proliferation's consequences will require comparable American leadership to identify the most critical threats, to fashion potential responses, and to win international support for them. With more widespread proliferation already on the horizon, it is none too soon for American policymakers and defense planners to turn their attention to this new set of problems for American security and global stability in the decades ahead.

Notes

1. This view is often expressed, for instance, by Roger Molander of the RAND Corporation.
2. Parts of the following discussion draw on Lewis A. Dunn, *Containing Nuclear Proliferation*, Adelphi Paper No. 263 (London: International Institute for Strategic Studies, Winter 1991). This analysis also has benefited from discussions with Gregory Giles, Barbara Gregory, James Tomashoff, and William Bajusz.
3. The best annual overview of nuclear proliferation trends is the volume produced by the Carnegie Endowment for International Peace. See, most recently, Leonard S. Spector with Jacqueline R. Smith, *Nuclear Ambitions: The Spread of Nuclear Weapons 1989–1990* (Boulder, Colo.: Westview Press, 1990).
4. See Frank Barnaby, *The Israeli Bomb* (London: I. B. Tauris & Co., 1989); and Seymour Hersh, *The Samson Option* (New York: Random House, 1991).
5. This description has been used by Marvin Miller.
6. The following discussion draws partly on discussions in Israel in January 1992. See also Avner Cohen and Marvin Miller, "Nuclear Shadows in the Middle East," *Security Studies*, vol. 1, no. 1 (Spring 1991), pp. 54–77.
7. Bill Gertz, "Israel Deploys Missiles for Possible Strike at Iraq," *Washington Times*, January 28, 1991, p. B7.
8. See the Inspection Reports issued by the United Nations Security Council. This assessment also reflects discussions with David Kay, a leader of several International Atomic Energy Agency (IAEA) inspections in Iraq, and with my colleague, Gregory Giles.
9. This judgment is based on the record of the IAEA special inspections conducted after Desert Storm.
10. In chapter 7, Philip Zelikow makes the useful distinction between "immature" and "mature" nuclear weapons programs. The latter would be very difficult for Israel or the United States to destroy fully, short of a major war and occupation.
11. This reflects my discussions with Barbara Gregory, whose recent research has highlighted such growing Arab resentment as a potentially dangerous nonproliferation trend in this region.
12. The author's own discussions indicated, for instance, that Seymour Hersh's claims about the size and characteristics of Israel's nuclear weapons program have been given wide credence among Egyptian officials and retired senior military men.

13. See David Hoffman, "Iran's Rebuilding Seen as Challenge to West," *New York Times*, February 2, 1992, p. A1.
14. See Statement by Algerian Minister of Defense Nezzar, reprinted in *Arms Control* (U.S. Joint Publications Research Service [JPRS], January 30, 1991), p. 16; "Mohajerani Discusses Islamic Nuclear Programs," *Abrar* (Tehran), October 23, 1991, reprinted in Foreign Broadcast Information Service FBIS–NES–91–214, November 5, 1991, pp. 73–76.
15. This discussion draws in large part on conversations in Cairo in January 1992.
16. For a discussion of steps that Israel could take to constrain its nuclear program, see Cohen and Miller, "Nuclear Shadows."
17. R. Jeffrey Smith, "Pakistan Official Affirms Capacity for Nuclear Device," *Washington Post*, February 7, 1992, p. A18; "What's News: Worldwide," *Wall Street Journal*, October 23, 1991, p. 1.
18. John Ward Anderson, "India Cool to U.S. Call for Nuclear Talks," *Washington Post*, March 11, 1992, p. A24.
19. Director of Central Intelligence Robert M. Gates. (Testimony before the U.S. Senate, Committee on Governmental Affairs, January 15, 1992.)
20. For a representative presentation of this line of argument, see "Pakistan: Open Debate on Nuclear Called For," *Nucleonics Week*, August 8, 1991, p. 13; General K. Sundarji, "The Nuclear Threat," *India Today*, November 30, 1990, p. 90.
21. See Elaine Sciolino, "C.I.A. Chief Says North Koreans Plan to Make Secret Atom Arms," *New York Times*, February 26, 1992, p. A1.
22. This public declaration matched an earlier statement by South Korea's President Roh Tae Woo. See Damon Darlin, "Roh's Nuclear-Free Pledge May Advance Effort to Inspect North Korean Facilities," *Wall Street Journal*, November 11, 1991, p. A10.
23. See David E. Sanger, "Koreas Sign Pact Renouncing Force in Step to Unity," *New York Times*, December 13, 1991, p. 1; Joint Declaration on Denuclearization of Korean Peninsula, February 19, 1992, as, "Denuclearization Declaration Issued," reprinted in FBIS–EAS–92–034, pp. 17–18.
24. The possibility that coercive measures could look quite different on the "receiving end" was pointed out to me by Philip Zelikow.
25. North Korea also stated that it had separated gram amounts of plutonium there. *Nuclear Fuel*, May 11, 1992, p. 13.
26. "Defector on North's Hidden Nuclear Facilities," *Korea Herald* (Seoul), reprinted in FBIS–EAS–91–216, November 7, 1991, pp. 26–27.
27. Several Japanese officials and academics have acknowledged to the author that North Korean acquisition of nuclear weapons would trigger such an intense debate in Japan.
28. Many observers believe that a unified Korea, brought about by North Korea's collapse, is conceivable by the end of the 1990s.
29. See "President on Joining Nonproliferation Treaty," *TASS* February 24, 1992, reprinted in FBIS–SOV–92–036. January 1, 1967, was the cutoff date by which a state had to have tested a nuclear weapon to be considered a "nuclear weapons state" by the NPT. In response to reminders that it was a Soviet weapon that was tested, Kazakh spokesmen argue that Kazakhstan

was fully involved in all aspects of the former Soviet nuclear weapon program.

30. Protocol to the Treaty Between the United States of America and the Union of Soviet Socialist Republics on the Reduction and Limitation of Strategic Offensive Arms, May 23, 1992, reprinted in *Arms Control Today*, vol. 22, no. 5 (June 1992), pp. 34–35.

31. See Barbara Crossette, "4 Ex-Soviet States and U.S. in Accord on 1991 Arms Pact," *New York Times*, May 24, 1992, p. A1.

32. See Nikolai Sokov, "Non-Proliferation in the CIS: The Quest for Survival of the NPT," unpublished manuscript, June 1992, p. 5. Sokov is the Deputy Director of the Office of Nonproliferation in the Russian Federation Foreign Ministry. This reflects Sokov's personal appraisal.

33. This is the view of officials and observers in each country, based on the author's discussions with them.

34. Ibid.

35. This reflects Robert Blackwill's conversations in Moscow in May 1992, and the author's discussions with Russian officials and observers in early June 1992.

36. This was pointed out to me by my colleague Burrus Carnahan and reflects his recent work in this area.

37. A particular problem is that detailed procedures and approaches are reportedly lacking in accounting for actual quantities of nuclear materials as opposed to accounting for the bulk items, such as drums of highly enriched uranium or numbers of warheads produced. This draws on discussions with U.S. scientists and officials familiar with the former Soviet Union's approach to accounting and control of nuclear materials in the civilian and military nuclear sectors.

38. See John R. Redick, "Argentina and Brazil's New Arrangement for Mutual Inspections and IAEA Safeguards," paper issued by Nuclear Control Institute, Washington, D.C., February 1992.

39. See Barnaby, *The Israeli Bomb*, pp. xiv, 13–21, 25; Hersh, *The Samson Option*, pp. 198–200.

40. On ballistic missile proliferation and countries' capabilities, see Martin Navias, *Ballistic Missile Proliferation in the Third World*, Adelphi Paper No. 252 (London: International Institute for Strategic Studies, Summer 1990).

41. On possible misuse of space launch vehicles, see Sidney Graybeal and Patricia McFate, "GPALs and Foreign Space Launch Vehicle Capabilities," unpublished manuscript, February 1992.

42. Also see the discussion of threats to U.S. interests in chapter 6 by Michèle Flournoy.

43. The classic examination of this aspect of the American tradition in foreign policy was written in the early years of the Cold War. See Robert Osgood, *Ideals and Self-Interest in American Foreign Policy* (Chicago: University of Chicago Press, 1954).

44. The importance of thinking partly in terms of a broader view of self-interest was suggested to me by my colleague William Bajusz.

45. The now classic contrary view is that of Kenneth Waltz, *The Spread of Nuclear Weapons: More May Be Better*, Adelphi Paper No. 171 (London: International Institute for Strategic Studies, Autumn 1981).

46. For a more extensive discussion, see Dunn, *Containing Nuclear Prolifera-tion*, pp. 23–25.
47. Quoted by Representative Les Aspin, Chairman of the House Armed Ser-vices Committee, "National Security in the 1990s: Defining a New Basis for U.S. Military Forces." (Speech before the Atlantic Council of the United States, January 6, 1992.)
48. Chapter 1 by Robert D. Blackwill and Albert Carnesale also speculates about the possible impact had Saddam Hussein possessed a nuclear weapon in 1990.
49. One useful description of the U.S. and global political, diplomatic, and mili-tary response to the Kuwait invasion is U.S. *News and World Report* Staff, *Tri-umph Without Victory* (New York: Times Books, 1992).
50. The following discussion partly reflects conversations with my colleague Jim Tomashoff, who has been working on scenarios involving nuclear use in pro-liferation contingencies.
51. For a more detailed presentation of the author's views on what a new and com-prehensive proliferation containment strategy would entail, see Dunn, *Con-taining Nuclear Proliferation*, passim.
52. See Thomas Graham, Jr., "Winning the Nonproliferation Battle," *Arms Control Today* (September 1991), pp. 8–13.

PART II

U.S. Diplomatic Efforts for Coping With New Nuclear Nations

CHAPTER THREE

Arms Control
for New Nuclear Nations

PAUL DOTY and STEVEN FLANK

Nuclear arms control is defined by the aggregate of treaties, agreements, declaratory statements, export controls, and restrictions that have come into force over the past three decades. The results of these measures may help in dealing with any new nuclear states that arise within the next decades.

This chapter will review the tools of arms control before examining the nuclear status of three categories of states: 1) those whose proliferation efforts have been rolled back, 2) those that have acquired nuclear weapons capability since the Nonproliferation Treaty came into force in 1970, and 3) those that have the potential and inclination to acquire a nuclear weapons capability within the next two decades. It will conclude with a consideration of U.S. policy options.

The same arms control measures cannot be promoted for all newly nuclear-capable states. U.S. policy toward a new nuclear state will depend, for example, on that nation's security goals, its past relations with the United States, the rate at which its nuclear developments are being pursued, the extent of the arsenal it is planning to build, and the likelihood that it will aid other proliferating states. But no arms control measures will be useful unless the new nuclear state finds them to be in its own self-interest. Meeting this condition in states without a consistent nuclear taboo may take years of diplomatic persuasion, overt pressure, or political evolution. The United Kingdom and the United States helped each other develop nuclear weapons, the Soviet Union helped China, France helped Israel, and help has been extended to several other current or potential nuclear states. Dilemmas will arise over whether to treat a new nuclear state as irreversibly nuclear and hence a member of the "club," or as a pariah deserving punishment and pressure to limit or undo its new-found capability.

U.S. policymakers must assess the role of arms control as a component of a much broader security policy pursued by diplomatic and, at times, military means. Most arms control measures will have to be pursued by a coalition in which the United States will play a key role, both in the negotiations and in the diplomacy that prepares the way.

THE TOOLS OF ARMS CONTROL

The many measures now restricting nuclear weapons are summarized in table 1. Almost all grew out of Cold War and nonproliferation efforts, but each of the objectives listed could also have a role in dealing with newly arrived nuclear states.

The Nonproliferation Treaty (NPT) and the International Atomic Energy Agency (IAEA)

The NPT forbids nuclear weapons states (defined as those that manufactured and exploded a nuclear device prior to January 1, 1967) to assist any nation in acquiring nuclear weapons, and forbids non-nuclear weapons member states from acquiring them. All parties must agree to use the IAEA and its system of full-scope safeguards to assure accountability of all nuclear weapons related materials.

For the NPT–IAEA regime to be an important player in future efforts to limit proliferation, there would have to be significant reforms. Recent experience in Iraq highlighted the NPT's inability to deal with a non-nuclear weapons member state whose nuclear program violates the Treaty. The upcoming 1995 NPT Review Conference should seek agreement on how to deal with such violations, and how to treat a violator over the long term. The United States should also promote Treaty changes that would permit progressively more severe sanctions to be instituted by the UN Security Council, rather than by individual countries, with participation in those sanctions being an obligation under the Treaty.

The 1995 Conference might consider a one-time admission of new nuclear weapons states (Pakistan, India, and Israel) to the Treaty, in return for a strengthened prohibition against the transfer of weapons or technology to non-weapons states, and for increased transparency for all nuclear programs. Lastly, although the NPT is not a permanent treaty, it could become so at the 1995 Conference.

The IAEA should be given explicit authority to evaluate compliance with the NPT, bringing that agency one step closer to becoming the verification and intelligence arm of an expanded global nonproliferation regime. In fact, the IAEA should be empowered to provide much broader coverage of all aspects of nuclear weapons management, such as detection, dismantlement, and safety. To become more aggressive in its search for possible clandestine nuclear weapons activities, it will need to expand its own intelligence capabilities and be assured access to the national intelligence capabilities of others. (Intelligence issues are discussed in detail in chapter 9 by Robert D. Blackwill and Ashton B. Carter.)

If a nuclear weapons state wants to renounce its nuclear arsenal, or has nuclear disarmament imposed upon it, the IAEA could be the implementing agency, overseeing the safeguarding and disassembling process. It can also provide assurance that denuclearization is happening as promised, to both outside powers who have conditioned their aid on denuclearization (as in the case of Ukraine), and to neighboring states who might otherwise initiate or continue a nuclear program of their own (as in the case of Brazil and Argentina).

The IAEA could also monitor compliance with the nontransfer provision of the NPT by establishing a new set of safeguard agreements that complement existing export controls. It could be instrumental in harmonizing export regulations, drafting model legislation, and furnishing technical assistance to countries attempting to implement their own controls. And it could become the core of a new international verification agency to help implement agreements between NPT member states.

Table 1

Present Nuclear Arms Control Measures

Objectives	*Application**
Multilateral Measures	
Prevent development, production and spread of nuclear weapons	NPT (1968)
Control of fissile materials; especially the diversion to weapons	Establishment of IAEA (1957) and its role in NPT compliance Physical Protection of Nuclear Materials Convention (1980)
Detect most but not all production sites and export of nuclear equipment	Satellite surveillance and other intelligence to detect nuclear weapons production
Nuclear weapons free zones (NWFZs)	The Antarctic Treaty (1959) Treaty of Tlatelolco (Latin America) (1967) Outer Space Treaty (1967) Seabed Arms Control Treaty (1971)
Limits on nuclear testing	Limited Test Ban Treaty (1963) Threshold Test Ban Treaty (1974) Unilateral moratoria on testing
Prohibitions on use of nuclear weapons	No-first-use declarations
Export controls to limit spread of weapons technologies	London (Nuclear) Suppliers Group (1978) Missile Technology Control Regime (MTCR) (1987) Coordinating Committee for Multilateral Export Controls (CoCom) (1949) Domestic implementing legislation
Openness concerning nuclear weapons and delivery systems	Country-by-country acceptance of IAEA safeguards Open Skies Treaty (1992)
Enforcement of UN Security Council sanctions	Elimination of Iraq's nuclear weapons capability (1991–)
Bilateral Measures	
Limits or bans on anti-ballistic missiles	ABM Treaty (1972)
Security guarantees to non-nuclear states by nuclear states	NATO U.S. implied guarantees to Israel and Japan

Table 1 (continued)
Present Nuclear Arms Control Measures

Objectives	Application*
Bilateral Measures (continued)	
Limits on strategic nuclear weapons	SALT Agreements (1972, 1979)
Elimination of intermediate range nuclear weapons	INF Treaty (1987)
Reductions of strategic weapons	START Treaty (1992) Reciprocal, unilateral reductions
Bilateral agreements not to attack nuclear installations	India–Pakistan agreement (1988)
Mutual inspection arrangement between nations that have not ratified the NPT	Four-party agreement (1991) among Argentina, Brazil, IAEA, and a bilateral control agency
Relevant Non-nuclear Measures	
Crisis communications	"Hot Line" Agreements (1963, 1971) Nuclear Risk Reduction Centers (1987)
Reductions in conventional forces that might otherwise justify nuclear weapons	Conventional Forces in Europe Treaty (1992)
Reduce the risk of surprise attack and build common trust	Confidence and Security Building Measures (CSBMs) mandated in 1989 have led to CSBM Talks in which agreements have been reached on limiting military deployments and exercises in Europe†

---

*Dates are those on which the treaty or agreement was signed.

†CSBMs refer either to agreements that arise from CSBM Talks under the Conference on Security and Cooperation in Europe (CSCE) that began as the Helsinki Review Conference (1975), or generically to measures taken anywhere, unilaterally or multilaterally, to reduce the risk of attack and to build common trust.

For all of these tasks, the IAEA will need new resources, specifically money and authority. Currently, the IAEA's authority and discretion are severely limited,[1] because its Board of Governors can include representatives of nonmember states as well as representatives of a nuclear industry that has substantial vested interests. To enhance its ability to operate in difficult situations, therefore, especially in states not party to the NPT, the United States should support placing the IAEA directly under the authority of the UN Security Council.

The second crucial resource is money. Even for its present missions, the IAEA is seriously underfunded and unable to respond to new demands.[2]

Nuclear Weapons Free Zones

While nuclear weapons free zones (NWFZs) cannot include nuclear weapons states, the zones may be useful in dealing with the consequences of proliferation. In cases where a country might want nuclear weapons because a neighboring country is going nuclear, NWFZs could provide a way out of such a security dilemma. In other cases, NWFZs can provide domestic political protection for a regime that would like to eliminate its arsenal. The chance to have neighboring countries give up their nuclear weapons can be a powerful argument for supporting denuclearization.

The most advanced weapons free zone is established by the Treaty of Tlatelolco (1967), which has thus far been signed by twenty-six of the thirty-two eligible states of Latin America. Other zones are under discussion for the Korean Peninsula, South Asia, southern Africa, and the Middle East (including northern Africa). In the Middle East, interest in a NWFZ has revived since the Gulf War, with supporters including the United States, Egypt, Iran, and Israel. As the last step in a Middle East peace process, after other central issues have been settled, a nuclear weapons free zone could allow the nuclear programs of Israel, and any other nuclear state that may arise, to be rolled back.

The United States can do little to directly foster NWFZs. It can, however, apply pressure in international negotiations, see to it that the IAEA is adequately funded, and offer its assistance in devising and implementing mechanisms for verification and enforcement. Such zones may provide the only long-term stability for regions that are nuclear-prone. Hence, vigorous advocacy and firm diplomatic pursuit of the conditions that will make NWFZs possible should be high on the U.S. agenda.

Limits on Nuclear Weapons Testing

The networks of monitoring devices that can detect violations of the Limited Test Ban Treaty (1963) and the Threshold Test Ban Treaty (1990) make it likely that any significant underground or atmospheric tests by a newly proliferating state would be noticed. Newly proliferating states, therefore, may prefer the advantage of ambiguity over the assurance that nuclear testing would provide. Only at a much later stage, if there is a move to thermonuclear weapons, might testing become important enough to outweigh the risks of detection.

If the United States is itself testing, it is not well positioned to argue strongly against it, especially if the United States opposed a Comprehensive Test Ban Treaty (CTBT) that was widely endorsed by other nuclear powers. In fact, a widely accepted CTBT could provide substantial leverage against proliferating states, and as testing by established nuclear states decreases, the prospect of reaching a broadly based CTBT increases.[3] The most promising formulation for the United States appears to be one that bans testing beyond a date several years ahead, or one that allows for only a very low rate of testing at low yield, ensuring the reliability and safety of weapons already in the arsenal but insufficient to permit any new weapons development.[4]

No-First-Use Pledges

Although the United States strongly opposed no-first-use pledges in the later years of the Cold War, it may now find reasons for reversing that position. As the prospects of a World War II–type war in Europe fade, and given the U.S. rejection of any use of nuclear weapons in its three recent wars (Korea, Vietnam, and the Gulf), it is unlikely to be tempted to use them in wars of the foreseeable future.

Indeed, the U.S. nuclear weapons doctrine has shifted from wide-ranging enhancement of U.S. security to last-resort deterrence. By further pursuing devaluation of nuclear weapons, the United States has an opportunity to take a lead in seeking broad support for no-first-use. A well-formulated pledge or treaty could win acceptance by new nuclear nations, heightening their awareness of the limits of nuclear weaponry and serving as a confidence and security-building measure.

Export Controls

Export controls over items clearly related to nuclear weapon production, as well as over dual-use items that may be so used, have been agreed to by the Zangger Committee (1974) with sixteen member states, and by the London Nuclear Suppliers Group (1978), which now has twenty-six members. While the aim has been to prevent proliferation, the unavailability of such items could also slow the rate at which a state could add to its nuclear arsenal. On the other hand, since many nuclear programs use indigenous technology, export controls might simply encourage states relying on foreign suppliers to develop indigenous technology as quickly as possible.

Nuclear-capable states might be persuaded to participate in export controls in return for market and technology access, development aid, and so on, perhaps as part of the Nonproliferation Treaty's nontransfer provisions described above. Efforts might shift from the ever-growing list of dual-use items to a concentration on clearly nuclear-related items: uranium, heavy water, tritium, and all enrichment and reprocessing technologies.[5] The United States should offer technical assistance to states willing to impose such controls.

Weapons-Grade Materials Production Cutoff

A materials production cutoff for new nuclear states provides a means of capping nuclear programs without even acknowledging their existence. For example, Israel might agree to shut down its reactor at Dimona in return for secure guarantees against weapons materials production in the Arab states. If weapons materials have been produced or treated at only a very few sites over a relatively short time, as is the case in South Africa, then verification of a cutoff is well within the IAEA's present capability. The production of highly enriched uranium and plutonium could also be brought to an end, as these items are not necessary in modern civilian power industries.[6] Power reactors can operate efficiently using uranium at much lower levels of enrichment than that needed for weapons. Stockpiles of plutonium are expanding because of the reprocessing of spent fuel, particularly from Japan and Europe, as well as from the destruction of nuclear weapons by Russia and the United States. Since decades will pass before this plutonium will find a use in power production, its stockpiles and ocean transport will be a tempting source of bomb material for newly proliferating states and must be carefully guarded.[7]

Negotiated Reductions of Nuclear Weapons and Missiles

The extensive negotiations between the former Soviet Union and the United States on limiting and reducing nuclear weapons and delivery systems are comparable to regional negotiations between two or more competing new nuclear states. In each case the critical step is to convince the participants of the advantage of such an undertaking. The models for doing this both with missiles and with weapons are established in the U.S.–Russian treaties and current negotiations.

Arguably, the most successful Cold War treaty was the Intermediate-range Nuclear Forces (INF) Treaty, completely eliminating U.S. and Soviet missiles with ranges between 500 and 5500 kilometers. To extend this treaty to include current and new nuclear states, admittedly an ambitious goal, would remove a great source of instability.

The Destruction of Nuclear Weapons Production and Stocks

In the future, newly proliferated states may be induced to roll back their nuclear forces and to destroy at least some of their nuclear weapons. The methodology of verified destruction could be based on earlier U.S. and Russian agreements.

An extreme example of a "rollback" was Iraq's Gulf War cease-fire agreement, which was actually the destruction of its nuclear weapons program as mandated by the UN Security Council. Such a case highlights the need for improved intelligence, the limits of high-precision bombing, and the value of on-site inspection. A UN Security Council resolution that authorized the destruction of a state's nuclear installations would put some of the lessons of the Iraq rollback to work. (This last-resort approach is treated in detail by Philip Zelikow in chapter 7.)

Confidence and Security Building Measures

Many of the confidence and security building measures (CSBMs) initiated at the Stockholm Conference (1986), which played an important role in establishing the trust and transparency with which the Cold War ended, apply to conventional arms: advance notice of military exercises, hot lines to help resolve crises or misunderstandings, limits on troop concentrations, preannouncement of missile tests, and military-to-military visits and exchanges. They could apply to nuclear weapons as well, by helping to relax tensions in regions where disputes have contributed to nuclear proliferation, thus paving the way toward more serious negotiations. (For examples, see the Bilateral Measures section of table 1.) Security guarantees by a nuclear state to a new nuclear state is another CSBM that might mitigate its nuclear incentives.

THE REVERSAL OF NUCLEAR WEAPONS PROGRAMS

The nuclear programs of proliferating states have been reversed and rolled back in four cases, although only one of these states had actually become nuclear-capable. Nonetheless, the steps involved in the reversals provide guidance on the role that arms control can play.

South Africa[8]

The discovery of a test site in the Kalahari desert in 1977 and a possible atmospheric test in 1979 alerted the world to South Africa's nuclear ambitions. By 1990 the UN Secretary General's expert team estimated that South Africa, with both reprocessing and enrichment capabilities on line, had accumulated enough fissile material for five to six weapons. That this weapons capability is now being eliminated voluntarily stands as the outstanding example of rollback.

South Africa's motives for building nuclear weapons were hardly rational, as they were not useful against the kind of attack that South Africa might have feared (from Angola or Namibia, for example). But this was ignored by a nationalistic regime that found itself cornered and isolated. In any case, disincentives were weak, since South Africa was already bearing the costs that would be imposed for violating nonproliferation norms. Because of global opposition to apartheid, it was already subject to sanctions, including the denial of technical assistance and expulsion from international organizations. As long as overt weaponization did not occur, it was unlikely that suspicions of a nuclear weapons program would make things worse.

Nevertheless, international pressures, increasing costs, and especially the prospect of mitigating apartheid led the new de Klerk government in 1990 to explore joining the NPT–IAEA regime, which it would have to do to return to normal international and trade relations. In particular it could look forward to rebuilding its uranium and enrichment markets that it lost in the 1980s. For the industrial and scientific communities that sustain the South African nuclear program, these incentives were more appealing than possession of the actual weapons. In addition, the winding down of the civil war in Angola and the establishment of an independent Namibia removed many of South Africa's security concerns. In September 1991, South Africa signed the IAEA safeguards agreement for the NPT. The IAEA inventory began in November 1991.

The IAEA's ability to respond quickly and verify the reversal of the weapons program was essential to its implementation. To be sure that South Africa's nuclear capability will not be bequeathed to a successor government or be put at risk in a civil war, the international community will have to help in rehabilitating South Africa's nuclear power industry, and in establishing a NWFZ in southern Africa. With appropriate funding and additional assistance from the leading NPT parties, this can be done.

Argentina and Brazil[9]

Argentina and Brazil engaged in a competition for nuclear arms in the 1970s and early 1980s stimulated by fervent nationalism, ambitious military regimes, and growing suspicions in both countries, although no credible security threat to either justified a nuclear deterrent. External pressures to desist were compromised by the sale of essential components from Canada, Germany, and the United States, usually justified by the needs of the nuclear power industries that were being developed at the same time.

The possibility of reversing this development came with the installation of civilian governments in Argentina in late 1983 and in Brazil in early 1985. In 1987, as mutual suspicions and domestic political pressures began to lessen, the two presidents initiated a series of exchange visits at nuclear installations. By 1990 these exchanges led to an agreement to restrict nuclear activities to peaceful uses, and to solicit IAEA inspection, even though neither was an NPT signatory. By December 1991, a four-party accord had been reached among Argentina, Brazil, the IAEA, and a Joint Argentina–Brazil Agency to administer procedures for the accounting and control of nuclear materials. This accord offers a model for instituting IAEA standards in other bilateral situations involving pairs of states not members of the NPT, such as India and Pakistan. Accession by Brazil and Argentina to the Treaty of Tlatelolco, making Latin America a nuclear weapons free zone, now seems possible.

Iraq

Iraq's experience follows a strikingly different course. Here, a belligerent state was forced to give up its facilities for producing weapons of mass destruction—nuclear, biological, and chemical weapons and missiles of more than 150-kilometer range—and to accept the most complete set of arms control measures ever imposed. Calling this "arms control" may be questionable, but it represents the reversal of the nuclear weapons program of a country impervious to negotiation, and such a situation may be repeated as new nuclear states arise.

Shortly after the Gulf War ended and after the failures of the NPT–IAEA regime had been revealed, the UN Security Council approved a resolution establishing a Special Commission to oversee on-site inspections and the destruction of Iraq's nuclear-weapons-related installations. While some destruction remains to be done and some equipment may remain undiscovered, the job done in one year has justified the critical importance of on-site "anytime, anywhere" inspections and long-term monitoring for arms control measures. It also provided invaluable hands-on experience for dealing with a proliferating state, especially a determined one.

The cost of inspection and nuclear installation destruction was to be paid by Iraq. It has partially complied, but substantial costs associated with the operation of the IAEA teams must be funded by the UN on a current basis. In October 1991, the IAEA Iraq program was $60 million in debt. The United States and the former Soviet Union were both late in paying their $65 million annual share to the IAEA. The eighth inspection had to be canceled because of lack of funds. The laxity in funding contrasts sharply with the dedication and risks borne both by the allied forces during the Gulf War and by the inspecting teams of the Special Commission. Greater fiscal discipline will be needed if the long-term monitoring of Iraq is to succeed or if similar demands arise elsewhere.

Finally, it should be noted that the motives for the Iraqi venture into proliferation—leadership of the Arab world, potential Iranian nuclear programs, Israeli nuclear weapons, and deterring external intervention—remain intact. Therefore, as long as the Iraqi leadership maintains its present orientation, the reversal of its determined push for nuclear weapons can be maintained only by the vigilance, commitment, and funding of a continuing UN consensus.

DEALING WITH RECENTLY PROLIFERATED STATES

It is widely agreed that since the NPT came into force in 1970, three nations (other than South Africa), have become nuclear weapons capable: Israel, India, and Pakistan. As none of these has joined the NPT, none has a formal obligation to limit nuclear developments. Yet other nations can bring pressure for them to do so in a variety a ways.

Israel

Israel's efforts to develop a nuclear capability began in the 1950s; its course was opposed by President Eisenhower but tolerated by all subsequent American presidents. Nuclear weapons neared completion by the early 1970s, and the arsenal has since grown to an estimated 100 weapons (by some estimates much more).[10] Israel has persisted in a policy of ambiguity, avoiding any admission of nuclear weapons capability, and leaving friend and foe alike free not to take overt counteractions.

For Israel, the reason for its nuclear weapons program is the threat of being pushed into the sea by an Arab attack. More recently, Israeli nuclear weapons are seen as a deterrent against Arab attacks either with chemical or biological weapons. Some observers argue that Israeli nuclear weapons could be a wasting asset, since they would stimulate Arab nuclear proliferation (a concern unrealized until the case of Iraq). With Iraq's program currently at a standstill, the next few years are the only ones in which it is fairly certain that there will be no nuclear weapons in the region except for Israel's. Hence this will be a unique period for working out a peace settlement which could remove the incentives for Iraq, Iran, Libya, and others to seek their own nuclear weapons. Converting the Middle East into a zone free of weapons of mass destruction is a daunting challenge for peacemaking, and requires arms control measures accompanying every step.[11]

Arms control measures are not new to this region. The Egypt–Israel Peace Treaty limited military activity in the Sinai and along the border between Egypt and Israel. In zones on either side of the Golan Heights, Israel and Syria have accepted limits on troops and tanks, with monitoring procedures that include U.S. satellite surveillance. Future steps should include finding ways to reduce the risks of war by miscalculation, to set deployment and weapons-testing limitations, to begin multilateral talks about weapons of mass destruction, and ways to set restraints on external supplies of military equipment.

If negotiations advance to core subjects, such as Palestinian autonomy or full normalization of Israel's relations with the Arab states, then more intrusive arms control measures could be possible, including demilitarized zones, peacekeeping forces, notification of military exercises, and surveillance and verification (perhaps with the aid of the Open Skies Treaty and foreign satellite data).

The final stage of this process would involve the removal of threats to Israel's existence: the renunciation of warlike acts, border guarantees, and planning for the transformation of the Middle East into a NWFZ. Here, arms control would enter the realm previously reached only in East–West agreements, involving successive reductions of weapons of mass destruction, a nuclear materials production cutoff, reductions of conventional forces, verified limits on arms production and on external arms supplies, and the verified destruction of biological and chemical weapons capabilities.

Even if the Arab–Israeli dispute were resolved, other Middle East wars are likely. Resentments run deep, opportunities for compromise are limited, resources such as water to sustain a rapidly increasing population are dwindling, and oil exports continue to fund large Arab and Iranian weapons purchases.[12] In the event of such wars, especially given the presence of nuclear weapons, the United States and other great powers might impose a settlement on the region that would include arms control measures aimed at reducing or eliminating nuclear capabilities.

India and Pakistan

India's decision to develop a nuclear option began in the 1960s following China's first nuclear test, and resulted in India's one and only nuclear test in 1974. Since then, India has developed a broadly based nuclear industry that maintained the nuclear weapons option. By 1985, it was reprocessing its own plutonium and building gas centrifuges for uranium enrichment. By the end of the decade, it had accumulated enough enriched uranium for up to fifty bombs and had successfully tested both short- and intermediate-range ballistic missiles.[13] It had acquired modern bombers, aircraft carriers, and a nuclear-powered submarine. With the growth expected in the next five years, India will clearly rank as a nuclear power with a considerable range of delivery.

Pakistan's program for a nuclear option began after its defeat in the 1971 India–Pakistan War. It achieved weapons capability in the late 1980s as a result of its acquisition from foreign sources, legally and otherwise, of the necessary components for nuclear weapons. Pakistan's principal motives were to counter India's nuclear program, to provide a deterrent against India's much larger conventional forces, and to enhance its image as the leading Islamic nation. By late 1989 the production of highly enriched uranium was believed to have reached the equivalent of two to three bombs annually. Sources were found for the tritium and beryllium needed for advanced fission weapons. Pakistan's status as a de facto nuclear state has been repeatedly confirmed, most recently by the director of the CIA and by the Pakistani foreign secretary.[14]

The potential India–Pakistan nuclear arms race differs from that now ended between Brazil and Argentina. India's and Pakistan's nuclear programs are much further advanced, and their hostility, amplified by three wars and continuing conflicts over Kashmir, is far greater. Moreover, the nuclear competition is not exclusive, because India must separately structure its nuclear posture vis-à-vis China, whereas Pakistan faces no such requirement.[15] India has summarily rejected numerous Pakistani arms control proposals based on equal constraints because they neglected the China dimension of India's security concerns.

Nevertheless, some progress has been made with confidence-building measures. In 1985 the two parties agreed not to attack each other's nuclear facilities; a formal agreement was signed in late 1988 and entered into force in January 1991. However, disputes have arisen over the completeness of the lists of sites to be exchanged. In 1987 troops were withdrawn from the Siachen glacier in Kashmir by mutual agreement, relaxing tensions that had impelled mobilizations on each side. Following this, agreement was reached on the advance notification of military exercises and the prevention of airspace violations by military aircraft. Thus CSBMs are beginning to play a role in reducing Indo–Pakistani tensions.

The latest effort was a Pakistani proposal in June 1991 for five-power talks in which the United States, the Soviet Union, and China would join India and Pakistan in discussing nuclear disarmament. Although India immediately rejected the proposal, officials in New Delhi suggested that India might agree to participate if certain assurances were forthcoming. Meanwhile, India is seeking more contacts in the United States through increased military meetings and more joint naval exercises, primarily to reduce conflicts over further nuclearization and to secure Western help for much-needed economic development. At the same time, tensions with Pakistan remain at a high pitch. Fighting over Kashmir might escalate to an all-out war, which might be nuclear. A New Delhi senior diplomat noted in early 1992 that "within the next five years both sides will have medium range missiles. Each side will have to assume the worst of each other."[16]

This brief examination leads to the conclusion that U.S. policy, like that of many other nations, has failed to affect the attainment of nuclear capability in these three states. The ground has not been prepared so that arms control measures could help much either in limiting or in reducing nuclear weaponry. In each case, however, CSBMs are beginning to soften the edges of mistrust.

DEALING WITH NUCLEAR WEAPONS STATES OF THE FUTURE

Diplomatic initiatives, arms control measures, and—in the case of Iraq—mandatory inspection and destruction have thus far succeeded in limiting the proliferation tendencies in the known new nuclear states. However, in ten to twenty years, others may arise, and with them the risk of nuclear wars. Plutonium may begin to become economically attractive as a fuel for nuclear power generation and thus become widespread in production and commerce. A new age of proliferation could be upon us if the intervening decades do not demonstrate ways to deal successfully with new nuclear states.

Northeast Asia

North Korea has undertaken gradual but determined development of a nuclear program. By operating its present reactors to maximize plutonium production, it could produce one or two bombs per year. Under pressure, North Korea did sign the NPT in 1985, but delayed until 1992 its ratification and IAEA safeguards agreement. This delay was widely interpreted as an effort to mark time so that it could exploit its largely indigenous nuclear industry for weapons production. It might have held out much longer but for several developments, including weakened cooperation by the former Soviet Union and China, skillful diplomacy by the United States, and the near collapse of its economy. Conditions for North Korea had radically changed since 1979 to 1980, when the decision to produce nuclear weapons was made.

Even after North Korea signed the IAEA safeguards agreement in January 1992, however, its delaying tactics continued. Nevertheless, the agreement was ratified on April 9, 1992, with mandatory inspections to begin within ninety days; the director general of the IAEA promptly visited much of the North Korean nuclear complex.[17]

These positive developments could unravel. First, under Kim Il Sung, or during the power struggles that could develop after his inevitable passing, a nuclear weapons goal could be reasserted and the NPT and IAEA agreements renounced. With intermediate-range missiles based on its Scud-C missiles and with material for perhaps a dozen weapons, North Korea would be a significantly armed nuclear state. South Korea and Japan would then be hard-pressed to resist going nuclear as well.

The other pessimistic scenario (described by Lewis A. Dunn in chapter 2) lies with the reunification of North and South Korea. Suspicious of Japan's technical capability and its accumulating stockpiles of plutonium, a unified Korea might decide to renounce the NPT and IAEA agreements and exploit its indigenous nuclear expertise, derived in part from South Korea's secret, short-lived nuclear weapons program in the 1970s and its advanced nuclear power base. Japan and possibly Taiwan might follow, completing the nuclearization of northeast Asia.

Most countries would join the United States in opposing the opening of this Pandora's box. The short-term goal would be to stay the present course in the hope that North Korea could be completely dissuaded from any nuclear weapons ambitions. Over the longer term, even if North Korea sees advantages in producing nuclear weapons, China, Russia, and the United States should strive to maintain a unified opposition: economic and political boycotts, trade embargoes, sea and air blockade, and perhaps even air strikes at North Korea's nuclear and military installations. (Philip Zelikow discusses the difficulties of the latter options in chapter 7.) Considering the North's weak economic condition, limited development, poor natural resources, and vulnerability to blockade, these actions could force North Korea to give up its nuclear weapons enterprise. Only then could arms control play a role, as the IAEA would become the focus of inspections and dismantlement.

One favorable circumstance should not be overlooked. The limits of North Korea's resources—in trained manpower, in economic and technological resources, and probably in outside help—would force a nuclear weapons program to grow slowly, allowing governments time to change and arms control alternatives to be explored. But once a state is convincingly nuclear weapons capable, hardball diplomacy backed by the threat of imposed arms control would be necessary to slow or stop further developments. The United States and like-minded nations must then face a decision: to live with a new nuclear state until major shifts in the political structure open new possibilities for mutual accommodation, or impose anything from "sanctions to bombing" to force the desired outcome.

The Middle East

Israel and Iraq are not the only nuclear-interested nations in the region; Iran and Libya are the major potential proliferators, but Algeria, Egypt, and Syria are also probably only two decades from achieving a nuclear weapons capability. Iran and Libya are of real concern because, like Iraq, their oil revenues provide an adequate base for funding and their hostility toward Israel and the West provides rationale for accepting the risks and costs involved.

Iran's nuclear weapons program was hobbled in the 1980s by political turmoil and the war with Iraq, but recent announcements reaffirm their intent.[18] If Iran utilizes indigenous technology to become a new nuclear state, U.S. arms control options would be limited. Although the United States would have almost no influence with any foreseeable Iranian government, it might still make use of arms control as an adjunct to a broader foreign policy, for example to reduce the risk of war in the region as a whole, with or without Iran's cooperation. But if dissuasion and CSBMs fail and the Middle East peace process flounders, then the harsh decision would have to be faced: to acknowledge and accept, or to form a coalition that would begin the sanctions route and carry it as far as necessary, perhaps even to the point of bombing.

Libya presents a different problem. Muammar Khaddafi has left no doubts about his desire for nuclear weapons. But his many efforts over the last two decades to initiate a nuclear program or to purchase nuclear weapons have thus far not succeeded. Libya's own limited technological development and its small population necessitate dependence on foreign nationals and imported components, making it easier for the rest of the world to follow any progress that Libya might make. But Khaddafi's success in constructing the massive Rabta plant for chemical weapons and in importing an arsenal of Scud-B missiles should warn against complacency in the nuclear case. Nonetheless, the high level of expertise required for nuclear weapons, the great cost and time needed to build the infrastructure, and the expected durability of the embargo against nuclear technology all create towering impediments.

The great worry lies in the clandestine purchase or theft of a complete weapon—the crisis of the terrorist's bomb. In that case extreme measures, quickly imposed, might be the only option. Arms control measures could only play a role after the threat is neutralized.

Belarus, Kazakhstan, and Ukraine

With the dissolution of the Soviet Union in 1991 there suddenly arose the possibility of three instant nuclear powers, armed with hundreds of high-yield warheads mounted on intercontinental range ballistic missiles or strategic bombers, as well as hundreds of smaller tactical weapons. After months of intense diplomatic activity, however, the three republics agreed to return all tactical nuclear weapons to Russia, and to eliminate the strategic missiles on their soil within the seven-year period prescribed by the START

Treaty. Moreover, these states have pledged to comply with existing agreements controlling nuclear, chemical, and conventional arms, to forgo reuse of fissile materials in weapons, to allow U.S. verification of weapons destruction, and to sign the NPT.

If these pledges are carried out during the seven years allowed for the complete removal of all nuclear weapons as planned, the risk of three new heavily armed nuclear states would disappear. Unfortunately, the main reasons for retaining the weapons remain. These include the prestige that nuclear arms confer; the bargaining chips they provide in negotiations concerning Western aid; and the deterrence they offer against Russian military aggression. At the same time, strong hostilities remain between each of these republics and Russia. If one or more of the republics were determined to become a nuclear power, it would probably dismantle the existing large warheads and reuse the fissile material in simpler and smaller nuclear weapons, a process that would require a considerable infrastructure and activities that would be difficult to conceal. Having already obtained the arms control commitments described above, the United States and its allies would almost certainly initiate a sequence of sanctions and, if necessary, countermeasures.

CONCLUSIONS

Arms control measures are the servants of larger policies, and they require diplomacy to establish some common ground between opposing national positions before they can be applied. The arms control measures that are applicable in dealing with new nuclear states fall into two distinct classes: minor, confidence-building measures, and major, intrusive ones. The former often relate to conventional rather than nuclear forces, and help create an atmosphere in which fundamental political, economic, military, and nuclear issues can be negotiated. The latter become important when new nuclear states become involved in security arrangements that require limiting, reducing, or eliminating their nuclear arsenals. The experience with Iraq adds another category of arms control, namely the imposition of invasive inspections to oversee the permanent destruction of nuclear weapons programs.

The arms control measures that may serve to restrain new nuclear states are listed in table 2. If U.S. policy seeks to limit, reduce, or roll back developments in new nuclear states, then it should support and promote all of the measures listed in table 2 and table 3. The importance of arms control becomes apparent whenever a common interest develops in reducing the likelihood of war, the damage war may cause if it occurs, and the costs that a large military enterprise require; otherwise, arms control is destined to remain in the background as new nuclear states arrive on the scene. As each such state reassesses the gains and losses of its new status, and as its neighbors and the rest of the world judge the new dangers created, the United States and its allies may seek to stabilize or reverse the course the new nuclear state has taken. Here arms control measures can come into play, and can contribute to a peaceful outcome like that accomplished over the decades of the Cold War.

Table 2
Arms Control Measures Relevant to New Nuclear States

Minor Measures Applicable to Early Stages of Arms Control

Confidence and Security Building Measures
    Advance notice of military exercises
    Troop deployment limitations
        Cap on troop concentrations
        Withdrawal from border areas
    Hot lines; crisis centers
    Announcing missile tests in advance
    Agreeing to prevent airspace violations by military aircraft
    Agreeing to exchange lists of nuclear facilities to be immune from bombing
    Military-to-military talks and exchange visits
    Token reductions of military forces
    Making military budgets public
    Undertaking joint military exercises
    Agreeing to talks on verified disposal of nuclear wastes
Accepting limited IAEA inspections
Agreeing to some limits on arms production and purchases
Pledging to accede to the Chemical Weapons Convention

Major Measures Applicable When Fundamental Security Issues
Are Under Negotiation

Agreeing to comply with Article 1 of NPT—no transfer of nuclear devices
If not a member, joining the NPT as a nuclear state and accepting IAEA
    Safeguards

Table 2 (continued)
Arms Control Measures Relevant to New Nuclear States

*Major Measures Applicable When Fundamental Security Issues
Are Under Negotiation (continued)*

If an NPT member, negotiating conditions for returning to member-in-good-standing status
Pledging no-first-use of nuclear weapons
If not a member, joining the Limited Test Ban Treaty
Pledging support for a Comprehensive Test Ban Treaty
Negotiating reductions in conventional forces
Negotiating limits on arms production and purchase
Beginning multinational talks on eliminating weapons of mass destruction
Supporting negotiations for a nuclear weapons free zone
Joining the Missile Technology Control Regime
Joining the London Nuclear Suppliers Group
Beginning regional negotiations on nuclear materials production cutoff

Table 3
Appropriate U.S. Arms Control Policy Options
for Dealing With New Nuclear States

Promoting reforms that make the IAEA more effective
Fully supporting IAEA funding
Promoting the use of the Open Skies Treaty to improve monitoring of developments in nuclear states
Supporting upgrading U.S. intelligence and information sharing on new nuclear states
Proposing rewards for important information on nuclear developments in new nuclear states
Supporting the revision of export controls to focus more effectively on nuclear weapons–related items
Agreeing to a Comprehensive Test Ban
Supporting a treaty that would pledge no-first-use
Urging new nuclear states to join a no-first-use pledge
Taking steps to induce new nuclear states to undertake nuclear restrictions
   Share satellite data
   Provide technical help to improve safety of nuclear weapons
   Provide security guarantees in critically important cases
   Support border agreements
   Provide help with nuclear power industry
Supporting the extension of the NPT in 1995
   Plan to propose changes that would enhance its effectiveness
Supporting the permanent members of the UN Security Council in their efforts to restrict arms trade
Supporting further aid to republics of the former Soviet Union to accelerate their destruction of nuclear weapons and the guarding of fissile materials

Notes

1. Paul L. Leventhal, "Plugging the Leaks in Nuclear Export Controls: Why Bother?" *Orbis*, vol. 36, no. 2 (Spring 1992), pp. 167–80.
2. In December 1991 the IAEA reported that $40 million in contributions were outstanding and that it expected a $25 million shortfall in 1991 and 1992. *The Arms Control Reporter, 1992* (Cambridge, Mass.: Institute for Defense and Disarmament Studies, 1992), p. 602.B.217.
3. Secretary of Defense Les Aspin had become a proponent while a member of Congress. See Les Aspin, "Three Propositions for a New Era Nuclear Policy," (MIT Commencement Address June 1, 1992); and Donna Cassata, "House Adds a Test Ban to Its Military Budget," *Boston Globe*, June 5, 1992, p. 3.
4. Steve Fetter, "Stockpile Confidence Under a Nuclear Test Ban," *International Security*, vol. 12, no. 3 (Winter 1987–88), pp. 132–67.
5. Leventhal, "Plugging the Leaks," p. 176.
6. Ibid., p. 178.
7. Lawrence Scheinman and David Fischer, "Managing the Coming Glut of Nuclear Weapons Materials," *Arms Control Today*, vol. 22, no. 2 (March 1992), pp. 7–12.
8. Leonard S. Spector, *Nuclear Ambitions* (Boulder, Colo.: Westview Press, 1990), pp. 269–81.
9. Ibid., pp. 223–63.
10. Seymour M. Hersh, *The Samson Option: Israel's Nuclear Arsenal and American Foreign Policy* (New York: Random House, 1991).
11. See Geoffrey Kemp, with the assistance of Shelley A. Stahl, *The Control of the Middle East Arms Race* (Washington, D.C.: Carnegie Endowment for International Peace, 1991), pp. 151–69.
12. In October 1991, Defense Minister Ahrens said, "The Middle East is marching toward a nuclear weapons era. This is the reality and we will have to live in and prepare for [it]." Ezer Weizman joined him in saying, "The next war will not be conventional. The nuclear issue is gaining momentum." *The Arms Control Reporter, 1991* (Cambridge, Mass.: Institute for Defense and Disarmament Studies, 1991), p. 453.B.124.
13. Sanjoy Hazarika, "India Successfully Tests a Medium-Range Missile," *New York Times*, May 31, 1992, p. 11.
14. *Arms Control Reporter, 1992*, pp. 454.B.150–51.
15. See Brahma Chellaney, "South Asia's Passage to Nuclear Power," *International Security*, vol. 16, no. 1 (Summer 1991), pp. 43–72.
16. *Arms Control Reporter, 1992*, p. 454.B.149.
17. Sheryl WuDunn, "North Korean Site Has A-Bomb Hints," *New York Times*, May 17, 1992, p. 1. For a critical view of IAEA Director General Hans Blix's assessment, see Gary Milhollin, "North Korea's Bomb," *New York Times*, June 4, 1992, p. A23.
18. Iran's deputy president was quoted in October 1991 as saying that "if Israel has nuclear capabilities, so should the Muslims. . . . This is feasible." "Mohajerani Discusses Islamic Nuclear Programs," *Abrar* (Teheran), October 23, 1991, pp. 1, 4, reprinted in *Foreign Broadcast Information Service Daily Report, Near East & South Asia*, November 5, 1991, pp. 73–76.

CHAPTER FOUR

Diplomatic Measures

JOSEPH S. NYE, JR.

Talk may be cheap, even when it comes to nonproliferation, but an effective policy to slow the spread of nuclear weapons can be costly in terms of the diplomatic frictions that may result. This is true especially when deterrence has failed and proliferation has occurred: what diplomatic cost should we pay for punishment, containment, or reversal? Are these objectives feasible? If so, are there diplomatic instruments with which to pursue them?

Nonproliferation is only one of the objectives of American foreign policy and must always be weighed against other objectives, such as regional security or human rights. The art of foreign policy is to obtain as much value as possible on as many objectives as possible in a given set of circumstances. For nonproliferation, like human rights or any other policy that rests on universalistic claims, trade-offs are particularly corrosive because they give rise to charges of hypocrisy. But diplomacy necessarily involves compromise. There are no easy answers to the compromise/hypocrisy dilemma. Nonetheless, there are both bilateral and multilateral diplomatic options that the United States can pursue once proliferation has occurred.

A BRIEF HISTORY OF PROLIFERATION

The United States already has experience in coping with proliferation. Five countries were grandfathered by the Nonproliferation Treaty (NPT) after it was signed in 1968. States that subsequently pursued nuclear weapons could be subject to sanctious, yet a cynic might also note that Israel, the first country to break the NPT monopoly, received more American military and economic aid than any other country in the world. Until 1990 and the end of the Cold War, Pakistan benefited from American military and economic aid as long as the United States gave a higher priority to defeating the Soviet Union in Afghanistan than to nonproliferation. India, which set off a so-called "peaceful" nuclear explosion in 1974, also continued to receive modest amounts of American aid. Of the four post-NPT proliferators, only South Africa was subjected to severe sanctions, and those were imposed largely because of its racial policies rather than its nuclear program. The United States did curtail nuclear assistance to all four countries, however, and three of the four suffered some constraints on the import of high technology dual-use products.

If history is any guide, American postproliferation policy will continue to be inconsistent. On the other hand, there are reasons to hope for stronger responses in the future: the end of the Cold War has reduced one of the main factors undermining an effective nonproliferation policy, and the collapse of the Soviet Union has heightened concern about the spread of nuclear technology. In addition, the scale of Iraq's covert nuclear program has added to U.S. concerns, and many of the would-be proliferators, such as Iraq and North Korea, are not regarded as friends. There is good reason to believe that nonproliferation may receive a higher priority in American diplomacy in the coming decade. But the dilemma still remains. What should we do if we fail to deter a country from developing nuclear weapons? Can our postproliferation diplomacy be consistent with our nonproliferation policy?

DIPLOMATIC OBJECTIVES

If the spread of nuclear weapons would produce stable deterrence and dampen regional conflicts, then nonproliferation policy would deserve only a low priority[1] and diplomatic compromises before or after proliferation would not be very costly. But there are several reasons to doubt that proliferation would have positive consequences. First, the nuclear stability that characterized the superpower relationship during the Cold War may not be replicable in many settings. Statistics show more conflicts, compared to the East–West arena of the Cold War, and a much higher incidence of governmental breakdown through military coups and civil wars in many of the regions where nuclear weapons might spread. Second, new nuclear weapons states might not be able to build enough survivable weapons to be confident of assured second-strike capability, and thus might increase the risk of preemptive attack against or by frightened neighbors. Third, few of the new nuclear powers could develop the elaborate system of command and control, special safety devices, and satellite verification that reduced the risk of accidental nuclear war between the superpowers. There may be some regional situations where conditions for stable nuclear deterrence would exist, but mainly the risk of nuclear instability would be very high. The concern behind nonproliferation policy is that as more countries develop nuclear weapons, the probability of their use increases, as well as the probability of their leakage into unauthorized hands or to terrorist groups.

Some analysts doubt the feasibility of nonproliferation policy. William Pfaff, for example, argues that "nuclear proliferation is a problem with no solution. It is too late now to stop it. By licit means or illicit, there are going to be more nuclear weapons states. Those of us who already live in well-armed states will have to make the best of it."[2] If this is true, we should worry less that postproliferation compromises might damage nonproliferation policy. But the view that the horse is out of the barn does disservice to clear thinking about postproliferation policy objectives.

To develop that metaphor, it matters how many horses are out of the barn and, once out, the speed at which they run. If the policy objective is to prevent any spread of technology, then surely the situation is hopeless. But if the policy objective is to slow the rate of spread so as to manage its destabilizing effects, then not only is the policy far from hopeless, but there have been a number of successes. More than forty countries have the capability to produce nuclear weapons, but fewer than a quarter of them have done so. This is a sharp contrast to President John F. Kennedy's 1963 prediction that there would be fifteen to twenty-five nuclear weapons states in the 1970s.[3]

One of the key questions for diplomacy is whether there should be continuity or discontinuity in policy objectives after proliferation has occurred. That is, should postproliferation diplomacy seek to preserve the nonproliferation regime, or rather to make radical adjustments to a changed world? The answer depends on the rate of proliferation and the number of nuclear weapons states. In a multiproliferated world, the existing regime and its restraints would clearly have failed, and a radically new set of diplomatic objectives might be appropriate. Over the coming decade, however, it seems more plausible to assume that the number of nuclear weapons states might increase from the current eight or nine to perhaps ten to twelve. This is not so significantly different a world that a wholesale revision of policy is called for. Thus, for the rest of this century, at least, continuity between nonproliferation and postproliferation policy is appropriate. Unless there is a major breakdown (such as a score of states building nuclear weapons), one of the major diplomatic objectives of managing proliferation in any particular case should be to contain the damage to the overall nonproliferation regime. In other words, our postproliferation response in a particular case must not undercut our general nonproliferation policy.[4]

Political scientists use the concept of "regime" to refer to the set of rules and norms and institutions that govern an international issue.[5] Like other aspects of international law, the basic norm in the nonproliferation regime restricts the *a priori* assumption that in a world of sovereign states any measure of self-defense is legitimate. The nonproliferation regime is centered in the NPT, but also includes institutions such as the International Atomic Energy Agency (IAEA) and regional arrangements such as the Latin American Nuclear Weapons Free Zone (the Treaty of Tlatelolco). Regimes affect both the domestic and international incentives of states. When proliferation is stigmatized as illegitimate, domestic groups and bureaucracies have more difficulty initiating a nuclear program. International treaty obligations make a nuclear program more costly to a state that violates its undertakings, and provide a basis for others to impose sanctions. Although the trade-offs may differ, the general policy objective for postproliferation diplomacy is the same as for preproliferation diplomacy: to slow, halt in place (or, in some cases, roll back) the rate of spread so as to manage the destabilizing political effects that might lead to violent conflict and nuclear use.

SPECIFIC OBJECTIVES

Within the context of this overall diplomatic framework, American diplomacy should pursue five specific objectives with regard to new nuclear states: 1) slow vertical proliferation; 2) no deployment; 3) no use; 4) no transfer; and 5) no leakage. In some cases, it may be appropriate to add a sixth objective: reversal. A possible seventh objective, keeping proliferation covert, is of more debatable usefulness.

Slowing Vertical Proliferation

The United States has an interest in keeping the arsenals of new proliferators limited. Large crude weapons are harder to deliver over long distances by conventional or unconventional means. Moreover, fewer weapons means fewer can be lost, stolen, or used, and allows for a greater prospect of reversal by diplomatic or military means. Furthermore, proliferation is more like descending a staircase than falling off of a cliff. While a reputed bomb or a crude explosion is a clear signal of major movement down the staircase, in terms of the international nonproliferation regime, there are, even after development or testing of a nuclear weapon, a number of significant steps before a country has a modern arsenal deliverable by conventional means. By using tritium to boost the yield of fission devices or by developing thermonuclear weapons, countries can reduce the size of their weapons and thereby increase their deliverability.

Proliferators can have a fair degree of confidence in their ability to explode a fission device without testing, but there is greater uncertainty about the success or yield of a fusion device. Thus diplomatic fictions (such as denial of possession) that inhibit testing, as well as formal test bans, may retard development of advanced nuclear devices and slow the march down the nuclear staircase, even after a weapons capability has been achieved. Since vertical (i.e., the deepening of a country's program) proliferation includes increasing the numbers of weapons, controls on the production of fissile materials can be useful even after a country develops an initial weapons capability.

Ballistic missile delivery systems can also be considered part of vertical proliferation. Of the potential delivery systems, missiles are more difficult to defend against and leave less time for diplomacy to work. Moreover, long-range missiles add to the vulnerability of the United States to threats from new proliferators. According to former CIA director William Webster, some fifteen countries may have the ability to produce ballistic missiles by the end of the century.[6] The majority of these countries, however, are still highly dependent upon external technology and only two—Israel and India—have significant programs to develop ballistic missiles with ranges beyond 1,000 kilometers.[7] (The Missile Technology Control Regime [MTCR] restrains the export of technologies for missiles with ranges beyond 300 kilometers, and thus limits the development of intercontinental capabilities by new proliferators.)

No Deployment

A second diplomatic objective is to discourage deployment of new nuclear weapons. One of the major dangers of nuclear proliferation in states with political instability and inadequate technological devices is loss of governmental control. While it is true that small and centralized arsenals may be more preemptable, there is still much to be said for centralization. The risk of preemption must be weighed against the more likely risk of losing control of weapons dispersed to the services or field commanders. Moreover, overtly deployed weapons may spur neighbors and adversaries to cross the nuclear threshold, further weakening the nonproliferation regime, and creating incentives for a regional nuclear arms race. From the American perspective, bombs in the basement of a small, weak state are better than bombs spread all over its front lines.

No Use

A third objective is to discourage the use of nuclear weapons. Nuclear weapons have not been used since 1945, and with time the taboo against their use has become stronger. The nonuse of nuclear weapons by the United States, Britain, and the Soviet Union in regional wars was important. In the Cold War, Soviet conventional superiority in Europe caused NATO to shy away from a doctrine of no-first-use of nuclear weapons, but since the collapse of Soviet power, NATO has been moving closer to a no-first-use posture. Whether in a multilateral or unilateral context, urging this position upon any new proliferator would have fewer costs for American diplomacy than was true in the past.

No Transfer

The fourth specific diplomatic objective is to discourage the transfer of nuclear weapons technology by a new nuclear weapons state. History is not encouraging in this respect. A French diplomat once observed privately that every country spreads the disease once before vowing celibacy: the United States to Britain; the Soviet Union to China; France to Israel; China to Pakistan; Israel to South Africa.[8] Most nuclear states learn the danger of proliferation too late. A major diplomatic objective with regard to a new nuclear weapons state should be to speed up its learning on how to provide disincentives for transferring nuclear technology.

No Leakage

One might assume that to the extent that new proliferators are rational, deterrence should work. It seems, for example, that Saddam Hussein was rational enough not to place chemical warheads on Scuds during the 1991 Gulf War.[9] But if nuclear weapons leak into terrorist hands, the threat to the United States increases. The logic of deterrence fails when there is no return address. Nuclear weapons can be smuggled into American cities via ships or air freight. Thus a major American objective must be to make sure that new proliferators have both incentives and capabilities to prevent leakage of weapons, materials, and technologies into unauthorized hands, whether they be other aspiring weapons states or terrorist groups.

Reversal

It is sometimes assumed that once proliferation has occurred, reversal is impossible. That is not necessarily the case. South Africa found it useful in 1991 to formally renounce the nuclear weapons option and sign the NPT, and it appears likely that Belarus, Kazakhstan, and perhaps Ukraine, will adhere to the Nonproliferation Treaty and give up the nuclear arsenals they "inherited" upon the disintegration of the Soviet Union.[10] Implementation of IAEA safeguards in some instances presents a thorny technical problem because of the difficulties in accounting for the previously produced stockpile of fissile materials, but the overall diplomatic gains seem worth the difficulties. By adroit and rapid diplomacy, the United States may be able to persuade new nuclear states to relinquish their status as nuclear weapons states.[11]

Covert vs. Open Programs

Should it also be an American diplomatic objective to encourage new nuclear weapons programs to remain covert? The diplomatic fiction of being a nonweapons state makes it more difficult for a new nuclear country to deploy them in war-fighting positions. This, in turn, may make it more likely that the weapons will be kept under tight central control. In India, for example, even the brief period during which weapons are assembled may add to stability in a time of crisis, as well as to greater protection against loss or theft. On the other hand, when nuclear weapons programs are secret, countries have less incentive to state a formal nuclear doctrine that makes clear what kinds of events, military or otherwise, might provoke their use. General K. Sunderji, India's retired chief of army staff, argues that "lack of doctrine is a very dangerous thing. The Indian High Command must think through that they should not go past a certain threshold, but they cannot be sure what Pakistan thinks the threshold is. One must go with impressions and guesses."[12] In short, covertness inhibits deployment and war-fighting doctrines, but it may also inhibit nuclear learning.

Israel has long had a declaratory policy of not being the first state to introduce nuclear weapons to the Middle East. Such a policy is justified as not inflaming Arab passions and not irritating the United States. The United States has a long tradition of accepting Israel's declaratory policy and turning a blind eye to the Israeli arsenal.[13] For example, in June 1991, Defense Secretary Dick Cheney said, "I don't know that Israel has any nuclear capability; they have certainly never announced it."[14] Yet Israel has been widely known to have an arsenal of a hundred or more nuclear warheads, certainly since a nuclear technician, Mordecai Vanunu, disclosed the critical information to a London newspaper in 1986. Geoffrey Kemp argues that "the best way to address the Israeli nuclear weapons program is to engage in a more open discussion of its existence and seek ways to limit its further growth, without, at this time, calling for its elimination. . . . [I]f Washington expects the Arab states to participate in arms control talks . . . such as a chemical weapons ban and a freeze on surface-to-surface missiles, the Arab states must be able to show that a sincere effort is under way to limit Israel's nuclear program."[15]

In short, there are pros and cons to U.S. collusion in covert nuclear programs. Since these pros and cons are likely to be closely balanced and to vary in different regions, the diplomatic objective will have to be established on a case-by-case basis.

BILATERAL DIPLOMATIC INSTRUMENTS

If these are the specific objectives that the United States wants to pursue in relation to new nuclear weapons states, what are the diplomatic instruments that can be used to achieve them? Among the most important are security guarantees, diplomatic realignment, technical assistance, sanctions, declaratory policy, and transgovernmental persuasion.

Security Guarantees

Bilateral security guarantees or alliances are important for preventing proliferation and remain important afterwards. Since states are often driven to acquire nuclear weapons by fear of their neighbors, they may be dissuaded from doing so by the reassurance offered through alliance or security guarantees. In return, the United States could require the new weapons state to slow its vertical proliferation and require it not to deploy, use, or transfer nuclear weapons. In some cases, the price of the guarantee might even be reversal, or relinquishment of nuclear weapons.

Except in the case of reversal, however, security guarantees would have a cost in terms of the overall objective of not damaging the nonproliferation regime. It might look as though the surest way to gain an American security guarantee would be to develop a nuclear weapons capability. In some cases, even a security guarantee might not provide sufficient leverage to overcome a deep-rooted sense of isolation and insecurity—for example, in Israel's position as a small, isolated state in a region with hostile neighbors. Furthermore, in South Asia, where acquisition of nuclear weapons is popular in domestic politics, American security guarantees would probably not be sufficiently credible or acceptable to lead to reversal.

Realignment

Another variant of the security guarantee could be called "help the neighbor." If a state develops a nuclear weapon, the United States could offer a bilateral security guarantee to neighboring countries to prevent them from following suit. Not only would such an approach break the chain of regional proliferation, but American realignment, where credible, would also punish the proliferator and reinforce the overall nonproliferation regime. In short, security guarantees to the neighbors might be more beneficial than security guarantees to the new proliferator.

Realignment, however compelling in the abstract, may run afoul of other diplomatic objectives. For example, what if the proliferator is close to the United States, while its neighbors have traditionally been hostile? Moreover, if a region is not a high priority to the United States, it may be impossible to extend a credible security guarantee. For example, the United States has been loath to offer Ukraine a security guarantee that might embroil the United

States in future conflicts between Ukraine and Russia, such as could happen in their dispute over Crimea. Finally, credibility may be a problem for any security guarantees if overall American diplomacy turns inward in the post–Cold War era.

Technical Assistance

Another bilateral diplomatic instrument is technical assistance (see chapter 5 by Steven E. Miller). New nuclear states will often need help in enhancing the safety and invulnerability of their new weapon. The United States might offer technical assistance for its own sake, that is, to provide local capabilities for improved control over nuclear weapons so that there would be no leakage into unauthorized hands. The United States might also offer technical assistance as an incentive to slow vertical proliferation, avoid deployments, and promise no use and no transfer.

In the 1950s, the United States provided technical assistance to Britain's nuclear weapons program, and, covertly, to France in the 1960s and 1970s.[16] Any leverage thus gained, however, seems to have been used for Cold War security objectives and to help France forgo atmospheric nuclear testing, rather than for nonproliferation policy per se.

Sanctions

Sanctions are an obvious bilateral diplomatic instrument. The United States could punish a new nuclear weapons state in a variety of ways, such as curtailing aid, blocking loans from the international financial institutions, restricting imports and travel to the United States, and through political actions ranging from covert operations to negative votes in international organizations. Sanctions could also be applied in response to deployment, transfer, or refusal to adopt a no-first-use policy.

Sanctions, however, are often a two-edged sword, hurting the sanctioning state as well as the sanctioned one. If the United States has diplomatic objectives other than proliferation, it may be reluctant to impose sanctions, as it was with Israel and Pakistan. Sanctions that are limited to a specific area or are tied to the nuclear program may be easier to apply. For example, the United States cut nuclear assistance to India, Israel, Pakistan, and South Africa. Similarly, sanctions would be easier to apply against hostile states like Libya and Iraq. As Michael Nacht has pointed out, the diplomatic costs will differ with four types of proliferators: major allies such as Japan and Germany; regional allies such as South Korea; states that are not formal allies such as Brazil; and adversaries such as Libya.[17]

Bilateral sanctions may not be effective in many cases in which there are alternative sources of supply or finance. In those instances only multilateral sanctions might work, and they in turn would depend upon other countries seeing the situation in the same way the United States does.

Even when the United States does not have an immediate overriding competing diplomatic objective in relation to a new proliferating country, it might have one in the future. In a sense, international politics is like a hockey game and sanctions are like putting a player in the penalty box. Everyone knows that the game will go on and eventually the punished player will reappear. Sanctions are of limited utility, but if they are used sparingly and effectively, they may help to preserve some of the rules of the game of nonproliferation and postproliferation (no use, no deployment, no transfer, no leakage) that the United States wants to encourage.

Declarations and Demarches

Declaratory policy can also play a significant role as a bilateral diplomatic instrument. What the United States says and how strongly it presses its displeasure can make a difference to a new proliferating state as to how willing it is to make accommodations. American declarations can range from general alarm to specific statements that we will target our own nuclear weapons against the new nuclear state.

Transgovernmental Persuasion

Political scientists use the term "transgovernmental relations" to refer to international contacts between units of governments that may not be under close central control.[18] Military-to-military talks and technical missions are examples of such ties where the United States can use its contacts as a bilateral diplomatic instrument. Since one of the goals of the United States is to educate new nuclear weapons states about the dangers and difficulties of control, encouraging international military education and training missions and allowing visits by military and nuclear energy personnel may be an effective way of speeding the nuclear learning process. On the other hand, more information may be conveyed in transgovernmental relations than the central authorities of either state desire.

MULTILATERAL DIPLOMATIC INSTRUMENTS

In a world where power is becoming more diffuse, multilateral instruments often provide leverage for American diplomacy. Among the most important are security guarantees, sanctions, development of new norms and revision of the regime, a comprehensive test ban, nuclear weapons free zones, and a broader role for the IAEA.

NATO Guarantees

NATO has served as an extremely important multilateral security guarantee, effective in slowing the incentives for the spread of nuclear weapons. In the post–Cold War period, the United States might try to persuade NATO to withdraw its guarantee from any alliance member that developed nuclear weapons, but this might conflict with other diplomatic objectives, including the desire to keep the alliance intact. Another possibility would be to extend NATO's guarantees to the neighbors of any new proliferators in Eastern Europe. If, following the collapse of the Soviet empire and the Warsaw Pact, countries that are capable of developing nuclear weapons chose to do so, a multilateral security guarantee to a threatened neighbor might be of value, though again the situation would probably be caught up in a complicated web of potentially conflicting diplomatic objectives.

UN Guarantees

The United States could also offer multilateral security guarantees through the United Nations. The permanent members of the UN Security Council could pledge to come to the aid of any country that was threatened by a new nuclear neighbor, but there would probably be doubts about its credibility. For example, if implementation of the pledge required coordinated UN action under Chapter 7 of the UN Charter, it would always be subject to veto by one of the five permanent members, thus making it less than totally reliable in the most critical cases.

UN Sanctions

Sanctions can also be imposed as a multilateral diplomatic instrument against proliferation, although they have been effective in only about a third of the cases in which they have been applied.[19] The UN has mandated them in regard to nuclear proliferation in Iraq. The United States might press for a UN Security Council resolution stating that henceforth any attempt to acquire nuclear weapons would be regarded as a threat to international peace under Chapter 7 of the UN Charter, making a proliferation-prone country subject to a range of sanctions, from economic to military.

Ad Hoc Sanctions

If UN-imposed sanctions were prevented by a veto, the United States might turn to smaller multilateral forums, for example the Group of Seven (G7) countries. This, however, might meet some resistance from countries unwilling to see the trade-oriented G7 further extend its reach into security problems. Another possibility would be to develop the London Nuclear Suppliers Group provisions on sanctions. Under Article 14 of the London guidelines, suppliers promise not to undercut sanctions taken by other member countries. This might be recast as a more positive pledge to impose sanctions on nuclear proliferating countries that have violated their treaty obligations. Yet another possibility would be to set up an ad hoc group of countries that would pledge to impose sanctions against a new nuclear weapons state that did not reverse its weapons program or, more modestly, that did not adhere to the widely shared objectives of no deployment, no use, and no transfer.

New Norms

Multilateral diplomacy could also pave the way for developing new norms against the acquisition of nuclear weapons, as well as for establishing standards of behavior for weapons states. UN resolutions could promote an attitude of illegitimacy about the spread of weapons of mass destruction so that ambiguous situations could be interpreted as threats to the peace or acts of aggression. Military efforts to reverse such efforts while arsenals are small are more likely to be effective (see chapter 7 by Philip Zelikow). If the presumption of legitimacy is strongly against the proliferator, preemptive actions might become more acceptable under Article 51 of the UN Charter which permits acts of self-defense. In addition, UN resolutions could help to promote norms against transfer, use, and testing that might eventually be applied to all nuclear weapons states.

NPT Revision

Another possible multilateral diplomatic instrument would be a revision of the Nonproliferation Treaty. In 1995, the NPT must be extended by a majority of its member states for a duration to be determined at the review conference. The treaty could be revised to recognize Israel, India, and Pakistan as weapons states, along with the five that were recognized in 1968. The benefit would be that the new nuclear weapons states would have to adhere openly to the provisions and obligations imposed by the treaty. Additional pledges (e.g., no-first-use and limited technical assistance to prevent leakage) might be written into the document. By starting the clock anew, the nuclear weapons states might escape from charges of hypocrisy about their blind eyes to covert proliferators.[20] The cost, however, would be to appear to create an incentive for others, on the presumption that the treaty would be open for membership to new nuclear weapons states in the future. The membership approach might work in South Asia where India and Pakistan both have nuclear weapons, but it might raise new problems in the Middle East. Would Arab states, for example, insist on equal status with Israel? Deputizing the outlaw has costs as well as benefits.

Instead of revising the NPT, a special protocol might be negotiated that would pledge states to declarations of no deployment, no use, no transfer, and no nuclear testing. It could be opened for all states to sign, whether full members of the NPT or not. It would be akin to offering associate status in the NPT as a multilateral means of promoting the specific objectives relating to new nuclear weapons states. But such a protocol would have many of the same regional problems as a revision of the treaty. A two-tiered system with a distinct regime for new nuclear states might be more appropriate for a multiproliferated world, should that occur. But if the rate of proliferation remains low, the costs of a distinct regime would probably be too high in terms of the adverse effects on the NPT. It might weaken its deterrent effect by showing that defiance can lead to a privileged status.

Comprehensive Test Bans

The Comprehensive Test Ban (CTB) is a specific arms control measure (see chapter 3 by Paul Doty and Steven Flank) that deserves mention here because it has taken on a larger diplomatic significance. The CTB has been a prominent demand of the non-nuclear weapons states at prior NPT review conferences but has been resisted, especially by the United States. During the Cold War, the United States worried about its ability to develop new nuclear weapons as well as its ability to test existing ones.[21] The issue was always whether a CTB would provide sufficient evidence of the nuclear weapons state's compliance with Article 6 of the NPT (pledging steps toward nuclear disarmament) that it would persuade other countries not to develop nuclear weapons.

Skeptics have pointed out that countries like Pakistan and Israel would have developed their own nuclear weapons regardless of whether the United States signed and adhered to a CTB or not. But apart from the prevention aspect, there is a postproliferation dimension of the CTB which may be even more important. Since a major objective at that point is to slow vertical proliferation, a formal test ban that retarded development of advanced nuclear devices and slowed the march down the nuclear staircase would take on additional value. The costs, on the other hand, would be a slightly diminished confidence in the reliability of the American nuclear arsenal and forgoing certain developments that might enhance the safety of existing nuclear weapons. Many analysts think, with the Cold War ended, that the balance now favors a CTB. Further proliferation might reinforce that view.

Nuclear Free Zones

Nuclear weapons free zones (see chapter 3 by Doty and Flank) are generally considered instruments of prevention, but they could also be relevant to reversal. In the case of Latin America, the Treaty of Tlatelolco has provided a useful supplement to the NPT regime. Not only does it include Brazil and Argentina, two states that have been reluctant to sign the NPT because of what they regard as its discriminatory nature, but it also provides a path for them to step back from their incipient nuclear arms race by agreeing to regional inspections. It could also provide a diplomatic framework for reversal if another Latin government was to develop a weapon.

In the Middle East, the Arabs and Israel have both proposed the idea of a nuclear free zone. Since Israel already has nuclear weapons, this device is less an arms control measure than a diplomatic one, but certainly useful for beginning discussions. A nuclear weapons free zone in the Middle East might proceed by stages. In the first stage, it might take the form of a regional test ban zone, a barrier which would be easily verifiable. A later stage might stop the production of fissile material, depending on progress in the larger peace talks. And if the peace talks produce a period of stable peace, eventually there might be denuclearization. In any case, prospects for a nuclear weapons free zone in the Middle East are more related to progress in regional diplomacy than to narrow arms control objectives per se.[22]

Expanded IAEA Inspections

A final multilateral diplomatic instrument is the International Atomic Energy Agency (IAEA). Heretofore, the IAEA has primarily had a preventive role as its inspectors visit declared nuclear facilities to confirm that they are being used for peaceful purposes. But the IAEA could be extended into postproliferation policy. For example, if the United States was to persuade a new nuclear weapons state to cut off the production of fissile material and to store its accumulated special nuclear materials rather than developing them into weapons, the IAEA could monitor the cutoff and inspect the plutonium storage facilities. Alternatively, such tasks could be assigned to new UN Special Commissions. There is some question about whether the IAEA, a large bureaucracy, could adapt its mission from prevention to management, but the issue deserves discussion.

A variety of existing bilateral and multilateral diplomatic instruments can be brought to bear after proliferation has occurred, and new ones can be invented. For example, one could imagine a group of countries pledging to take any actions necessary to reverse future cases of proliferation. But all instruments must be seen in the context of larger diplomatic objectives. If the next case of proliferation turned out to be an important ally like Japan, it is doubtful that the United States would honor (or wish to be locked into) a binding pledge of sanctions or military action. Even if the next case is North Korea, American actions are likely to be affected by the desires of South Korea (and Japan) to escape retaliation by North Korea for an American armed attack. There are no automatic formulas, no diplomatic equivalent of a silver bullet.

The likelihood of inventing radically new diplomatic instruments and international regimes will also depend in part upon the health of the existing regime. In a multiproliferated world, radical alternatives will be less costly because the NPT regime will clearly have failed. Until that occurs, one of the central problems for postproliferation policy will be to deal with new facts without undercutting existing norms. For the next decade, both postproliferation and preproliferation policy should pursue the same objective of slowing, halting in place, or reversing the rate of spread so as to manage its destabilizing effects. This is a realistic objective which encompasses a number of more specific objectives on which a range of bilateral and multilateral instruments can be brought to bear. Diplomacy alone is not a sufficient postproliferation policy.

Notes

1. Kenneth Waltz, *The Spread of Nuclear Weapons: More May Be Better*, Adelphi Paper No. 171 (London: International Institute for Strategic Studies, 1981).
2. *International Herald Tribune*, January 30, 1992.
3. John F. Kennedy quoted in Glenn T. Seaborg, *Kennedy, Khrushchev, and the Test Ban* (Berkeley: University of California Press, 1981).
4. This case is made well by Thomas W. Graham, "Winning the Non-Proliferation Battle," *Arms Control Today*, vol. 21, no. 7.
5. Joseph S. Nye, Jr., "Maintaining a Non-Proliferation Regime," *International Organization*, vol. 35, no. 1 (Winter 1981).
6. *New York Times*, February 10, 1989.
7. Aaron Karp, "Controlling Ballistic Missile Proliferation," *Survival*, vol. 33, no. 6 (November/December 1991).
8. Bertrand Goldschmidt, personal conversation, 1979.
9. See David Ignatius, "Madman's Bluff: Why Deterrence Still Works," *Washington Post*, May 10, 1992.
10. "Program for Promoting Nuclear Non-Proliferation," *Newsbrief*, no. 15 (Autumn 1991).
11. Kurt Campbell, Ashton B. Carter, Steven E. Miller, and Charles A. Zraket, *Soviet Nuclear Fission: Control of the Nuclear Arsenal in a Disintegrating Soviet Union* (Cambridge, Mass.: Center for Science and International Affairs, 1991). See also Barbara Crossette, "Ex-Soviet States and U.S. in Accord on 1991 Arms Pact," *New York Times*, May 24, 1992.
12. K. Sundarji quoted in S. Coll, "In India and Pakistan, the Nuclear Trigger Still Gleams," *Washington Post*, National Weekly Edition, October 7–13, 1991. See also Avner Cohen and Ben Frankel, "Opaque Nuclear Proliferation," *Journal of Strategic Studies*, vol. 13 (September 1990).
13. Seymour Hersh, *The Samson Option: Israel's Nuclear Arsenal and American Foreign Policy* (New York: Random House, 1991).
14. Richard Cheney quoted in Stephen Rosenfeld, "Time to Talk About Israel's Bomb," *Washington Post*, National Weekly Edition, December 8–14, 1991.
15. Geoffrey Kemp, *The Control of the Middle East Arms Race* (Washington, D.C.: Carnegie Endowment for International Peace, 1991).
16. Richard Ullman, "The Covert French Connection," *Foreign Policy*, no. 75 (Summer 1989).
17. Michael Nacht, "The Future Unlike the Past," *International Organization*, vol. 335, no. 1 (Winter 1981).

18. Robert O. Keohane and Joseph S. Nye, Jr., *Transnational Relations and World Politics* (Cambridge, Mass.: Harvard University Press, 1970).
19. Gary Hufbauer, Jeffrey Schott, and Kimberly Elliott, *Economic Sanctions Reconsidered* (Washington, D.C.: International Institute for Economics, 1985).
20. Ambassador Robert F. Goheen has suggested such an approach. See "Letter to the Editor," *New York Times*, May 18, 1992.
21. Steve Fetter, "Stockpile Confidence Under a Nuclear Test Ban," *International Security*, vol. 12, no. 3 (Winter 1987–88).
22. United Nations General Assembly, "Establishment of a Nuclear-Weapons-Free-Zone in the Region of the Middle East" (New York: United Nations, October 1990), Document A/45/435.

CHAPTER FIVE

Assistance to Newly Proliferating Nations

STEVEN E. MILLER

T he full range of American policy responses to nuclear proliferation includes the option of providing assistance to the nuclear
weapons programs of newly emerged nuclear powers. This option is
not merely hypothetical, but one that the United States has already
exercised with Britain, France, and most recently the newly independent republics of the former Soviet Union. While there has been
considerable analysis of specific nuclear relationships (particularly on
the Anglo–American connection),[1] there is little general analysis of
this policy option.[2]

This chapter examines the advantages and disadvantages of
nuclear assistance, the various constraints on the ability of the
United States to provide it, the kinds of assistance that the United
States might be willing to extend, and some of the factors that are
likely to affect the decisions of U.S. policymakers. Assessment of the
nuclear assistance option suggests that it cannot be dismissed out of
hand. Despite the real costs and difficulties associated with it, there
may be cases and conditions in which it is the preferred policy.

WHETHER TO HELP?

Pros

The core logic of the case for providing help is simple: if nuclear proliferation does occur despite U.S. and international efforts to prevent

it, the resulting nuclear capabilities should be made as safe, secure, and stable as possible, to minimize risks of accident, theft, or unauthorized use. Any measures to facilitate stability would reduce the risk of nuclear use as a consequence of traditional preemptive or preventive incentives, thereby minimizing the dangers associated with regional crises or wars.

There is little reason to assume that new nuclear powers will promptly or reliably achieve the desired attributes in their nuclear forces in the absence of outside help. Safety and security may initially be secondary to creating effective weapons and meeting operational military requirements.[3] Thus, for example, UN inspectors found that Iraq had designed a weapon that was quite unsafe and could detonate as a consequence of even minor accidents or mishandlings.[4] Even the United States, which has made major efforts to ensure weapons safety and has resources to devote to this that are well beyond the means of most potential proliferators, has some observers concerned that its own stockpile is not as safe as it could be.[5] Such worries could be more intense in the case of nuclear weapons states that attach lower priority to safety and security and have more limited technical and financial resources to devote to their achievement. Further, organizational and procedural safeguards may be more difficult to put durably in place in societies subject to political and social instability; this could increase the importance of technical safeguards.[6] There are likely to be cases, in short, in which nuclear assistance can help proliferators attain desirable degrees of safety and security in their nuclear programs.

Similarly, regional nuclear instability may arise because new nuclear weapons states could have difficulty achieving levels of survivability in their nuclear forces sufficient to offer credible retaliatory threats. Even the United States has suffered repeated vulnerability crises despite its expensive and complex nuclear capability. The problem would be much more acute for states in possession of only a few weapons and delivery systems, deployed in a small number of locations, with hostile neighbors nearby and conflict a real possibility.[7] Such capabilities could be vulnerable even to conventional attack, particularly if imprudently deployed;[8] assuring survivability in the face of nuclear threats is considerably more difficult. Even Israel, which is regarded as having one of the more substantial nuclear capabilities, lies only ten minutes flying time from hostile air bases, has only a small number of bases of its own, has only limited territory to exploit for dispersal and mobility, and has a nuclear complex that is inevitably heavily concentrated. These circumstances lead most analysts to the conclusion that nuclear stability is unattainable in the Middle East.[9]

Since the United States has invested heavily in the safety, security, and stability of its own nuclear forces, it has relevant technology, procedures, and expertise that could be constructively transferred to new nuclear weapons states. Such transfers could spell the difference between safe and unsafe, or stable and unstable; they could permit reassuring levels of safety, security, and stability to be reached more quickly; or they could enhance the efforts of the recipients in these areas and thereby strengthen confidence that desirable levels had been achieved. What is furthered by such transfers, the argument goes, is the general interest in seeing that the potentially adverse consequences of proliferation are contained as much as possible. These arguments apply to the nuclear programs of hostile as well as friendly states.

A second rationale for providing nuclear assistance is diplomatic: if the proliferating state is an ally or close friend, then a program of nuclear cooperation can be part of a broader framework of defense collaboration. This has been a powerful tendency in U.S. policy, especially in the cases of NATO allies Britain and France.[10] In neither case did the United States initially welcome the nuclear efforts of the ally, but in both cases the desire for good relations and alliance collaboration eventually prevailed. With the end of the Cold War, the inclination to provide nuclear assistance to friends and allies may wane. But in the past, nuclear assistance was regarded as appropriate and useful for friendly states.

A third rationale for providing help to new nuclear programs is the possible benefit of access to and potential influence over the proliferator's program. Efforts to acquire nuclear weapons are usually secret and often leave U.S. policymakers uncertain about the extent and direction of the programs, as illustrated by the murkiness associated with the North Korean, Pakistani, and Indian programs.[11] Nuclear assistance could provide the U.S. government with a better—if not complete—understanding of proliferators' weapons programs. Similarly, it might give the United States influence over programs that would otherwise develop autonomously, perhaps in directions that the United States regards as unfortunate or dangerous. With some input, the United States might be able to steer programs toward more stabilizing deployments or more prudent custodial arrangements, or away from destabilizing, wasteful, or inefficient steps.[12]

Nuclear assistance can also provide the United States with a more general instrument of influence in bilateral relationships. Like any other source of leverage, it can be wielded in a manner that serves other American interests. In return for nuclear assistance to France, for example, the United States received what was regarded as a substantial "payment": the quiet alteration of French policy toward NATO, allowing much more integration of French military capabilities into NATO and U.S. warplans.[13] Programs of nuclear assistance could provide the basis for other bargains with other states.

Finally, nuclear assistance could be an asset in U.S. diplomatic efforts to influence regional affairs, and particularly to resolve or pacify regional tensions and hostilities. In this context, assistance could be regarded as a potential payoff to participants in a regional peace process. Israel, for example, might feel that it needs assurances of nuclear cooperation with the United States if it is to give up occupied territories that it regards as important to its defense; without the territories, it would almost certainly feel more dependent on nuclear weapons as the ultimate guarantors of its security. While Israel's rivals would be unlikely to find this an ideal component of a settlement, if the choice were between Israel with nuclear weapons *and* the territories, or Israel with nuclear weapons but without the territories, the latter might be tempting.

Similarly, Pakistan might be more willing to work out a settlement with India if a nuclear weapons capability undergirded its security position. The United States could contribute to Pakistan's confidence in the adequacy of its nuclear deterrent. Again, this would not please India, but it might be preferable to the alternative of a Pakistani nuclear capability without U.S. involvement. If it were believed that nuclear cooperation with the United States would introduce prudence and stability into the regional nuclear balance, even rivals might be willing to tolerate it. There is no indication that nuclear assistance has actually been proposed in the context of regional peacemaking efforts in the Middle East or South Asia, but this is a context in which the question of nuclear assistance might arise for U.S. policymakers.

There are, in short, arguments for regarding nuclear assistance to proliferators as a serious policy option that can provide visible benefits in terms of U.S. interests. Set against these arguments, however, is an array of potential costs and disadvantages.

Cons

An obvious liability of nuclear help is that it collides with the strong nonproliferation policy that the United States has pursued. Giving assistance to new nuclear powers could appear to reward proliferators, suggesting to others that if they can attain a nuclear weapons capability the United States will cease to lean against them and instead offer tangible support. Indeed, the prospect of help could create an incentive for near-nuclear states to cross the threshold. The potential for undermining the international nonproliferation regime is obvious. The United States has shown itself to be sensitive to this cost. It refused, for example, to transfer even nuclear reactor safety equipment to India because India has not signed the NPT.[14]

Nuclear assistance could also cause diplomatic friction in U.S. relations with those states that felt themselves threatened by the nuclear capability in question. The Soviet Union, for instance, long felt threatened by the British and French nuclear capabilities that were benefiting from nuclear cooperation with the United States; this was a recurrent problem in U.S.–Soviet strategic arms control negotiations. Similarly, U.S. help to a nuclear Taiwan would almost surely cause repercussions in U.S. relations with China. Even more difficult might be cases in which the United States offered nuclear assistance to a state hostile to U.S. friends or allies.[15] While the United States could make the argument that enhancing safety and security of nuclear weapons is in everyone's interest, opponents and neighbors of the proliferator may believe or fear that U.S. help will make the nuclear force in question more affordable, sophisticated, or effective. Alternatively, they could suspect that the nuclear relationship is more extensive than the United States is willing to admit. Clearly, then, nuclear assistance policies are not cost-free in diplomatic terms.

A third argument is that certain kinds of help may remove or complicate preventive or preemptive military options that the United States or its allies might prefer to retain.[16] It is unlikely in individual cases that U.S. policymakers would simultaneously pursue stability assistance and denuclearization via military action. But efforts to help stabilize regional nuclear balances could produce nuclear forces that were more resilient against attack, which would prove problematic if changes in internal or regional politics were to put the military option on the agenda.[17]

A fourth factor that could weigh against the nuclear assistance option is the concern that sharing U.S. technologies or procedures for safety, security, and stability may diminish the safety, security and stability of the U.S. arsenal. However, this is probably more properly regarded as a limitation on the ability to help rather than a general argument against helping, because the United States could refrain from sharing information or transferring technologies that might compromise its own systems or safeguards.[18]

A related point is that some assistance might entail the sharing of information (e.g., weapons design parameters) that the United States prefers not to disclose. Even allies have periodically shown sensitivity about divulging information, as was evidenced by the U.S. refusal to share nuclear information with any other state after World War II, even with Britain.[19] But again the United States would be in a position to decide how much and which information to share, so that this may also be regarded as a limit on the ability to help rather than as an argument against helping.

In sum, there are clear disadvantages to a policy of nuclear assistance. Some of the potential costs, however, can be controlled by U.S. policymakers; others are more problematic. The heart of the case against nuclear help is the risk of undermining the nonproliferation regime, and the potential complications associated with entanglement in the nuclear programs of proliferators.

WHO, HOW MUCH, HOW SECRETLY?

At least three other factors will influence U.S. decisions. First, choices will depend on the identity of the potential recipient. Historically, U.S. reactions to proliferation have been determined by the character of its political and security relationship with the proliferator[20]—is it a friendly or a hostile nation? In the case of close allies, the United States has been willing to involve itself in a rather full nuclear embrace; indeed, it may find it difficult to refuse nuclear help to allies without damaging valued relationships.[21] Assistance to hostile proliferators has been extremely limited, but the fact of hostility has not precluded all nuclear assistance.

Another important distinction is between those polities that are stable and those that are not. While domestic instability increases the likelihood that U.S. help will fall into undesirable hands, it also increases worries about the safety and security of nuclear weapons. For example, the United States has been eager to help authorities in the former Soviet Union take steps to minimize the threat that internal chaos might pose to the nuclear arsenal. But U.S. help to unstable societies will generally be more cautious and more limited than help to stable proliferators. While these are only some of the distinctions that might matter, they suffice to make the point that "whether" will depend on "who."[22]

Second, decisions about whether to help will be strongly influenced by how much help is under consideration. Help can be offered formally or informally, officially or unofficially; it can entail everything from discussion of concepts and philosophy, to limited information or technology transfers, to extensive technology sharing or nuclear collaboration.[23] In the early 1960s, for example, the U.S. government decided that it was desirable that Soviet nuclear weapons be well protected against the possibility of unauthorized use. It therefore made a point of publicizing its own efforts in this regard, drawing attention to permissive action link (PAL) technology that involved the use of coded locks to ensure proper control.[24] It also encouraged private individuals to highlight this issue in their contacts with Soviet counterparts. U.S. scientists communicated the contours of the U.S. program to Soviet scientists at a Pugwash meeting in 1963 and made available an unclassified training tape about the two-man rule for nuclear release.

This "assistance" was indirect, informal, unofficial, unclassified, and involved little transfer of information and no transfer of technology.[25] It involved nothing more than an effort to nudge the Soviet nuclear weapons program in a desirable direction. Given the high level of friction that existed between the two nations at the time, this example suggests the possibility of, but also the substantial limits on, nuclear help to hostile proliferators. This model may be applicable in the future, although mere nudging may be insufficient when dealing with hostile proliferators who lack the resources and expertise of the Soviet nuclear complex, or the essential commitment to stability.

At the other end of the spectrum is the Anglo–American nuclear relationship. Product of a formal agreement between the British and American governments, it has entailed detailed sharing of information about nuclear weapons design and fabrication, cooperation in testing, exchange of weapons components and special nuclear materials, transfer of delivery systems, extensive intelligence cooperation, and even some integrated targeting.[26] A nuclear relationship of this sort is motivated not only by concerns about safety, security, and stability, but perhaps even more by a desire to strengthen the military capabilities of a major ally.

Many cases are likely to fall between the two extremes. Most would involve tangible but circumscribed help to address specific safety, security, or stability concerns. The more modest help options would typically be the easiest to offer, the most likely to be deemed appropriate when dealing with hostile proliferators, and perhaps also the natural starting place for nuclear relationships with friendly proliferators, which might grow more extensive with the passage of time.

Third, decisions about whether to help may be influenced by the prospect of being able to do so covertly. The secrecy option could eliminate or minimize the costs associated with nuclear assistance. Invisible help should not undermine the nonproliferation regime or disturb U.S. relations with neighbors and enemies of the proliferator. Insofar as a policy of covert assistance can be successfully implemented, it would allow the United States to gain the benefits of nuclear assistance without incurring the costs, thus dramatically altering the balance between pros and cons. At least one known precedent suggests that this is plausible: U.S.–French nuclear collaboration was a closely held secret for more than fifteen years.[27] But secrets rarely stay secret forever, and the covert option adds the risk of eventual exposure and scandal to the list of potential disadvantages. If it is assumed that covert assistance will sooner or later be revealed, then secrecy only postpones the costs of assistance rather than eliminating them. There may be cases in which the advantages of stabilizing a situation in the short run are sufficiently high to warrant risking a day of reckoning down the road. But if the eventual cost is the erosion of the global nonproliferation regime, such reasoning may in the end appear to be shortsighted.

In sum, the questions of "whether," "who," "how much," and "how secretly" will be tightly interconnected in U.S. decision-making about nuclear assistance.

CONSTRAINTS ON THE ABILITY TO HELP

The United States does not possess an unfettered ability to provide nuclear assistance. An array of legal, political, and other factors will constrain and shape U.S. nuclear help options.

Laws, Norms, Commitments

Several bodies of domestic legislation bear on the U.S. ability to assist the nuclear weapons programs of new proliferators. Most directly germane is the legislation that governs U.S. nuclear information and assets. The foundation is the Atomic Energy Act of 1946 (the McMahon Act), which established a fundamentally restrictive approach. Responding in part to a belief that the atomic secret was critically important to the United States and in part to a mounting hysteria over nuclear espionage, the McMahon Act prohibited any transfer of nuclear information or materials to any other state on pain of severe penalties.[28] The passage of the McMahon Act contravened several earlier agreements and understandings between the United States and Britain on the subject of nuclear cooperation, much to the dismay of the British government. For more than a decade after its passage, it prevented the development of full-fledged Anglo–American nuclear cooperation. The British, however, conducted a relentless campaign for the restoration of nuclear collaboration,[29] and during the 1950s, Congress passed two amendments to the McMahon Act which permitted the Anglo–American nuclear relationship to reemerge. The first, the Atomic Energy Act of 1954, permitted the United States to transfer to allies information on nuclear weapons effects and about the external characteristics of weapons; it was inspired in part by a desire to facilitate the nuclearization of NATO's defense posture in Europe.[30] The second, in 1958, permitted the transfer of "restricted data" to allies—that is, information about nuclear weapons design and fabrication. This allowed extensive nuclear cooperation, and was followed shortly by the U.S.–UK "Agreement for Cooperation on the Uses of Atomic Energy for Mutual Defense Purposes," which became the basis for the special Anglo–American nuclear relationship.[31]

While the United States can create the domestic legal foundations for nuclear assistance, the legislation of the 1950s was created with NATO in mind and is in a number of particulars explicitly or implicitly specific to the U.S.–UK relationship. It does not necessarily provide the legal basis for nuclear help to regional proliferators, and the transfer of nuclear weapons know-how or technology would probably require congressional authorization. This would not be an insuperable obstacle, but one that could be incompatible with secrecy.

Second, many varieties of help that the United States might provide to the nuclear weapons program of a proliferator (for example, delivery systems, radars, command and control equipment, as well as storage facilities or other types of military construction) might be constrained by existing domestic controls on conventional arms exports.[32] One of the legal grounds for rejecting a proposed conventional arms transfer, for example, is concern that it will contribute to the nuclear program of the recipient. This guideline conflicts with potential arms transfers intended to assist a nuclear program. Further, it provides a basis for bureaucratic and legislative opposition to arms transfers. Both the executive and legislative branches of government are tending toward more restrictive attitudes about anything connected to the spread of unconventional technologies (including chemical and biological as well as nuclear weapons); this tendency was substantially reinforced by the experience of the Gulf War and its aftermath, which revealed the extent of Iraq's nuclear, chemical, and ballistic missile capabilities. Existing legislation confers on Congress a substantial role in U.S. arms transfer decisionmaking, requiring congressional scrutiny and approval of all significant arms transfers. While this role tends to become prominent only in unusual or controversial cases, instances of "arms transfers as nuclear help" are likely to be regarded as unusual and controversial. Likely politicization may render nuclear assistance more difficult to bring about and could be an additional impediment to secrecy.

Third, policies of nuclear help could run afoul of U.S. nonproliferation legislation. The Nuclear Nonproliferation Act of 1978, for example, establishes stringent nonproliferation criteria for all U.S. nuclear exports.[33] This law is clearly intended to govern commerce in nuclear energy technologies rather than nuclear weapons technologies, but the spirit of its guidelines for nuclear exports would be breached by nuclear assistance arrangements. Arguably, nuclear help could be construed as "nuclear exports" and hence illegal; this argument might give members of Congress another political basis for opposing nuclear assistance. How, it will be asked, can the United States insist on the vigorous general application of nonproliferation safeguards when it is providing nuclear help to new proliferators?

To these domestic constraints must be added several international commitments deriving from legal obligations or from U.S. support for international norms and guidelines. The most fundamental of these derive from the adherence of the United States to the Nonproliferation Treaty (NPT) as a nuclear weapons state. Article I of the NPT unambiguously proscribes transfer of nuclear weapons: "Each nuclear-weapon State Party to the Treaty undertakes not to transfer to any recipient whatsoever nuclear weapons or other nuclear explosive devices or control over such weapons and devices directly or indirectly; and not in any way to assist, encourage, or induce any non-nuclear-weapon State to manufacture or otherwise acquire nuclear weapons."[34] Also important in assessing the implications of the NPT for policies of nuclear assistance is Article IX, Paragraph 3 of the Treaty, which defines a nuclear weapon state as "one which has manufactured and exploded a nuclear weapon or other nuclear device prior to January 1, 1967."[35] By this definition, all states except the United States, the Soviet Union, Britain, France, and China are, in the legal framework of the NPT, non-nuclear-weapon states, even if they acquired nuclear weapons subsequent to January 1, 1967. Hence, it is apparent that the passage which enjoins the nuclear weapon states "not in any way to assist . . . any non-nuclear-weapon state to manufacture or otherwise acquire nuclear weapons" would apply to aid to any new proliferator. Consequently, nuclear assistance to post-1967 proliferators involving information about, technologies pertaining to, or testing of nuclear weapons would be not merely a potential threat to the NPT regime but a breach of U.S. obligations under the NPT, even if inspired purely by concerns about safety and security.[36]

Also complicating U.S. nuclear assistance efforts are its commitments under strategic arms control agreements not to circumvent bilateral provisions by transfers to other states. Both the SALT II and START treaties contain noncircumvention restrictions. Article XVI of the START treaty, for example, is sweeping: "To ensure the viability and effectiveness of this Treaty, each party shall not assume any international obligations or undertakings that would conflict with its provisions." It also explicitly provides for consultations in START's Joint Inspection and Compliance Commission "to resolve any ambiguities that may arise in this regard."[37] Further, in the Agreed Statements that accompany the Treaty, both parties agree "not to transfer strategic offensive arms subject to the limitations of the Treaty to third states."[38] This prohibits transfer of intercontinental ballistic missiles (ICBMs), sea-launched ballistic missiles (SLBMs), heavy bombers, and long-range, air-launched cruise missiles (ALCMs), since these capabilities are all subject to limitation in START.

In both SALT and START, the United States sought to shelter its nuclear relationships with Britain and France from these provisions by insisting that treaty obligations would not affect "existing patterns of cooperation."[39] Left unclear, however, was any precise definition of what would constitute a circumvention in the context of other nuclear relationships. U.S. nuclear assistance to regional proliferators around the periphery of the former Soviet Union could be construed as circumvention of START to the extent that the proliferators were friendly to the United States and threatening to the republics of the former USSR. With independent Kazakhstan now a party to the START agreement, for example, it could regard nuclear assistance to Pakistan to be a circumvention of the Treaty; Russia might feel the same about U.S. nuclear help to any number of states, including Germany, Japan, and Ukraine.

An additional source of possible difficulty for U.S. nuclear help options is the weak but evolving regime of voluntary restraint emerging out of the discussions of the five permanent members of the UN Security Council on arms transfer controls.[40] These discussions have produced communiqués in which the states declare themselves against nuclear proliferation and pledge to seek effective nonproliferation measures. More importantly, at their meeting in London in October 1991, the permanent five declared their intention "to observe rules of restraint" and to "act in accordance with" a set of guidelines for conventional arms transfers. These guidelines include several criteria that could prohibit or inhibit certain varieties of nuclear help,[41] particularly agreement not to undertake conventional arms transfers that "contravene . . . other relevant internationally agreed restraints to which they are parties." In addition, the United States is pushing for agreement on disclosure of past sales, advance notification of future sales, and the option of meaningful consultation about them.[42] If these proposals are incorporated into the guidelines, they could preclude secret assistance and permit international consultations on U.S. nuclear help policies.

Another potential source of constraint is U.S. participation in the Missile Technology Control Regime (MTCR).[43] Because the MTCR involves voluntary adherence to nonbinding and not very restrictive guidelines, it is not a strong restraint on U.S. choices. Nevertheless, the main intent of the regime, which the United States strongly supports, is to inhibit the proliferation of nuclear weapons (and other weapons of mass destruction) by limiting access to one very effective means of delivery. Thus, suspicion that missiles would be used as nuclear delivery vehicles by a recipient is grounds for rejecting a proposed missile transfer. Under current guidelines, the MTCR applies only to cruise and ballistic missiles with a range of at least 300 kilometers and a payload of 500 kilograms or more, so many existing missile systems are outside its mandate. But some earlier U.S. nuclear-related missile transfers to allies, such as the sale of Polaris and Trident submarine launched ballistic missiles (SLBMs) to Britain, would not have met MTCR criteria of acceptability. The MTCR would inhibit transfers that the United States might wish to make to enhance the survivability of a proliferator's nuclear force, such as sea- or air-launched cruise missiles. It is hard to see how the United States could make the case for nuclear assistance–related exceptions to the guidelines without undermining the regime.

In short, two legal regimes—domestic legislation on atomic energy and the NPT—place direct limits on the U.S. ability to provide nuclear help. Several other laws, agreements, or guidelines also represent potential complications for nuclear assistance. Since the United States is not only an adherent, but a strong promoter, and in many instances the initiator, of these regimes, it will inevitably be sensitive to the problems and contradictions that can be raised by policies of nuclear help. Only if it were willing to be contumacious could the United States design nuclear assistance programs that ignore these constraints.

Political Constraints

Programs of nuclear help will need support domestically; they will need to be agreeable to the proliferator-recipient; and they will need to be palatable to those states whose interests are affected by the actions of the proliferator.

Domestically, a decision to offer any substantial degree of nuclear assistance will be a major policy issue. Elements within the bureaucracy may strongly oppose specific aspects of a proposed nuclear assistance program (as the U.S. Navy did when the French were interested in help with anti-submarine warfare), or there may be more broadly based resistance. Thus, while Nixon and Kissinger were eager to establish a close nuclear relationship with France in the early 1970s, the Pentagon was more reluctant and often slowed and hindered the implementation of the policy, much to the frustration of the French.[44]

Congress can also play a large, and legally mandated, role in nuclear assistance decisions. Throughout the nuclear era, Congress has maintained a vigorous and influential involvement in issues relating to the civil and military use of the atom.[45] Congress's role in U.S. relations with Pakistan provides a good example. In 1985, prompted by concerns that Pakistan might be developing a nuclear weapons capability, Congress passed the Pressler Amendment, which required the president to certify annually, as a prerequisite to the sale of arms or the provision of aid, that Pakistan did not possess a nuclear explosive device.[46] Presidents Reagan and Bush, desiring to preserve traditionally close relations with Pakistan, repeatedly provided such certification, but with growing difficulty in the face of mounting evidence of Pakistan's nuclear ambitions. In 1991, acting on the wide acknowledgment of Pakistan's progress toward acquisition of nuclear weapons, Congress cut off $570 million dollars of assistance.[47]

Congress acted in opposition to the preferences of the executive branch,[48] demonstrating that decisionmakers cannot assume a free hand in choices about nuclear assistance, even to friendly states. Pakistan had a long record of close ties to the United States, and its strategic importance was high during the 1980s because of Soviet involvement in the war in Afghanistan. Nevertheless, the Pressler Amendment prohibited nuclear help in the case of Pakistan. How could an administration certify the non-nuclear status of Pakistan as a condition for providing assistance to its nuclear program?

But Congress is not consistently negative toward nuclear assistance. In November of 1991, for example, the Senate took the lead in urging nuclear assistance to the former USSR and authorizing money for this purpose.[49] Congress passed the "Soviet Nuclear Threat Reduction Act of 1991" by overwhelming margins and appropriated $400 million to "facilitate on a priority basis the transportation, storage, safeguarding, and destruction of nuclear and other weapons in the Soviet Union . . . and to assist in the prevention of weapons proliferation."[50] While this may be a unique case, the example of nuclear help to the former USSR shows how safety, security, and proliferation worries can produce political will to provide nuclear help.

Even if the United States is prepared to offer help, there is no guarantee that new proliferators will be prepared to accept it. States that are motivated to acquire nuclear weapons partly by considerations of status may be unwilling to accept the appearance (or the reality) of dependence. Thus, in 1963 French president Charles de Gaulle rejected the Kennedy administration's offer of nuclear assistance, proclaiming that France would opt for true independence by building its own nuclear deterrent.[51] Similarly, during World War II, some British decisionmakers opposed moving the atom bomb project to the United States out of fear of becoming dependent on Washington.[52] Moreover, any significant degree of nuclear collaboration requires a high level of trust on the part of the proliferator that its program will not be jeopardized by giving the United States access to information about technical characteristics, facilities, and deployment patterns. It is hard to imagine that North Korea, Iran, or Libya would provide the United States with significant access to or influence over its nuclear weapons program. Thus, with respect to nuclear assistance to hostile states, hesitation and circumspection is likely to exist on both sides, with the United States reluctant to help, and the proliferator reluctant to accept help.

A final political inhibition on U.S. nuclear help options is the probable reaction of regional neighbors of the new proliferator. (Covert assistance obviously would eliminate this complication.) Any state that felt threatened by a proliferator's nuclear capability might protest any American assistance, especially if such assistance would (or was thought to) improve the effectiveness of the proliferator's nuclear forces.[53] If the objecting state is a friend or ally of the United States, it may have considerable capacity to influence U.S. policy by exploiting diplomatic channels, lobbying Congress, and mounting public relations campaigns. Indeed, this dynamic operates even with respect to significant conventional arms transfers.[54] If the experience with conventional arms transfers is any guide, the combination of regional and congressional opposition to a proposed transfer is potentially powerful. Thus, nuclear help policies may have to overcome external as well as internal resistance.

Cultural and Technological Constraints

The United States may not be able to provide help that is suitable for the proliferator, in part because technological levels vary. The most advanced safety devices or designs may not be compatible with the less sophisticated capabilities likely to be characteristic of most new proliferators.

Technology also has a sociological dimension: its characteristics and appropriateness are a function of the political setting in which it must operate, the organizational styles that produce and use it, and the techno-economic context out of which it emerges.[55] This suggests that transplanting a given technology from one social and organizational context to another can be complicated and difficult. Thus, a piece of technology designed specifically for the vast U.S. nuclear arsenal in the half-century-old $10-billion-per-year U.S. nuclear weapons complex may not be adaptable to the Iranian or North Korean or Pakistani nuclear programs. Moreover, strategy has a cultural component.[56] Other states and societies may not see security problems in the same way, prefer the same solutions, or behave the same way as the United States. They may define stability differently, for example, or attach less priority to safety and security, or be more sanguine about nuclear use. Variations in national strategic style may influence a proliferator's receptivity and its capacity to absorb nuclear help.

WHEN TO HELP?

The United States opposes nuclear proliferation and aims to discourage aspiring proliferators; pursuing the nuclear help option will require a reversal of this policy. The timing of this reversal will be one of the basic dilemmas confronting U.S. policymakers. They must decide at what point U.S. policy should cease to oppose a proliferating state and begin instead to assist it.

Several criteria might guide the timing of the U.S. policy reversal,[57] but there will inevitably be a tension between a concern for giving help too early, and for giving it too late.

Not Too Early

A basic fear is that providing help too soon will encourage proliferation. One sensible threshold, therefore, is weaponization. Until a potential proliferator actually has nuclear weapons, the United

States should remain in a nonproliferation posture. Premature assistance may have the counterproductive effect of helping a proliferator cross the line to nuclear weapons status.

Even in cases where an advanced nuclear acquisition effort exists or a nuclear weapons capability has been achieved, the United States will probably prefer that the proliferator's nuclear decision be reversed rather than consolidated. In view of steps taken in recent years by Argentina, Brazil, and South Africa to abandon their nuclear weapons aspirations, and more recently Pakistan's apparent retreat from the brink of weaponization, reversal does not seem an unattainable objective, provided the international community continues to press strongly against proliferation. Hence, the United States ought not to consider the nuclear help option until a nuclear program seems clearly irreversible. Often, however, this will not be an easy judgment to make, especially since many proliferators may deny and hide their programs. Moreover, a nuclear decision could be reversed at any time, even in the case of well-established nuclear programs.[58] Still, the United States will probably not reverse its antiproliferation policy so long as it believes that there is some hope of reversing the proliferator's policy.

This line of reasoning leads to consideration of further indicators of the consolidation of the proliferator's nuclear capability. One such threshold is the operational deployment of weapons, when the proliferator has moved beyond creating or testing an explodable nuclear device to the deployment of usable weapons in operational military units. This threshold could be set at low or high levels of operational capability.

If the fear of helping prematurely predominates, the general rule would be: when in doubt, wait. If this were the only consideration at stake, it would be that simple.

Not Too Late

Set against this analysis, however, is the concern over helping too late. According to this logic, a basic trigger for U.S. consideration of the nuclear help option ought to be evidence of safety, security, and stability risks. These risks are most likely to be associated with new and immature programs. It is at the beginning that a proliferator's nuclear capability is likely to be small, vulnerable, and lacking in technical and procedural safeguards. It is at the beginning also that help may be needed most and may matter most. U.S. policy will need to strike a balance between helping later to avoid being too early and helping early to avoid being too late. There is no clear-cut solution to this dilemma.[59]

Ask and (Maybe) Ye Shall Receive: The Proliferator's Initiative

The timing of U.S. decisions about nuclear assistance may be affected if the proliferators themselves initiate the process by asking for help. Depending on their relationship with the United States, they could do so at any point in the process of nuclear acquisition, whether before or after a weapons capability had been achieved. Britain, for example, insistently pursued nuclear collaboration with the United States throughout its weapons development program. Other U.S. allies may feel it appropriate to seek assistance particularly if changes in the international environment (e.g., nuclear acquisition by neighbors or adversaries, or the appearance of a dire conventional threat) seemed to justify the nuclear quest. In proliferator-initiative scenarios, the United States loses some control over the timing of nuclear help decisions. It retains the right to say no (as it did to Britain between 1946 and 1958), but only at some cost to its relations with the proliferator. Once a proliferator puts the nuclear help issue on the agenda, though, U.S. policymakers will find it necessary to decide whether to help, how much, and when.

HOW TO HELP? AN INVENTORY OF POSSIBLE ASSISTANCE MEASURES

If the United States actually gets to the point of providing nuclear assistance, what sort of help might it provide? Several possible categories exist, reflecting the purposes of addressing safety, security, and stability concerns. In addition, some categories of nuclear assistance may serve to enhance the nuclear capabilities of close allies.[60]

Safety: Preventing Accidents

Nuclear weapons will be moved, handled, maintained, involved in exercises, flown in combat aircraft, loaded and unloaded, or be otherwise exposed to the risk of accident. Hence, it is important that they not be prone to detonate or to disperse nuclear materials if dropped, burned, or crashed. New proliferators should be made aware of the necessity for stringent safety criteria incorporated into design parameters and weapons-handling procedures. U.S. weapons design, for example, has followed the so-called "one point safety" rule, whereby weapon designs are required to meet the test that there is less than one chance in a million that the detonation of the high explosive in the warhead due to fire or other unusual stimulus will result in a nuclear yield exceeding four pounds TNT equivalent. The United States has developed elaborate procedures for, and has vast experience with, the handling of nuclear weapons, and it could offer training in such matters to new proliferators.

In addition, the United States has developed several technological answers to the risk of accident. Environmental sensing devices (ESDs), for example, prevent detonation unless the weapon has already experienced the physical parameters associated with its means of delivery. Thus, a nuclear artillery shell would have to sense the acceleration and velocity associated with being fired out of an artillery tube or its arming mechanisms would not function. The United States has also developed insensitive high explosives whose "unique insensitivity to extreme abnormal environments," including heat, pressure, and shock,[61] greatly reduces the risk of non-nuclear detonation in the event of accident. Further, the United States has emphasized weapons design features that ensure that weapons are disabled in the absence of proper arming signals. The most advanced of these is known as the Enhanced Nuclear Detonation Safety system (ENDS). Weak links, designed to fail in the event of an accident, are incorporated into the electrical arming and fusing mechanisms. Also available are fire resistant pits (FRP), meant to prevent the spread of molten or gaseous fissile material in the event of fire.

Such accident prevention technologies could be transferred to new proliferators. Those having to do with weapons design, however, would probably require close collaboration with the nuclear program of the recipient and are arguably incompatible with the NPT. In addition, advanced safety technologies may be incompatible with the more primitive systems likely to be in the possession of proliferators. U.S. safety procedures and technologies from the 1950s may be more appropriate as solutions to the problem of safety in new nuclear forces. For example, during the 1950s, a basic technique for increasing the safety of U.S. weapons was to store the fissile core separately from the high explosive assembly.[62] Although more advanced weapons designs are safer, this technique may be more appropriate for new proliferators.

Security: Preventing Unauthorized Use

Another chronic fear associated with nuclear weapons is that they will be used in an unauthorized manner or otherwise fall into the wrong hands. This concern may be especially acute if the new proliferators are countries that lack sober leadership or constitutional procedures for the peaceful transfer of power, or are prone to instability, coups d'etat, civil war, ethnic strife, or other internal turbulence. Hence, it is strongly desirable that new nuclear forces be resistant to illicit seizure or use.

There are several ways that the United States might help a proliferator address the security problem. One is to provide permissive action link (PAL) technology, which prevents the use of nuclear weapons unless a code is generated by the proper chain of command. A second approach involves the design and construction of safe storage facilities that provide multiple layers of security, including coded doors and specialized weapons containers. In addition, weapons, facilities, and transporters can be booby-trapped. Weapons, for example, can be fitted with tamper proofing or command disable devices that cripple a weapon not handled according to normal procedures. Facilities can be designed to produce a variety of unpleasant surprises to intruders who fail to follow proper entry procedures. Transporters can be designed to require secret codes, to withstand collision, and to immobilize those who attempt to breach the system. The United States could make such technologies available to other states.[63]

The United States could also provide training and education in physical security and personnel reliability programs, including such procedures as the two-man rule (designed to ensure that no one person can cause a nuclear detonation), to minimize security risks.

Stability: Minimizing Nuclear Vulnerability

Because vulnerable forces invite attack and produce preemptive pressures, the United States has made an enormous investment in survivable forces. The basic options for enhancing force survivability are few and well known: the force can be made larger; it can be made more diverse; it can be dispersed; it can be prepared to escape attack by alert and evacuation measures; or it can be defended, either passively through sheltering or actively through air or missile defenses.

There will be real limits to U.S. willingness to assist in these areas. It is very unlikely that the United States will provide its strategic delivery systems to new proliferators, for example, not least because this would contravene its commitments under START. It will probably not want to help enlarge and diversify regional nuclear forces, lest it encourage regional nuclear arms races. And it would be reluctant to promote the spread of long-range nuclear delivery systems that could pose a threat to its own security.

On the other hand, it is patently undesirable for regional nuclear forces to remain vulnerable to conventional or nuclear attack. The existence of such instabilities in regions marked by high levels of hostility and conflict would greatly increase the dangers of crises and thus the likelihood of nuclear use. Hence, as a general rule, the United States might wish to consider what minimum of nuclear assistance would meaningfully reduce nuclear vulnerabilities in regional settings.

Several considerations figure in such a calculation. First, new proliferators should themselves be strongly motivated to minimize the vulnerability of their nuclear capabilities in order to avoid offering their adversaries a preemptive option. Many steps toward this end—sheltering, dispersal, covert basing, and so on—ought to be within the grasp of determined proliferators and are not likely to require U.S. advice or technology. The United States, therefore, should consider whether or how much help is really necessary when considering stability-enhancing nuclear assistance. Second, if a new proliferator is structuring its force imprudently or recklessly, and thereby permitting force vulnerabilities to exist (as the Soviet Union seems to have done into the 1960s), the United States should weigh in against such policies and encourage the proliferator to decrease its own risks before offering any assistance. The United States should not foster the notion that it will take responsibility for stabilizing regional balances, thus allowing regional nuclear powers to avoid or neglect such responsibility or, worse, creating incentives for proliferators to allow or induce instabilities as a route to U.S. nuclear assistance.

While there may be some cases in which the United States does not need to help, a third consideration has to do with the opposite possibility: that U.S. help cannot make a significant difference in reducing force vulnerability. Some new nuclear powers may face intractable problems: small arsenals in small states may at some level be irreducibly vulnerable to nuclear attack. Hence, the United States ought to consider whether nuclear assistance is adequate to make an appreciable difference to the survivability of a proliferator's force.

Fourth, the United States should be careful that it does not increase the vulnerability of rival states while attempting to reduce the vulnerability of a proliferator. If regional nuclear stability is the goal, then all parties should end up with confidence in the survivability of their deterrent force. This result could be undermined if the United States were to transfer delivery systems for the sake of reducing vulnerability that also provided the recipient with enhanced offensive options. For example, cruise missiles are a logical delivery system for a vulnerable proliferator because they are small and easily hidden, they are relatively affordable and hence can be bought in considerable numbers, and they can be deployed on a number of different platforms, thus multiplying the difficulties for any potential attacker.[64] On the other hand, as a nuclear delivery system, cruise missiles can be hard to detect, difficult to shoot down, accurate, and capable of short-warning attacks in regional settings where distances are usually not great. Thus, while the recipient of such capabilities might feel more secure, its rivals would feel less so, generating destabilizing fears of preemptive and preventive attack. The fact of regional instability would be unchanged.

In sum, the goal of regional nuclear stability does not suggest any straightforward guidance for U.S. nuclear assistance policy. For the reasons described above, it should not be U.S. policy to try to remedy nuclear vulnerabilities wherever it sees them. But neither can it ignore persistent instabilities in regional nuclear balances if it wishes to minimize the likelihood of nuclear use.

Nuclear "Services": Supporting Nuclear Arsenals

There is more to having a meaningful operational nuclear capability than just possessing nuclear weapons and delivery systems. An array of "support services" are required, especially in the areas of testing, command and control, and intelligence. The United States possesses a nuclear command and control and intelligence infrastructure that would be impossible for most new proliferators to replicate. Its capabilities in these areas give rise to two possible varieties of nuclear assistance: first, it could provide proliferators with the advice and technical assistance needed to set up their own nuclear support capabilities; second, it could allow access to some of its own capabilities. Help of either sort would generally take place only in the context of substantial nuclear cooperation, particularly if the help involved access to U.S. intelligence or command and control assets.

In the area of nuclear testing, for example, precedent for U.S. cooperation with other states is found in its partnership with Britain. Indeed, more than half of Britain's forty-four nuclear tests were done jointly with the United States at the Nevada test site.[65] Similarly, the French have been allowed to participate in U.S. tests, have been offered (but refused) the use of the Nevada test site, and received U.S. advice in creating their own underground nuclear test site in the South Pacific.[66] There are at least two potential advantages to providing help in testing. First, it would ensure that testing was safe and environmentally sound, particularly if the alternative to exploiting U.S. underground test facilities was above-ground tests. Second, this could facilitate the development of safer and more secure weapons designs.

Reliable communications are as necessary as reliable nuclear forces if the forces are to be effective and responsive to political control. Vulnerable communications can be as destabilizing as force vulnerabilities if a successful attack against them would render the forces unusable.[67] In the case of Britain and France, just to offer one example, there are hints in public sources that the United States provided help in the area of submarine communications.[68]

The United States also possesses a tremendous intelligence capability for nuclear threat assessment, targeting, and warning. U.S. intelligence information has clearly been shared with Britain and France. Israel has received imagery from the U.S. KH-11 reconnaissance satellites, and there are allegations that this information was used to inform Israeli nuclear targeting.[69] U.S. intelligence can also be used for the verification of regional arms control agreements, an application which is especially important in countries where lack of verification capabilities prevents regional restraint.[70] There are obvious risks associated with sharing intelligence, but it is another form of nuclear assistance that the United States could provide.

Dialogue and Dollars

The most modest form of nuclear assistance involves dialogue on matters of mutual concern. Even with hostile proliferators, it has been possible for the United States to find ways of communicating concerns about safety, security, and survivability. Because the United States has half a century of experience with all aspects of nuclear possession, it has much to impart to new proliferators confronting many of these issues for the first time. There would probably be a tendency in such nuclear consultations to focus on safety, security, and survivability issues. But nuclear consultation could include discussion of the implications of nuclear doctrine and operations, the role of arms control in structuring nuclear balances,[71] and advice on the management of a nuclear arsenal, including guidance on the norms of responsible custodianship and appropriate forms of civil–military relations.[72]

Among the recent illustrations of the wide feasibility and potential value of dialogue are the discussions of nuclear weapons safety and security in U.S.–Chinese military-to-military contacts (before these were interrupted as a consequence of the U.S. reaction to the Tiananmen Square massacre).[73] Even more striking have been the intensive discussions between the United States and authorities in the former Soviet Union,[74] in which near-term concerns over nuclear safety and security, as well as the longer-term issue of fashioning a new nuclear relationship, have been addressed.

The case of the former Soviet Union raises another possible form of "nuclear" assistance. The U.S. Congress has appropriated $400 million to help pay for what the United States regards as sensible steps in coping with the "Soviet" nuclear arsenal. When a scarcity of financial resources prevents or inhibits sensible steps in nuclear custodianship, the United States could undertake to provide monetary help. The domestic politics of this may not be easy, but the logic of doing so seems straightforward.

CONCLUSION: WHETHER AND HOW MUCH TO HELP?

Nuclear assistance has figured prominently in U.S. policy toward other nuclear powers. With NATO allies Britain and France, there has been an extensive and intimate pattern of nuclear cooperation. With adversaries such as the former Soviet Union and China, there was at least occasional modest cooperative interaction, mostly in the form of dialogue, on issues of mutual interest and concern. Concern over the conjunction of large numbers of nuclear weapons and high levels of internal instability in the former Soviet Union has again put nuclear assistance high on the U.S. policy agenda. Thus, toward states that have actually acquired nuclear weapons, U.S. nuclear assistance is more the norm than the exception. While U.S. attitudes toward proliferation may have toughened to the extent that the future will be unlike the past, it is still likely that nuclear assistance will remain an element of U.S. policy.

Under what circumstances is the United States likely to choose the nuclear assistance option? The record suggests two clear conditions: the first is if the proliferator is a close friend or ally of the United States. There the instinct to help is likely to prevail over the instinct to punish. This category is especially important because it is the one most likely to lead to extensive nuclear cooperation; it is also the category in which nuclear help may be motivated as much or more by a desire to enhance the recipient's nuclear capabilities as by concern about safety, security, and stability.

The second condition in which the nuclear assistance option is likely to seem compelling is one in which nuclear weapons exist in an environment of internal or international instability. If it seems that nuclear weapons could fall into the wrong hands or that gaping force vulnerabilities could lead to hair-trigger postures that make the probability of nuclear use seem uncomfortably high, then this too could be regarded as a justification for nuclear assistance. An immediate example is the former USSR, but similarly worrying circumstances could also arise in the Middle East, in South Asia, on the Korean Peninsula, or even in China.

There will be incentives to provide nuclear assistance and cases where to do so is a sensible policy choice. However, it cannot be provided except at the cost of eroding the nonproliferation regime, possibly creating incentives for near-nuclear states to cross the nuclear threshold, and entangling the United States in the nuclear programs and foreign policy rivalries of recipients. These costs are sufficient to compel the conclusion that the United States ought not have a liberal policy of nuclear assistance. Indeed, it is preferable as a general matter not to help. It further seems prudent to conclude that U.S. nuclear assistance should be as limited as possible, so that proliferation does not come to be regarded as a route to American nuclear largesse; this may be hard to observe in nuclear relations with allies, but should guide U.S. transfers to other states.

Fortunately, U.S. nuclear help options are circumscribed in two ways: first, by a range of domestic and international legal commitments and norms, and second, by the political hostility of many of the most troubling proliferation-prone countries—North Korea, Iran, Iraq, and Libya. The fact of hostility does not preclude the desirability or the feasibility of nuclear assistance, but it does suggest that such assistance will be quite limited.

The United States should also adopt stringent criteria for assessing whether and how much help is needed. It should be persuaded, for example, that the potential recipient is taking all feasible measures toward the achievement of a safe, secure, and survivable nuclear capability, since these objectives are in the interest of any government possessing a nuclear capability. It should not provide measures, resources, or technologies that the recipient ought to be able to provide for itself. Nor should U.S. nuclear assistance be the cure for imprudent policies adopted by new proliferators, except insofar as that assistance takes the form of advice about more sensible policies. U.S. nuclear help should not be allowed to become the ransom in a game of instability blackmail.

In addition, the United States ought to take into account other potential sources of nuclear assistance. Indeed, it is unusual for a nuclear weapons program to develop in complete isolation; nuclear cooperation relationships are common, including not only relations between proliferators and the United States or Soviet Union, but also such groupings as China and Pakistan, or Israel, Taiwan, and South Africa.[75] This could, however, have a number of potentially contradictory implications. For example, U.S. policymakers could conclude that if a proliferator is going to get nuclear assistance, it is better that it come from the United States. On the other hand, if a proliferator is already getting nuclear assistance from somewhere else, this could diminish the U.S. motivation to help. This latter alternative might involve some loss of American influence in countries that the United States cares about, but the alternative would be to lose control of U.S. nuclear assistance policy or make it vulnerable to blackmail. Thus the United States should tread cautiously in cases where other suppliers are involved.

Finally, the United States should consider the feasibility of mixed strategies that combine assistance with resistance. As noted, it would be extremely difficult to combine any substantial program of nuclear assistance with punitive or coercive policies. But it may be more plausible to mix modest levels of nuclear help with continued objection to the proliferator's nuclear program.

In sum, nuclear help should be regarded as a serious, but circumscribed and highly conditional, policy option. It is unlikely to remain merely a hypothetical option if further nuclear proliferation occurs. A world in which the United States is deep into the business of providing nuclear assistance is clearly unappealing; a proliferated world of unsafe or unstable nuclear arsenals is even less attractive.

Notes

1. For a useful survey of this literature, see Ian Clark and Philip Sabin, "Sources for the Study of British Nuclear Weapons History," *CISSM Occasional Paper* (Nuclear History Program), Center for International Security Studies, University of Maryland, 1989.

2. Noteworthy is Lewis A. Dunn, *Containing Nuclear Proliferation*, Adelphi Paper No. 263 (London: International Institute for Strategic Studies, Winter 1991), especially pp. 23–25 and 46–55. See also Rodney W. Jones, "Small Nuclear Forces and U.S. Security Policy," in Rodney W. Jones, ed., *Small Nuclear Forces and U.S. Security Policy: Threats and Potential Conflicts in the Middle East and South Asia* (Lexington, Mass.: Lexington Books, 1984), esp. pp. 248–50; Albert Wohlstetter et al., *Moving Toward Life in a Nuclear Armed Crowd?* (Los Angeles: Pan Heuristics, 1976), esp. pp. 149–52; and John J. Weltman, "Managing Nuclear Multipolarity," *International Security*, vol. 6, no. 3 (Winter 1981/82), pp. 192–94.

3. See, for example, Mark D. Mandeles, "Between a Rock and a Hard Place: Implications for the U.S. of Third World Nuclear Weapon and Ballistic Missile Proliferation," *Security Studies*, vol. 1, no. 2 (Winter 1991), pp. 244–45, which claims that "there is no indication that use control technology has been a high priority for Third World weapons designers."

4. Gary Milhollin, "Building Saddam Hussein's Bomb," *New York Times Magazine*, March 8, 1992, p. 32. One UN inspector said of the Iraqi design, "I wouldn't want to be around if it fell off of the edge of this desk."

5. Panel on Nuclear Weapons Safety, Committee on Armed Services, House of Representatives, *Nuclear Weapons Safety* (Washington, D.C.: U.S. Government Printing Office [USGPO], December 1990), pp. 1–2, 8. Excerpts from this report can be found in "Nuclear Weapon Safety: How Safe Is Safe?," *Bulletin of the Atomic Scientists* (April 1991), pp. 35–40. See also George Leopold, "Warheads From Canceled MX May Go to Minuteman III," *Defense News*, March 9, 1992, p. 10.

6. On the organizational and procedural basis for safe and secure handling of nuclear weapons, see Kurt Campbell, Ashton B. Carter, Steven E. Miller, and Charles A. Zraket, *Soviet Nuclear Fission: Control of the Nuclear Arsenal in a Disintegrating Soviet Union* (Cambridge, Mass.: Center for Science and International Affairs, Harvard University, November 1991), pp. 12, 16. On risks associated with internal instability, see Leonard Spector, *Going Nuclear* (Cambridge, Mass.: Ballinger, 1987), pp. 57–62.

7. Geoffrey Kemp, *Nuclear Forces for Medium Powers: Strategic Requirements and Options*, Adelphi Paper No. 107 (London: International Institute for Strategic Studies, Autumn 1974), pp. 7–14, assesses the effect of anticipated force vulnerability on the nuclear force requirements of medium nuclear powers. Wohlstetter et al., *Moving Toward Life in a Nuclear Armed Crowd?*, pp. 116–42, emphasizes (in the hypothetical case of Japan) the cost and difficulty for medium nuclear powers of achieving and maintaining a secure second-strike capability. In both these analyses, however, the nuclear adversary is the Soviet Union, which obviously posed far more daunting challenges than would be found in purely regional settings. Addressing the

regional question more directly is Rodney W. Jones, "Small Nuclear Force Delivery Systems," in Jones, ed., *Small Nuclear Forces and U.S. Security Policy*, esp. pp. 53–54. Jones argues that while force fragilities will initially exist, the local threat to small nuclear forces is so circumscribed that new nuclear weapons states ought to be able to achieve adequate levels of survivability. I suspect that this understates the preemptive risks associated with these forces. Less sanguine is Dunn, *Containing Nuclear Proliferation*, pp. 16–27, who suggests that emerging nuclear arsenals lack many of the technical and political attributes that made for stability in the Soviet–American context. Leonard Spector provides an extensive survey of proliferator delivery systems in *The Undeclared Bomb* (Cambridge, Mass.: Ballinger, 1988), pp. 23–66, and touches on their destabilizing characteristics (pp. 49–53).

8. This was true of Soviet and American nuclear capabilities during the first fifteen years of the nuclear age because both countries neglected substantial force vulnerabilities.

9. See, for example, Peter Pry, *Israel's Nuclear Arsenal* (Boulder, Colo.: Westview Press, 1984), pp. 113–16. As Pry notes, even those who argue that nuclearization could stabilize the Middle East acknowledge the potential vulnerability of the Israeli force. A good example is Shai Feldman, *Israeli Nuclear Deterrence: A Strategy for the 1980s* (New York: Columbia University Press, 1982), p. 93.

10. Peter Malone, *The British Nuclear Deterrent* (New York: St. Martin's, 1984), pp. 45–82; and Richard Ullman, "The Covert French Connection," *Foreign Policy*, no. 75 (Summer 1989), pp. 3–33.

11. See Avner Cohen and Benjamin Frankel, "Opaque Nuclear Proliferation," *Journal of Strategic Studies*, vol. 13, no. 3 (September 1990), pp. 14–44.

12. See Richard E. Neustadt, *Alliance Politics* (New York: Columbia University Press, 1970), pp. 30–55.

13. Ullman, "The Covert French Connection," p. 3. Similarly, the British offered Holy Loch, Scotland, as a forward operating base for U.S. ballistic missile submarines as quid pro quo for U.S. help to Britain's nuclear weapons program. Neustadt, *Alliance Politics*, pp. 34–35.

14. Brahma Chellaney, "South Asia's Passage to Nuclear Power," *International Security*, vol. 16, no. 1 (Summer 1991), p. 65, 67n.

15. The diplomatic complexities associated with nuclear assistance can cause difficulties even among friendly states. In the early 1960s, for example, the Kennedy administration miffed the British by extending the same nuclear assistance to France that it had already offered to Britain, but simultaneously irritated the French by first having reached agreement with the British. Neustadt, *Alliance Politics*, pp. 53–55.

16. For Philip Zelikow's analysis of the military option, see chapter 7.

17. On the other hand, proliferators may fear that accepting U.S. involvement in their nuclear program would increase their vulnerability by revealing the location and character of their facilities and forces.

18. When the French wanted help in submarine technologies in order to make their ballistic missile submarines less vulnerable to Soviet SSNs, for example, the United States refused on the grounds that the survivability of U.S. ballistic missiles submarines was too important to permit any sharing of information on

that subject. For the French example, see Ullman, "The Covert French Connection," pp. 16–17.

19. See Margaret Gowing, "Prologue: Early Western Nuclear Relationships," *CISSM Occasional Paper*, No. 4 (Nuclear History Program), Center for International Security Studies, University of Maryland, 1989, p. 13. Gowing also notes earlier uneasiness in Britain from 1939 to 1940 regarding information-sharing and nuclear cooperation with the United States; see p. 6.

20. See, for example, Michael Nacht, "The Future Unlike the Past: Nuclear Proliferation and American Security Policy," in George Quester, ed., *Nuclear Proliferation: Breaking the Chain* (Madison: University of Wisconsin Press, 1981), pp. 193–202.

21. Lewis Dunn has discussed the complications associated with proliferator-allies in "Aspects of Military Strategy and Arms Control in a More Proliferated World," in John K. King, ed., *International Political Effects of the Spread of Nuclear Weapons* (Washington, D.C.: USGPO, April 1979), p. 157; and in Dunn, *Controlling the Bomb: Nuclear Proliferation in the 1980s* (New Haven, Conn.: Yale University Press, 1982), pp. 155–57.

22. Nacht, in "The Future Unlike the Past," p. 210, suggests four categories of potential proliferators: major allies such as Germany or Japan; regional allies such as South Korea or Taiwan; states that are neither allies nor adversaries, such as Brazil and Argentina; and states that are adversaries of the United States or its allies.

23. Dunn, *Containing Nuclear Proliferation*, pp. 50–51, also highlights the range of possible assistance measures.

24. Peter Stein and Peter Feaver, *Assuring Control of Nuclear Weapons: The Evolution of Permissive Action Links*, CSIA Occasional Paper No. 2, Center for Science and International Affairs, 1987, pp. 83–84; and Dunn, *Containing Nuclear Proliferation*, p. 49.

25. At the SALT I negotiations in 1971, the United States did formally raise the PAL issue with the Soviets, but they declined to discuss the subject.

26. For a concise overview of this range of activities, see Malone, *The British Nuclear Deterrent*, pp. 58–74. The text of the nuclear cooperation agreement between the United States and Britain can be found in John Baylis, *Anglo–American Defense Relations, 1939–1984* (New York: St. Martin's 1984), pp. 112–25.

27. Ullman, "The Covert French Connection," pp. 27–31. In the U.S.–French case, the motives for secrecy seem to have been primarily domestic in both cases.

28. Richard Hewlett and Oscar Anderson, *A History of the United States Atomic Energy Commission (Volume I): The New World, 1939–1946* (University Park: Pennsylvania State University Press, 1962), pp. 428–530.

29. See Margaret Gowing with Lorna Arnold, *Interdependence and Deterrence: Britain and Atomic Energy, 1945–1952 (Volume I): Policy Making* (New York: St. Martin's, 1974), pp. 104–23; Gowing, "Prologue: Early Western Nuclear Relationships," pp. 13–17; Malone, *The British Nuclear Deterrent*, pp. 52–59; and Martin Navias, *Nuclear Weapons and British Strategic Planning, 1955–1958* (Oxford: Clarendon Press, 1991), pp. 188–239.

30. Ian Clark and Nicholas Wheeler, *The British Origins of Nuclear Strategy, 1945–1955* (Oxford: Clarendon Press, 1989), p. 219.

31. See Navias, *Nuclear Weapons and British Strategic Planning*, pp. 219–20.
32. In this section, I draw on Ian Anthony, "The United States," in Ian Anthony, ed., *Arms Export Regulations* (Oxford: Oxford University Press, 1991), pp. 183–202.
33. I am relying here on Frederick Williams, "The United States Congress and Non-proliferation," *International Security*, vol. 3, no. 2 (Fall 1978), pp. 45–50.
34. U.S. Arms Control and Disarmament Agency (ACDA), *Arms Control and Disarmament Agreements: Texts and Histories of the Negotiations* (Washington, D.C.: USGPO, 1990), p. 99.
35. ACDA, *Arms Control and Disarmament Agreements*, p. 101.
36. Dunn also notes the conflict with NPT obligations. See *Containing Nuclear Proliferation*, p. 48.
37. *Treaty with the Union of Soviet Socialist Republics on the Reduction and Limitation of Strategic Offensive Arms (The START Treaty)*, U.S. Senate, Treaty Document 102–20 (Washington, D.C.: USGPO, 1991), p. 46.
38. From the First Agreed Statement in the Annex to the START Treaty. See *The START Treaty*, p. 48.
39. On the noncircumvention issue in SALT II (Article XII), see Ullman, "The Covert French Connection," pp. 28–29; Ullman speculates that part of the Soviet motivation in raising the issue was a concern about the "covert" assistance program between the United States and France. Article XVI in *The START Treaty*, p. 46, says: "The Parties agree that this provision does not apply to any patterns of cooperation, including obligations, in the area of strategic offensive arms, existing at the time of the signature of this Treaty, between a Party and a third state."
40. See "Perm Five Experts Faced With Difficult Arms Trade Issues," *BASIC Reports on European Arms Control*, no. 20 (February 19, 1992), pp. 1–5; and "Arms Transfers and Non-Proliferation," Policy Statement 69/91, British Information Services.
41. Ibid.
42. The UN General Assembly in December 1991 created a registry of international arms transfers, intended to increase the transparency of global arms flows. While nonbinding, it too embodies the emerging norm that arms transfers ought to be accompanied by notification and consultation. See William Epstein, "Write Down Your Arms," *Bulletin of Atomic Scientists* (March 1992), pp. 11–12.
43. See Ian Anthony, "The Missile Technology Control Regime," in Anthony, ed., *Arms Export Regulations*, pp. 219–27.
44. Ullman, "The Covert French Connection," pp. 12, 16.
45. See Harold Green and Alan Rosenthal, *Government of the Atom: The Integration of Powers* (New York: Atherton Press, 1963), p. 20. A recent example is the congressional push to pass the Nonproliferation Act of 1978, described by Williams, "The United States Congress and Non-Proliferation," p. 45.
46. For an informative account of the nuclear issue in U.S.–Pakistani relations, see Leonard Spector with Jacqueline Smith, *Nuclear Ambitions: The Spread of Nuclear Weapons, 1989–1990* (Boulder, Colo.: Westview Press, 1990), pp. 93–112.

47. This prompted Pakistan to admit finally the existence of its nuclear weapons program and to pledge that it had not built and would not build any nuclear bombs. See Paul Lewis, "Pakistan Tells of Its A-Bomb Capacity," *New York Times*, February 8, 1992.

48. The dispute between Congress and the Bush administration over military sales to Pakistan erupted again in March 1992, when it was revealed that the administration held an interpretation of the Pressler Amendment that permitted commercial sales of weapons and spare parts, and had accordingly authorized more than $100 million in arms sales to Pakistan. This prompted charges from Congress that the law had been violated. See Steve Coll and David Hoffman, "Shipments to Pakistan Questioned," *Washington Post*, March 7, 1992, p. A19.

49. See Sam Nunn and Richard Lugar, "Dismantling the Soviet Arsenal," *Washington Post*, November 22, 1991.

50. See also Eric Schmitt, "Senate Votes Funds for Moscow to Dismantle Nuclear Weapons," *New York Times*, November 26, 1991.

51. Neustadt, *Alliance Politics*, p. 55.

52. Gowing, "Prologue: Early Western Nuclear Relationships," p. 6.

53. Dunn also notes the tendency of nuclear assistance to improve recipient capabilities. See *Containing Nuclear Proliferation*, p. 49.

54. Israel, for example, has regularly objected to U.S. arms sales to Arab states, and it has often delayed, complicated, or altered U.S. policy. Andrew Pierre, "Beyond the Plane Package: Arms and Politics in the Middle East," *International Security*, vol. 3, no. 1 (Summer 1978), p. 148, reports Israeli dismay at U.S. willingness to supply advanced aircraft to Saudi Arabia and Egypt. On the recurrent pattern of Israeli opposition to U.S. arms transfers to other states in the Middle East, see David Pollock, *The Politics of Pressure: American Arms and Israeli Pressure Since the Six Day War* (Westport, Conn.: Greenwood Press, 1982).

55. A pioneering work on this subject is Donald MacKenzie, *Inventing Accuracy: A Historical Sociology of Nuclear Missile Guidance* (Cambridge, Mass.: MIT Press, 1990), which suggests that "technological knowledge is social through and through" (p. 11).

56. See Ken Booth, *Strategy and Ethnocentrism* (New York: Holmes and Meier, 1979); and Colin S. Gray, "National Style in Strategy: The American Example," *International Security*, vol. 6, no. 2 (Fall 1981), esp. pp. 21–23.

57. Dunn, *Containing Nuclear Proliferation*, p. 51, is the only source that I have found which addresses this issue.

58. During the 1980s, for example, there was recurrent but ultimately unfulfilled speculation that Britain might forsake its nuclear capability on grounds of cost and public opposition. See Lawrence Freedman, "Britain: The First Ex-Nuclear Power?" *International Security*, vol. 6, no. 2 (Fall 1981), pp. 80–104.

59. Dunn, *Containing Nuclear Proliferation*, p. 51, warns that "to wait too long may be to wait too late."

60. This discussion draws on: Donald R. Cotter, "Peacetime Operations: Safety and Security," in Ashton B. Carter, John D. Steinbruner, and Charles A. Zraket, eds., *Managing Nuclear Operations* (Washington, D.C.: The Brookings

Institution, 1987), pp. 17–74; Panel on Nuclear Weapons Safety, Committee on Armed Services, House of Representatives, *Nuclear Weapons Safety*; Gregory F. Giles, "Safety and Control of New Nuclear Forces," unpublished manuscript, SAIC, September 10, 1991; Thomas A. Julian, "Nuclear Weapons Security and Control," in Paul Levanthal and Yonah Alexander, eds., *Preventing Nuclear Terrorism* (Lexington, Mass.: Lexington Books, 1987), pp. 169–90; Mahlon E. Gates, "The Nuclear Emergency Search Team," in Levanthal and Alexander, eds., *Preventing Nuclear Terrorism*, pp. 397–402; Stein and Feaver, *Assuring Control of Nuclear Weapons*; Mason Willrich and Theodore Taylor, *Nuclear Theft: Risks and Safeguards* (Cambridge, Mass.: Ballinger, 1974); Robert S. Norris, "The Soviet Nuclear Archipelago," *Arms Control Today*, January/February 1992, pp. 24–31; Richard Garwin, "Post–Soviet Nuclear Command and Security," *Arms Control Today*, January/February 1992, pp. 18–23; "Testimony by the Honorable Reginald Bartholomew," Senate Armed Services Committee, February 5, 1992; "Testimony of Stephen J. Hadley," Senate Armed Services Committee, February 5, 1992; and Campbell, Carter, Miller and Zraket, *Soviet Nuclear Fission*, pp. 5–34.

61. Panel on Nuclear Weapons Safety, Committee on Armed Services, House of Representatives, *Nuclear Weapons Safety*, p. 14.

62. Chuck Hansen, *U.S. Nuclear Weapons: The Secret History* (New York: Orion Books, 1988), pp. 225–26. Arming of early U.S. nuclear weapons deployed on bombers required inflight insertion of the fissile core.

63. Much of the discussion of nuclear assistance to the former USSR, for example, has involved issues of safe transport and storage. See, for example, "Testimony of Stephen J. Hadley."

64. For discussion of the pros and cons of cruise missiles as delivery systems for small nuclear forces, see Rodney W. Jones, "Small Nuclear Force Delivery Systems," in Jones, ed., *Small Nuclear Forces and U.S. Security Policy*, pp. 52–53.

65. "Known Nuclear Tests Worldwide, 1945–December 31, 1991," *Bulletin of Atomic Scientists*, April 1992, p. 49.

66. Ullman, "The Covert French Connection," pp. 13–15.

67. See Ashton B. Carter, "Communications Technologies and Vulnerabilities," and Carter, "Assessing Command System Vulnerability," both in Carter, Steinbruner, and Zraket, eds., *Managing Nuclear Operations*, pp. 217–81 and 555–610, respectively.

68. See Senate Armed Services Committee, *Department of Defense Authorization for Appropriations for Fiscal Year 1986*, Part 7, (Washington, D.C.: USGPO, 1976), pp. 3511–12.

69. Hersh, *The Samson Option*, pp. 3–17. It is unclear from this account how much U.S. policymakers were aware of the extent of Israel's access to KH-11 intelligence or of the uses to which it was put in Israel. But see the comment that former CIA Director William Casey "was prepared to show them [the Israelis] a little thigh" (p. 13).

70. Chellaney, "South Asia's Passage to Nuclear Power," pp. 65–66, makes this point with respect to South Asia.

71. See Dunn, *Containing Nuclear Proliferation*, pp. 50–57.

72. This point is developed in more detail in Campbell, Carter, Miller, and Zraket, *Soviet Nuclear Fission*, pp. 88–89.
73. I am indebted to Professor John Lewis of Stanford University for suggesting this example.
74. Described in "Testimony of Stephen J. Hadley" and "Testimony by the Honorable Reginald Bartholomew."
75. On the China–Pakistan nuclear connection, see, for example, Ashok Kapur, *Pakistan's Nuclear Development* (London: Croom Helm, 1987), pp. 244–48. Regarding Israel's alleged nuclear entanglements, see Pry, *Israel's Nuclear Arsenal*, pp. 36–38; and Hersh, *The Samson Option*, pp. 263–68.

PART III

U.S. Military Means for Coping With New Nuclear Nations

CHAPTER SIX

Implications for U.S. Military Strategy

MICHÈLE A. FLOURNOY

This chapter focuses on how nuclear proliferation may influence four distinct but related aspects of U.S. military strategy:[1] 1) how the United States defines its interests and commitments around the world; 2) the posture of U.S. military forces; 3) U.S. military options (deterrence, preventive war, preemption, and defense) in confronting new nuclear weapon states; and 4) securing the necessary domestic and international support for a chosen course of U.S. military action.[2]

Rather than attempt to deduce specific implications from a series of hypothetical cases, this chapter seeks to construct a framework for thinking through the impact of nuclear proliferation on U.S. military strategy. While the chapter may raise as many questions as it answers, it should also offer a context for analyzing the military options available to the United States in coping with new and potentially hostile nuclear weapon states.

DEFINING U.S. INTERESTS

The spread of nuclear weapons will inevitably cause a reevaluation of U.S. interests and commitments in the post–Cold War world.[3] By creating new threats to friends, allies, and forces, nuclear proliferation will compel the United States to distinguish anew those interests worth the risk of nuclear confrontation from those that are not.

The acquisition of nuclear weapons by additional countries may alter both the list of U.S. vital interests and the nature of the U.S. commitment to them. Whether and how Washington's perception of its interests in a given region may change will depend on two key factors: 1) whether the proliferator is perceived to be friendly or hostile, and 2) who is threatened by the proliferation—a staunch U.S. ally, a friend, a neutral country, or an adversary.

If the proliferator is an important U.S. ally or friend, past experience with Britain, France, and Israel suggests that its acquisition of nuclear weapons will not have any significant effect on its long-term relations with the United States. However, the United States might strengthen its commitment to defend or assist the "friendly" proliferator in the hope of reducing the likelihood that its newly acquired nuclear arsenal would ever be used; in other cases, the United States might choose (or be asked) to reduce its defense commitment in light of its ally's new-found nuclear sufficiency. In addition, proliferation by friends could sound a wake-up call for the United States, energizing its efforts to stop the spread of nuclear weapons to others in the region whose agendas may be less coincident with U.S. interests.

If the proliferator is perceived to be a potential adversary, and its acquisition of nuclear weapons appears to threaten important U.S. allies, the United States might reaffirm or even strengthen its commitment to their security. For example, if North Korea crossed the nuclear weapons threshold, the United States could be expected to reaffirm its nuclear guarantee to Japan, and perhaps offer to share U.S. ballistic missile defense technology. If the country threatened by a proliferator's bomb was one of the United States' stranger Cold War bedfellows, Washington might opt to weaken or withdraw prior security commitments. In short, nuclear proliferation should force the United States to reassess its interests in a new and harsher light, strengthening the ties that truly bind, while weakening or perhaps breaking those that are merely legacies of now outmoded Cold War relationships.

In addition, reversing the spread of nuclear weapons may well take on greater importance as a U.S. foreign policy objective in and of itself. Public opinion polls taken prior to Desert Storm suggested that most Americans saw the destruction of Saddam Hussein's nuclear, chemical, and biological weapons capabilities as one of the most important reasons for the United States to go to war with Iraq.[4] Although the United States is unlikely to declare "rollback" a universal aim given its demonstrated willingness to tolerate proliferation in some cases, it may well become a U.S. priority in instances where a proliferator is governed by an undemocratic regime, has demonstrated its willingness to challenge the sovereignty or borders of other countries, or supports international terrorism.

How the United States defines its interests and objectives in the face of proliferation will also be influenced by domestic public opinion, world opinion, and bureaucratic politics. And public opinion will be shaped by a number of factors, including: 1) perceptions of a new nuclear weapon state's leadership—whether it is a dictatorship or a democracy, whether it is believed to sponsor terrorism, whether it is perceived to respect human rights;[5] 2) perceptions of what the United States stands to gain or lose in a given region; and 3) views of opinionmakers, as expressed in public pronouncements, the release of intelligence data, stories in the media, and so on. World opinion will be molded by similar considerations— whether the proliferator is an upstanding member of the international community, a pariah, or something in between; how much is at stake in the region; and by public and private diplomacy. As channels through which significant pressure may be brought to bear on the White House, both domestic and international opinion have the potential to act as serious constraints on how U.S. interests are defined. Further limits are imposed by bureaucratic politics, especially disputes between the National Security Council, the Defense Department, the State Department, the various intelligence agencies, and within the White House. Here, the determining questions could include: Whose agenda would be served or harmed if the United States were to embrace a particular interest? How much power do the champions or opponents of a particular interest bring to the bureaucratic bargaining table?

In sum, the spread of nuclear weapons can be expected to push the United States to clarify, and in some cases to change, the definition of its national interests and the objectives of its foreign policy.

REORIENTING U.S. MILITARY POSTURE

During the Cold War, the military was a central instrument of U.S. foreign policy. U.S. military posture, although defensive in its primary aim of containing the Soviet Union, was highly assertive in character. Its hallmarks included frequent intervention, direct and indirect, in regional conflicts; forward deployments of ships, troops, and weapons around the globe; and peacetime operations designed, in part, to make the U.S. presence felt far and wide. This assertiveness enabled the United States to draw its line of defense thousands of miles from its borders and to communicate this fact to potential adversaries on virtually a daily basis.

Now that the Cold War is over, the basic role and orientation of the U.S. military are undergoing fundamental reassessment. Should the military retain its primacy as an instrument of U.S. foreign policy, or should other instruments, such as diplomacy and trade, now take the lead in promoting U.S. interests and objectives? Must the United States military be as engaged and omnipresent now that the Soviet threat has vanished, or can it afford to draw its line of defense closer to home? The acquisition of nuclear weapons by additional countries will inevitably figure into how these vital questions are ultimately answered.

Some will undoubtedly argue that the continued spread of nuclear weapons calls for the U.S. military to remain at the center of U.S. grand strategy and for it to retain an assertive posture in support of a new policy of nuclear containment—containing nuclear proliferation, by military means if necessary. U.S. public opinion polls taken prior to Desert Storm imply that the American people would, at least in some cases, enthusiastically support such a policy.[6] Nuclear containment, however, would run counter to several post–Cold War trends in the U.S. military, such as reduced operating tempos for overseas forces and declining deployments of nonstrategic nuclear weapons. If such a policy was adopted, these moves might be reversed.

Others, however, will undoubtedly argue that greater emphasis should be placed on nonmilitary instruments of foreign policy and that the U.S. military should disengage from regions where proliferation has occurred. In this case, the United States might step up diplomatic activity aimed at a new nuclear weapon state while adopting a more conservative military posture in the area and avoiding military intervention in the region. (Indeed, one hope of would-be proliferators is that their acquisition of nuclear weapons will enable them to deter the United States from intervening in their regional affairs.) Still others will argue for a general policy of isolationism and total military disengagement.

If the U.S. interests at stake in a proliferated region are deemed vital, the U.S. military posture there is likely to remain somewhat assertive, even in the face of nuclear danger. It is, for example, difficult to imagine the United States radically reorienting its military stance in Europe or the Middle East in response to the acquisition of nuclear weapons by, say, Ukraine or Iran. If the U.S. interests are less than vital, the outcome is more difficult to predict.

Like the redefinition of U.S. interests, the relative emphasis placed on the military as an instrument of U.S. foreign policy and the character of its posture will be shaped by bureaucratic politics and public opinion. For example, as the U.S. defense budget declines in the wake of the Cold War, the Pentagon has emphasized the threat posed by proliferation in an effort to justify new military missions and to give some threatened procurement programs a new lease on life.[7] Arguments for an assertive military response to proliferation are also being raised in opposition to calls for a more isolationist American foreign policy. And military policies aimed at containing nuclear proliferation could help the U.S. maintain an active role in the proclaimed "new world order."

Domestic public opinion will also figure into the equation. The greater the public's concern over a specific country's acquisition of nuclear weapons, the more assertive a military posture they are likely to support. Whereas the American people would probably not lose much sleep over Sweden's or Australia's acquisition of nuclear weapons, the same would not be true if Iran or Libya went nuclear. Public opinion is, however, neither static nor impervious to persuasion. U.S. policymakers must therefore consider not only where public opinion stands on a particular case of proliferation, but also the extent to which it can be led to support a new U.S. military posture.

The views of other countries must also be considered, lest the political costs of an operation outweigh the military gains. For example, if the United States were to adopt a highly assertive military posture off the Korean peninsula or in the Middle East despite widespread objections from the international community, it would risk being branded as provocative and ultimately blamed for any confrontation that ensued. Thus nuclear proliferation highlights an essential element of U.S. leadership in the post–Cold War world: the ability to muster and sustain multilateral consensus in support of U.S. military action (discussed below).

Finally, the nature of a proliferator's nuclear weapons capabilities will also be weighed in U.S. calculations. How many deliverable weapons does the new nuclear weapon state have? Against whom can these be used? Can the proliferator be deterred from using them? Are they vulnerable to destruction? Can they be defended against with any success? The particulars of a proliferator's nuclear weapon capabilities and judgments about whether their use can be prevented or neutralized will go a long way toward defining the parameters of U.S. military posture in a given region or crisis.

MILITARY OPTIONS

During the Cold War, nuclear deterrence—threatening nuclear retaliation to forestall an attack—became the preferred U.S. military option for confronting nuclear-armed adversaries.[8] Although preventive war—in this case, using military force to keep the Soviet Union from acquiring nuclear weapons—was given serious consideration in U.S. military circles in the late 1940s (when the USSR was acquiring atomic weapons) and again in the early 1950s (when the USSR was acquiring thermonuclear weapons), the idea was discarded by both the Truman and Eisenhower administrations. Preemption—the use of military force to destroy an adversary's military (in this case, nuclear) capabilities before they can be used—remained a central strand in U.S. nuclear war planning and procurement, in the form of damage limitation and counterforce, but was used largely in pursuit of deterrence.[9] Similarly, the option of defending the United States against large-scale Soviet ballistic missile attack gained currency during some periods of the Cold War, first in the late 1960s and again in the 1980s, but it never eclipsed deterrence as the focus of U.S. military strategy toward its nuclear-armed nemesis.

It would, however, be shortsighted and perhaps even dangerous simply to transplant this long-standing policy preference into a post–Cold War world of new proliferators. Secretary of Defense Les Aspin has noted that "there is no single analogue to deterrence as a nuclear policy in the new era."[10] In thinking through its strategy for confronting nuclear-armed adversaries other than the former Soviet Union, the United States must take a fresh look at the full range of military options, from preventive war to defense.[11] What made sense in the Soviet context may no longer work in the context of a particular new nuclear weapon state; and what did not work against the Soviets might well be feasible against a new proliferator.

These options—deterrence, preventive war, preemption, and defense—are examined below.[12] Although their feasibility and appropriateness must be determined on an adversary-by-adversary basis, one can construct a framework for making case-specific judgments.

Deterrence

Can the United States deter new nuclear weapon states from using their newly acquired nuclear weapons against U.S. interests? Few questions are likely to be more central in the new nuclear age.

Given the role that deterrence has played in keeping all of the former Soviet Union's 30,000 nuclear weapons unused for more than four decades, there is reason to believe that the United States should be able to deter an adversary that possesses a smaller nuclear arsenal. The United States will have unquestionable nuclear superiority over any new nuclear nation, quantitatively, qualitatively, and operationally. It will probably also have a substantial edge in conventional military capabilities. And while its own nuclear forces would be invulnerable to a disarming strike by a proliferator, the converse may not be true. These advantages suggest that the United States should be able to deter any new nuclear weapon state that emerges. Nevertheless, conditions conducive to credible deterrence may not always be present.[13]

The types of nuclear use the United States might seek to deter include a warning or demonstration shot, an attack on U.S. forces overseas, an attack against U.S. allies or friends, or a strike against U.S. territory. The United States might seek to deter a proliferator from using its nuclear weapons first or in retaliation; in crisis or in war; by means of aircraft, missiles, or unconventional modes of delivery. In each case, the requirements of deterrence may be somewhat different. For example, the seriousness of U.S. intent to retaliate in response to a nuclear attack on its allies might be more difficult to establish than it would in response to an attack on American soil. Similarly, it could be more difficult to deter a proliferator from using those weapons remaining after a first strike than to deter it from using its weapons first in a crisis, depending on such factors as the nature of the initial attack on the proliferator, the value it places on surviving assets still held at risk, and judgment as to whether its remaining nuclear weapons would be useful for either bargaining or revenge.

Nevertheless, one can point to a handful of conditions that both in theory and in practice increase the likelihood that the United States could deter an adversary from using nuclear weapons.[14] Most, if not all, of them were operating in the U.S.–Soviet context during the Cold War, but some might be missing in a future U.S. encounter with a new nuclear weapon state.

1. The identity of the adversary threatening nuclear use is known.

2. The adversary is rational—that is, it makes decisions based on a reasonable calculation of the expected costs and benefits associated with a specific course of action.

3. The nature of the behavior to be deterred and the commitment to punish the transgressor (or deny its aims) is carefully defined and clearly communicated by the United States.

4. The adversary believes that the United States possesses both the means and the resolve to carry out its deterrent threat.

In order for deterrence to be effective, the United States must be able to determine who its object of retaliation would be if deterrence failed; it must know whom to threaten with reprisal. However, in a proliferated post–Cold War world, the identity of an adversary might be unknown or unclear. Imagine a scenario where the White House receives an anonymous but credible nuclear threat: a nuclear device will be detonated in New York if the United States intervenes in an Arab–Israeli war that Israel is beginning to lose. In this scenario, the United States believes that Iran, Libya, and Syria all have undeclared nuclear weapons capabilities and a desire to keep the United States out of the conflict. The U.S. intelligence community might not be able to determine the origin of the threat in time to support U.S. efforts to deter the threatened action. Hostile proliferators might well be willing to gamble that this would be the case and might believe that they could engage in nuclear blackmail while ultimately escaping nuclear retaliation.

Similarly, if the United States were unable to identify or locate a terrorist group issuing a nuclear threat, deterrence would not be a viable option. Even if the group and its location (or valued assets) could be identified, a deterrent threat might founder if the United States were perceived to lack the will to attack the group's host country.

The second condition conducive to deterrence—that the adversary is rational—is not as straightforward as it seems. The debate on future threats to U.S. security is divided among those who believe that new proliferators are likely to be irrational and therefore undeterrable[15] and those who argue that they will be both rational and predictable when faced with clear and overwhelming threats of retaliation.[16] This debate obscures a more important point, namely that a proliferator's reasoning may not be amenable to deterrence theory's cut-and-dried distinction between rational and irrational actors. The proliferator might weigh the same expected costs and benefits of a given action, but weigh them differently than U.S. leaders would, based on different values. For example, a dictator might be willing to accept higher levels of civilian deaths and societal destruction as the price of his actions than an American president would. Alternatively, the proliferator might make cost-benefit calculations based on a different set of factors than U.S. leaders would.[17] Or the proliferator's reasoning might be based on something other than cost-benefit calculations, such as religious beliefs, ideology, or cultural norms.

If a proliferator's style of reasoning is not readily perceived or understood in Washington, opportunities for effective deterrence could be missed. Therefore, with the help of the intelligence community, U.S. decisionmakers must strive to see the situation through a particular proliferator's eyes as well as through their own.[18] The chances of misperception are likely to be higher in the proliferation context than they were in the Cold War because the United States will almost certainly be less familiar with a new nuclear weapon state's needs, aims, worldview, and attitudes toward nuclear weapons than it was with those of the Soviet Union. Under such circumstances, the United States may lack the keys to "unlock the strategic personality" of the proliferator.[19] What is its foreign policy agenda? What domestic pressures are influencing that agenda? How do nuclear weapons fit into this picture? Under what circumstances would the country's leadership be willing to use nuclear weapons? How would it use them? And what carrots and sticks, if any, could prevent such use? Answers to these questions could help the United States avoid the pitfall of misperceiving a rational and potentially deterrable leader of a new nuclear weapon state as an irrational, undeterrable one. Gaining such understanding presents a daunting but essential task for U.S. intelligence.

The possibility of misperception cuts both ways, however. For example, a new nuclear weapon state may fail to recognize a U.S. commitment to defend a specific country or set of interests. Signaling intent may be particularly difficult across cultural lines or between adversaries who lack a shared frame of reference.[20] What the sender believes to be a clear message may be misinterpreted by or entirely lost on the recipient,[21] especially if the sender chooses (for political or other reasons) to shroud its message in purposeful ambiguity, hinting that nuclear weapons might be used in retaliation but not saying so explicitly.[22] Furthermore, with the end of the Cold War, there is more ambiguity in any case: spheres of interests are less clear, the U.S. commitment to defend some former Cold War allies is more uncertain, and there is greater room for miscalculation.

Alternatively, a proliferator may doubt the U.S. resolve to carry out its deterrent threat. Such doubt could be rooted in its perception of past U.S. actions or in its belief that the U.S. interests at stake are not as vital as its own. Although new nuclear weapon states may be less prone to doubt U.S. resolve in the wake of the Gulf War, they may nevertheless do so in a given instance if some degree of U.S. retrenchment or waffling is perceived. In addition, it may be difficult for some countries to believe that something 1,000 or 10,000 miles from the United States but only 10 miles from their border is seen by the United States to be as vital to its interests as to their own.

Finally, deterrence might be undermined by a proliferator's unwillingness to accept a basic tenet of "responsible nuclear custodianship"[23]: that the possession of nuclear weapons—given their unique military, strategic, and political characteristics—imposes certain restrictions on state behavior. Most fundamentally, it may not respect the long-standing taboo against the use of nuclear weapons.

In some cases, therefore, deterrence may work simply because of the tremendous asymmetry in military capabilities between the two powers; in others, the conditions for deterrence may not be present. What U.S. decisionmakers can do in the face of this uncertainty is to increase their ability to distinguish deterrable adversaries from potentially undeterrable ones. Specifically, they should keep the following principles in mind:

- Know thy adversary. Seek to understand its intentions, capabilities, needs, ends, worldview, and attitudes toward nuclear weapons, especially toward their use.

- Know thy potential adversary. Develop an understanding of the "fingerprints" of a range of potential enemies—their agendas, modes of operation, hardware, and so on—in an effort to minimize the chances that the identity of an anonymous threat maker could remain concealed.

In the event that the United States chooses to rely on deterrence in dealing with a particular new nuclear weapon state, several key decisions would have to be made: 1) What should the nature of the U.S. deterrent threat be? 2) If a proliferator is threatening a U.S. ally (rather than U.S. territory or forces), should the United States provide the ally with the instruments of deterrence? 3) What should U.S. declaratory policy be?

The Nature of the Deterrent Threat

Defining the nature of a deterrent threat encompasses several distinct but related issues. First, what is the specific action to be deterred? It is difficult to imagine a situation in which the United States would seek to deter anything less than every offensive use of a proliferator's nuclear weapons against U.S. interests. Second, should the United States make its deterrent threat unilaterally or in concert with other states? To the extent possible, the United States would be wise to seek multilateral support; it should, however, stop short of moves that would effectively give others veto power over U.S. actions, as this could undermine the credibility of deterrence. Third, what kind of retaliation should be threatened? The targets to be held at risk will depend on what installations a particular proliferator values most and on the nature of its nuclear arsenal.

U.S. planners must also give careful consideration to the instruments of retaliation. The United States might threaten and actually execute nuclear retaliation in response to a proliferator's use of nuclear weapons in order to ensure that its deterrent threat is taken seriously, and that subsequent proliferators would think twice before using their nuclear weapons. However, it is important that the nuclear taboo be upheld or, if violated, be restored as quickly as possible. It would be counterproductive and politically disastrous to launch an extensive or prolonged nuclear attack. In most cases, conventional munitions could do the job, and should be relied on as much as possible to achieve U.S. aims.

Providing Others With the Instruments of Deterrence

In cases where the primary threat posed by a proliferator is to a U.S. ally or friend rather than to U.S. troops or territory, the United States must, in relying on deterrence, be prepared to decide whether it is prepared to provide others with the means to deter a proliferator's use of nuclear weapons. This could involve basing U.S. nuclear weapons on allied soil, as in Western Europe, or transferring nuclear weapons or weapons technology to other countries. Since the latter would violate U.S. obligations under the Nuclear Nonproliferation Treaty and would undermine U.S. nonproliferation efforts, the key question is whether deploying U.S. nuclear weapons in a given theater would significantly strengthen the credibility of a U.S. nuclear guarantee.[24] For example, would a nuclear-armed North Korea be more likely to be deterred by U.S. nuclear-capable aircraft based in South Korea than by U.S. strategic bombers based in the continental United States, or long-range missiles on U.S. submarines at sea? Any gain in credibility would have to be weighed against the potential downside risks of deploying U.S. nuclear weapons on foreign soil, such as political discord or tensions with the host country. U.S. weapons could also become targets of preemption or subject to pressures for early use during a conflict.

Declaratory Policy

Finally, taking these considerations and uncertainties into account, what should U.S. declaratory policy be with regard to deterring new nuclear weapon states? By remaining silent, the United States could keep its options open, keep the lid on controversy, and keep proliferators guessing. But saying nothing could be costly. In declining to state a policy, the United States would lose a valuable opportunity to put new nuclear weapon states on notice that they risk devastating retaliation if they use nuclear weapons against U.S. interests. It might even lose an opportunity to prevent such use.

U.S. policy, therefore, should negotiate a middle path between specificity and ambiguity: It should be specific enough to relay a strong message to proliferators, but ambiguous enough to avoid constraining U.S. freedom of action in the event that nuclear weapons are in fact used. Washington should open doors to specific options, such as nuclear retaliation, without committing itself to walking through any of them. For example, the United States could publicly declare that it reserves the right to use any means at its disposal to inflict an unacceptable level of damage on any proliferator who uses a nuclear weapon in a manner detrimental to U.S. interests. Such a general pronouncement could be further defined as needed according to the particular situation.

Preventive War and Preemption

Preventive war—the use of military force to destroy an adversary's capability to develop or deploy nuclear weapons—and preemption, the use of military force to disable or destroy an adversary's nuclear weapons before they can be used, are two additional options for the United States against a new proliferator. Preventive war and preemption are treated together because they raise many of the same questions for U.S. decisionmakers (see also chapter 7).

In contrast to deterrence, relatively little thought has been devoted to preventive war and preemption as means of dealing with nuclear-armed adversaries.[25] Offensive military action was not given a high priority during the Cold War; although preemption thinking influenced U.S. nuclear war planning, it was essentially subsumed under the central mission of deterring the Soviet Union. Because scenarios in which the United States might confront a nuclear-armed adversary other than the Soviet Union were considered "lesser included cases" in the Cold War paradigm, these scenarios, in which both preventive war and preemption might have been more feasible, were given scant attention in U.S. military planning.[26]

The United States now needs to take a fresh look at the feasibility and desirability of both the preventive war and preemption options against new nuclear weapon states. Their nuclear programs or arsenals will certainly be smaller than those of the former Soviet Union; they may be more vulnerable to attack; and they may not include weapons that could retaliate against the United States even if they survived a first strike. Although these are not grounds for advocating offensive military action, they are reasons to reconsider these options, especially for proliferators who may be difficult to deter.

In evaluating whether or not preventive war or preemption should be considered, the United States would need answers to at least six questions. These questions would probably arise not just once but many times as a country's nuclear program develops:

First, is enough known about the adversary's nuclear capabilities, defenses, and military operations to launch a disarming strike with high confidence of success? Accurate and reliable information would be needed on such matters as the size and composition of the proliferator's nuclear program or arsenal; the location of its key nuclear facilities, its weapons, its weapons components; the location and nature of any vital command and control nodes; whether and how its nuclear assets would be defended if attacked; and how its peacetime nuclear operations might change in time of crisis (see chapter 9).

Second, what are the goals of the strike? U.S. aims could be as limited as destroying a particular set of nuclear weapons facilities, or as ambitious as unseating the leader of a new nuclear weapon state.

Third, does the United States have the military capabilities to do the job? Both preventive war and preemption would require not only weapons capable of destroying chosen targets but also adequate reconnaissance, delivery, damage assessment, refueling and support capabilities (see chapter 7).

Fourth, what is the likelihood of success, not only in short-run military terms but also in long-run strategic terms? Can a strike be expected to decrease a proliferator's nuclear ambitions or to intensify its pursuit of those ambitions, with greater attention to survivability and secrecy?

Fifth, what is the likelihood of retaliation, and what kind of retaliation might be expected? If a proliferator had the nuclear delivery capabilities to threaten the most valued U.S. interests, U.S. planners would need enormously (perhaps prohibitively) high confidence in the success of a preventive or preemptive strike; if the proliferator lacked these capabilities, the United States would still have to worry about the delivery of a nuclear device by unconventional means, such as a civilian airliner, truck, or fishing boat.

Sixth, what kind of public reaction, domestic and foreign, could be expected? If the United States were already at war with a new nuclear weapon state, public opinion might well support its efforts to destroy the nuclear arsenal before it could be used.[27] A preventive war in the absence of a larger crisis would be less likely to receive popular support and would raise some profoundly unsettling moral questions: Would the United States be justified in initiating hostilities for the sole purpose of denying an adversary a nuclear weapons capability? Would the amount of force required to accomplish this, and the damage it could cause, be proportionate to the objectives involved? Domestic political reaction will depend on who the adversary is, what else has been tried, and how skillful U.S. leaders are in leading public opinion to support their preferred course of action.

Internationally, there appears to be a broad consensus in favor of reversing proliferation where possible; there is far less agreement on the wisdom of using of military force to do so. Any preventive war is, therefore, likely to be highly controversial. Even in cases where a proliferator is widely seen as a pariah, such as North Korea or Libya, building a multilateral coalition to support preventive war could prove difficult, if not impossible. It is, therefore, important that U.S. decisionmakers think past the Gulf War experience of preventive strikes in the context of a war already begun, and the tremendous international support they received, to the far more difficult dilemmas of determining whether to start a preventive war in peacetime. They must try to imagine how the U.S. bombing of Iraqi nuclear facilities might have been received by the international community had Iraq not invaded Kuwait.[28]

Can the United States afford not to use military force to destroy an adversary's nuclear capabilities? If preventive war appears to be too hard, too risky, or too unpopular a military action, U.S. decisionmakers must decide whether they are willing to live with the consequences of failing to destroy a proliferator's nuclear capabilities. Launching such a war would presumably be a last resort to reverse proliferation once diplomatic measures had failed. Therefore, in declining to use force in a given case, the United States would have to take a close look at the short- and long-term implications of allowing a new member into the nuclear club.

Finally, do the anticipated benefits of preventive war or preemption against a particular proliferator—both strategic and political—outweigh the anticipated costs?

The answers to these question should help determine whether or not preventive war or preemption are judged to be feasible, desirable, and appropriate in a given case. Several additional issues, similar to those raised with regard to deterrence, would also have to be addressed.

The United States would have to consider whether to launch the contemplated strike on its own or in cooperation with other powers. It would be in a stronger position politically if it were acting as part of a group of states, but it would have to be careful not to compromise operational security. It would also have to decide whether nuclear or conventional weapons, or some mix of the two, should be employed. U.S. military planners must consider more than purely technical factors, such as the hardness of certain targets and the destructive capability of particular weapons; they must also be sensitive to important political considerations, especially the international taboo against the use of nuclear weapons. Great pains should be taken to preserve this inhibition of almost five decades' standing and to avoid increasing the perceived utility of nuclear weapons in the eyes of potential or actual proliferators. Therefore, as a rule, U.S. decisionmakers should rely on conventional weapons exclusively in preventive strikes and primarily in preemption, resorting to nuclear weapons if and only if they believe beyond a reasonable doubt that a proliferator is about to use its nuclear weapons, that the conventional weapons available are inadequate to do the job, and that the use of U.S. nuclear weapons would have a high probability of success. These conditions set a very high standard that few if any scenarios would meet; they thus ensure that nuclear weapons will remain weapons of last resort.

Should the United States provide another country with the means to carry out a preventive or preemptive attack? A U.S. friend or ally might be directly threatened by the nuclear capability of a new nuclear weapon state but lack the means to destroy or defend itself against it. Transferring nuclear weapons to another country would run counter to U.S. nonproliferation policy and, once discovered, would undoubtedly trigger an international uproar; however, intelligence sharing or a transfer of sophisticated conventional arms useful for preventive war could be less controversial. Although such an arms transfer would have many of the advantages and disadvantages of arms transfers for other purposes and would need to be evaluated on those grounds, it would also present some particular dilemmas. On one hand, it would have the political advantage of unburdening the United States of direct responsibility for starting a preventive war. Washington could enable without having to execute. On the other hand, if the proliferator in question posed a serious and direct threat to U.S. forces or interests, the United States might not want to trust the job to any but its own military, particularly if it risked being a target of retaliation. In addition, the transfer of such offensive capabilities to the neighbor of a new nuclear weapon state, if publicly known, could be highly destabilizing, heightening regional tensions and placing "use 'em or lose 'em" pressures on the proliferator in a crisis.

What, then, should the stated U.S. policy on preventive war and preemption be? The United States could choose to say nothing. In so doing, it would avoid bringing the politically volatile subject of disarmament by force into the public spotlight. It would, however, also forgo the chance to caution existing and potential proliferators that their nuclear weapons capabilities may be fair game for a disarming strike if they pose a threat to U.S. interests. U.S. decisionmakers must send a clear signal to new nuclear weapon states without constraining U.S. freedom of action. For example, the United States, preferably together with other like-minded nations, might reserve the right to use whatever military force is necessary to destroy the nuclear weapons facilities and associated infrastructure of any country whose acquisition of nuclear weapons would threaten regional or international stability and the prospects for peace. Such a statement would issue the warning of a preventive strike under some circumstances but would not commit the United States to disarming any and all new nuclear weapon states by force. The United States might also reserve the right to use whatever military force is necessary to destroy a country's nuclear weapons if their use is judged to be offensive and imminent. Again, such a statement would lay down a marker for the United States and its partners without tying their hands. It would add the prospect of a disarming strike to the list of disincentives a proliferator would have to consider before crossing the nuclear threshold, making a nuclear threat, or using a nuclear weapon.

Defense

Another military option available to the United States in confronting a new nuclear weapon state is defense (see also chapter 8).

What questions would have to be answered before defense is deemed a viable policy option?

In contrast to most Cold War scenarios of nuclear use, in which the Soviet Union attacked the United States or its NATO allies with thousands of nuclear weapons, post–Cold War scenarios of nuclear use generally involve relatively few weapons. In most cases, a new proliferator is assumed to have fewer than ten weapons, and to be capable of threatening U.S. allies or overseas forces but not, at least for the time being, the U.S. homeland. Under these circumstances, defending against nuclear attack would appear to be more feasible. This widespread impression has been reinforced by the perceived success of the upgraded Patriot air defense system against Scud missiles during the Gulf War.[29] In addition, there are those who see defense as more necessary in a proliferated world in which new nuclear weapon states may be more willing to use their arsenal than their predecessors were.[30] These arguments have refueled the U.S. debate over defenses and have changed its direction.

Whether or not to employ defense in confronting new nuclear weapon states would depend on the answers to several questions:

1. What interests does the United States care most about defending? The list is straightforward: the U.S. homeland, U.S. forces deployed overseas, U.S. allies, U.S. friends, and particular U.S. interests (such as an embassy or an oil field). More difficult is distinguishing between those that are worth defending, all things considered, from those that are not.

2. What is the spectrum of threats against which U.S. defenses must be arrayed? One proliferator may possess only unconventional means of delivery for a crude nuclear device, whereas another may possess nuclear-capable fighter-bombers, ballistic missiles or cruise missiles. These threats require substantially different sorts of defenses, yet the current U.S. defense budget cannot accommodate a comprehensive defense against the full range of threats. The United States will, therefore, have to make some difficult choices, eliminating one vulnerability while leaving another exposed. This outcome has been likened to "buying insurance against lightning but not against fire or theft."[31]

3. How successful need a defense be in order to be worth building? Any plausible defense will have some estimated rate of leakage associated with it; the key issue is whether a particular defense system can keep leakage to a "tolerable" level. U.S. notions of what is and is not "tolerable" will vary according to the interest at stake and may differ from those of its allies.

4. Is defense a technically feasible option? Building a "traditional" ground-based ABM defense would be easier than constructing a defense that would essentially seal all U.S. borders against unconventional means of delivery. Building a defense against aircraft would be far less challenging than erecting one against cruise missiles. However, the greatest challenges to a particular system's feasibility may stem not from inherent technological hurdles but from external responses, such as an adversary's use of countermeasures. Furthermore, there is no guarantee that the most feasible defense will also be the most appropriate, and vice versa.

5. Are defenses affordable? Does the United States have the resources to build the defenses it desires? Are the American people willing to commit those resources to that cause?

6. What impact would defenses have on strategic stability? One of the strongest arguments against a nationwide U.S. ballistic missile defense during the Cold War was that it might threaten deterrence by undermining the Soviet Union's confidence in its retaliatory capability, thus fueling an offense–defense arms race between the superpowers. Now that the Cold War is over, the stability question bears reassessment. The impact of other types of defenses on stability should also be examined (see chapter 8).

7. Should the United States provide defenses to others? During the Gulf War, the United States provided upgraded Patriot air defenses to both Saudi Arabia and Israel to protect them from attacks by Iraqi Scud missiles. Since then, the United States has agreed to sell the Patriot system to several foreign countries, and is jointly developing the Arrow antitactical ballistic missile with Israel. Defenses may become one of the most popular

forms of U.S. military cooperation in the future. Although seemingly more benign than transfers of offensive arms, these transactions could in some cases also undermine stability and spur regional arms races, particularly if, by minimizing the damage that could be caused by retaliation, defenses were perceived as making offensive military action more likely.

In sum, while defense may appear to be a more attractive military option in the post–Cold War security environment, it is one with many faces, each of which must be evaluated. The public debate surrounding the feasibility and desirability of defense for coping with new nuclear weapon states also serves as a reminder that the United States must be able to build the necessary political support for whatever military options it ultimately chooses.

POLITICAL SUPPORT FOR U.S. MILITARY OPTIONS

The spread of nuclear weapons can be expected to affect the U.S. ability to secure domestic and international support for specific military policies. Proliferation can help or hinder the political process of coalition building.

The near possession by Saddam Hussein's Iraq of nuclear weapons galvanized support at home and abroad for U.S.-led military action against Iraq. But what if Iraq had already crossed the nuclear threshold? Fear of nuclear retaliation might have prevented an effective coalition and divided opinion about a forceful response to Iraq's invasion of Kuwait. An adversary's possession of nuclear weapons can easily cause dissension in alliances; countless NATO policy debates were sparked by the threat of Soviet nuclear use in Western Europe and fueled by the perception that alliance members on the opposite sides of the Atlantic faced markedly different levels of nuclear risk. Similar concerns and dynamics might have come into play during the Gulf War if the United States and its allies had faced a nuclear-armed Iraq with missiles capable of striking neighboring states and Europe but not the continental United States.

An adversary's possession of nuclear weapons can aid or impede coalition building, depending on the perceived importance of the interests threatened by a proliferator's nuclear capabilities, and the degree of international consensus supporting this perception. The nature of these capabilities also matter—can they deliver a nuclear weapon to U.S. territory, to U.S. allies and friends, or to U.S. forces? Can this capability be defended against? Is it vulnerable to destruction?

These questions suggest not only the potential lines of division between allies but also the importance of timing in determining success or failure in coalition building: mustering political support for military action against a new nuclear weapon state is likely to become increasingly difficult as the perceived capabilities of its nuclear arsenal grow. A window for internationally supported military action against a proliferator may close as the country gains the capability to retaliate against additional countries at greater distances.

The importance of the interests at stake and the specifics of a proliferator's nuclear capabilities might also influence whether a "free rider" effect could endanger coalition building. If potential partners believe that the United States will ultimately take military action with or without them, they might opt to take a "free ride" by declining to become coalition members and possible targets of retaliation, while enjoying the benefits of the U.S. action. The United States might be able to neutralize this effect by making a country's support for a particular U.S. military action a condition for its receipt of future U.S. protection and assistance.

A third factor likely to affect coalition building is the strength of international norms against the acquisition, production, testing, deployment, threatened, and actual use of nuclear weapons. The stronger these are when military action is being considered, the greater the level of international support the United States can expect to command. Thus, strengthening the norms against proliferation should be viewed not only as an instrument of nonproliferation but also as an instrument of coping with proliferation—a means of garnering greater political support in the event that military action against a new nuclear weapon state must be pursued as a last resort.[32] Building such a normative consensus in advance, before a real-world need for coalition building arises, could prove essential to forming effective coalitions in a crisis.

CONCLUSION

Like a lens that brings objects into sharper focus, nuclear proliferation will force a fundamental reassessment, and in some cases a revision, of how the United States sees its interests and commitments around the world. It will also play a significant role in determining how assertive U.S. military posture will be now that the Cold War is over.

Perhaps most important, nuclear proliferation will require U.S. decisionmakers to consider seriously, for the first time in decades, a much broader range of military options in confronting nuclear-armed adversaries. In the context of proliferation, the primacy of deterrence is no longer a given. Although deterrence may ultimately emerge as the preferred option in a particular instance, other approaches—such as preventive war, preemption, and defense— will deserve equally serious study and evaluation. Furthermore, building coalitions in support of a chosen military course of action will present the United States with potentially unprecedented leadership challenges.

The choice of options will depend in large part on what the United States can learn about the new nuclear weapon state. Proliferation will put a premium on detailed and accurate intelligence assessments of the intentions, capabilities, perceptions, and behavior of new nuclear nations. Decisionmakers will need to know more about a given adversary as well as about a greater number of adversaries. How, and how well, we ultimately cope with new nuclear weapon states may ultimately come down to what we know, how much we know, and when we know it.

Notes

1. In this chapter, "U.S. military strategy" denotes the principles and guidelines governing the use of military power in support of U.S. national interests and objectives, as well as specific military options and missions.
2. The author is grateful to McGeorge Bundy, Howard Griffiths, Teresa Johnson, Leo Mackay, and the other contributors to this volume for their helpful comments on this chapter.
3. It is beyond the scope of this chapter to determine what U.S. foreign policy goals

and interests should be in the post–Cold War world. The debate on this subject is voluminous, fierce, and ongoing. See, for example, Stephen Van Evera, "Why Europe Matters, Why the Third World Doesn't: American Grand Strategy After the Cold War," *Journal of Strategic Studies*, vol. 13, no. 2 (June 1990), pp. 1–51; Samuel P. Huntington, "America's Changing Strategic Interests," *Survival*, vol. 33, no. 1 (January/February 1991), pp. 3–17; Ted Galen Carpenter, "The New World Disorder," *Foreign Policy*, no. 84 (Fall 1991), pp. 24–39; Earl Ravenal, "The Case for Adjustment," *Foreign Policy*, no. 81 (Winter 1990–1991), pp. 3–19; Robert J. Art, "A Defensible Defense: America's Grand Strategy After the Cold War," *International Security*, vol. 15, no. 4 (Spring 1991), pp. 5–53; and Alan Tonelson, "What Is the National Interest?" *The Atlantic*, vol. 268, no. 1 (July 1991), pp. 35–52. Whatever the ultimate outcome of this debate, it is safe to assume that for the foreseeable future the United States will remain committed to defending at least some key interests and friends beyond its own borders.

4. See John Mueller, "American Public Opinion and the Gulf War: Trends and Historical Comparisons," unpublished paper presented to the Conference on the Political Consequences of War, The Brookings Institution, Washington, D.C., February 28, 1992.

5. A March 1991 poll conducted by Americans Talk Issues indicates that most Americans believe the following kinds of dictators to pose a serious threat to international security and to the United States: those who sponsor terrorism around the world (92 percent), those who acquire chemical, biological, and nuclear weapons (91 percent), and those who violate human rights (91 percent). See "The New World Order—What Peace Should Be," *Americans Talk Issues*, Survey No. 15, March 19–24, 1991, p. 41.

6. See, in particular, the *Los Angeles Times* polls of November 14, 1990, and January 8–12, 1990, and the Gallup poll of November 15–16, 1990, as reprinted in Mueller, "American Public Opinion and the Gulf War."

7. For example, in his *Report of the Secretary of Defense to the President and the Congress* of February 1992 (Washington, D.C.: United States Government Printing Office [USGPO]), Secretary of Defense Dick Cheney argues that the proliferation of weapons of mass destruction underlines the need for continued investment in defense assets ranging from GPALS (p. 66) to Special Operations Forces (p. 100).

8. This chapter focuses on immediate deterrence as opposed to general deterrence. Immediate deterrence denotes specific attempts to prevent an anticipated challenge to a well-defined and publicized commitment, whereas general deterrence is based on a broader power relationship and denotes attempts to prevent an adversary from seriously considering any kind of military challenge because of its anticipated adverse consequences. See Richard Ned Lebow and Janice Gross Stein, *When Does Deterrence Succeed and How Do We Know?* CIIPS Occasional Paper No. 8, February 1990, p. 9; and Patrick M. Morgan, *Deterrence: A Conceptual Analysis*, rev. ed. (Beverly Hills, Calif.: Sage Library of Social Science, 1983).

9. Much has been written about the role of counterforce in U.S. nuclear strategy. See, for example, Charles L. Glaser, "Nuclear Policy Without an Adversary: U.S. Planning for the Post-Soviet Era," *International Security*, vol. 16, no. 4

(Spring 1992), pp. 34–78; and Desmond Ball, "Development of the SIOP, 1960–1983," in Desmond Ball and Jeffrey Richelson, eds., *Strategic Nuclear Targeting* (Ithaca, N.Y.: Cornell University Press, 1986).

10. Les Aspin, *From Deterrence to Denuking: Dealing With Proliferation in the 1990s,* unpublished working paper, February 18, 1992, p. 9.

11. This section deals exclusively with military options for confronting new nuclear weapon states that the United States views as implacably hostile adversaries. It does not evaluate the options that might be available to the United States in coping with more friendly proliferators, as these would probably not be military in nature.

12. Greater emphasis will be placed on deterrence in this chapter, while more in-depth analysis of preemption is provided by Philip Zelikow in chapter 7, and of defense by Albert Carnesale in chapter 8.

13. As chairman of the House Armed Services Committee, Les Aspin argued that the new threat to U.S. interests is the nondeterrable, terrorist state armed with nuclear weapons. See Les Aspin, "National Security in the 1990s: Defining a New Basis for U.S. Military Forces," *Comments Before the Atlantic Council of the United States* (Washington, D.C.: USGPO, January 6, 1992), pp. 7–10. Similarly, former Secretary of Defense Cheney argued that U.S. strategy must shift its focus from "a unitary, rational actor with full knowledge and respect for the consequences of nuclear war" to "states or leaders [that may] perceive they have little to lose from employing weapons of mass destruction." See *Report of the Secretary of Defense to the President and the Congress* (Washington, D.C.: USGPO, February 1992), p. 59.

14. The classics of deterrence literature include Bernard Brodie, *Strategy in the Missile Age* (Princeton N.J.: Princeton University Press, 1959); William W. Kaufmann, *The Requirements of Deterrence* (Princeton: Center for International Studies, 1954); and Thomas Schelling, *The Strategy of Conflict* (New Haven, Conn.: Yale University Press, 1960).

15. See, for example, Aspin, "National Security in the 1990s," pp. 7–8.

16. See, for example, David Ignatius, "Madman's Bluff: Why Deterrence Still Works," *Washington Post*, May 10, 1992, pp. C1, C4.

17. Its reasoning might, for example, be "need-driven"—based on its strategic vulnerabilities or domestic political needs—rather than "opportunity-driven"—based on an inclination to exploit opportunities to make gains. See Lebow and Stein, *When Does Deterrence Succeed and How Do We Know?*, pp. 60–61, 64–69.

18. For example, if U.S. decisionmakers fail to see, whether rightly or wrongly, that a new nuclear weapon state perceives itself to be the defender rather than the challenger in a given deterrence encounter, they could easily misinterpret its actions. Although deterrence theory often defines these two roles as mutually exclusive and assumes that their proper identification is obvious to all, this is not necessarily so, as Lebow and Stein point out in *When Does Deterrence Succeed and How Do We Know?*, pp. 73–75.

19. The phrase is that of Ashton B. Carter and Robert D. Blackwill. See their discussion of this issue in chapter 9 on intelligence.

20. See Richard Ned Lebow's discussion of barriers to signaling in "Conclusions" in Robert Jervis, Richard Ned Lebow, and Janice Gross Stein, eds., *Psy-*

chology and Deterrence (Baltimore, Md.: Johns Hopkins University Press, 1985), pp. 204–11.

21. It is easy to imagine, for example, a carefully worded U.S. deterrent threat getting lost amid the hyperbolic rhetoric of the Middle East. Lebow cites several examples of failed signaling in numerous historical cases, including the 1948 Berlin crisis, the Korean War, Vietnam, and the Falklands conflict. Ibid., pp. 204–11.

22. A recent example of such purposeful ambiguity was President Bush's January 5, 1991, letter to Saddam Hussein just prior to Operation Desert Storm. As described in McGeorge Bundy, "Nuclear Weapons and the Gulf," *Foreign Affairs*, vol. 70, no. 4 (Fall 1991), pp. 83–94, the letter warned Saddam against "unconscionable acts" like "the use of chemical or biological weapons," saying that "the American people would demand the strongest possible response," and "you and your country would pay a terrible price." But the letter refrained from making an explicit nuclear threat. When asked at a press conference a month later whether the United States might retaliate against any Iraqi use of chemical weapons with its own weapons of mass destruction, President Bush replied, "I think it's better never to say what you may be considering." It is impossible at this point to say definitively whether this threat, operational constraints, or other factors actually kept Saddam Hussein from using the chemical weapons at his disposal.

23. The phrase is from Kurt M. Campbell, Ashton B. Carter, Steven E. Miller, and Charles A. Zraket, *Soviet Nuclear Fission: Control of the Nuclear Arsenal in a Disintegrating Soviet Union*, CSIA Studies in International Security No. 1 (Cambridge, Mass.: Center for Science and International Affairs, November 1991).

24. The United States has been moving away from in-theater nuclear deterrence, withdrawing tactical nuclear weapons from Europe, South Korea, and ships at sea, leaving 500 or so bombs deployed in Europe. See, for example, Jonathan Kauffman, "NATO to Cut Nuclear Arms 80%," *Boston Globe*, October 18, 1991, p. 1; Don Oberdorfer, "U.S. Decides to Withdraw A-Weapons from S. Korea," *Washington Post*, October 19, 1991, p. A1; and Michael Gordon, "Navy Phasing Out Nuclear Rockets for Close Combat," *New York Times*, April 30, 1989, p. A1.

25. Early U.S. thinking on preventive war is reviewed in Marc Trachtenberg, "A 'Wasting Asset': American Strategy and the Shifting Nuclear Balance, 1949–1954," *International Security*, vol. 13, no. 3 (Winter 1988/89), pp. 7–11; Russell D. Buhite and William Christopher Hamel, "War for Peace: The Question of an American Preventive War Against the Soviet Union, 1945–1955," *Diplomatic History*, vol. 14 (Summer 1990), pp. 367–84; and David Alan Rosenberg, "The Origins of Overkill: Nuclear Weapons and American Strategy, 1945–1960," *International Security*, vol. 7, no. 4 (Spring 1983), pp. 3–71.

26. By contrast, preemption has long been an important option in Israeli military strategy, as the June 7, 1981, bombing of the Osiraq reactor evidenced. See Shai Feldman, "The Bombing of Osiraq Revisited," *International Security*, vol. 7, no. 2 (Fall 1982), pp. 114–42; and Shlomo Nakdimon, *First Strike: The Exclusive Story of How Israel Foiled Iraq's Attempts to Get the Bomb*,

Peretz Kidron, trans. (New York: Simon and Schuster, 1987).

27. See "The New World Order—What the Peace Should Be," p. 38.

28. It is instructive to recall international reaction to Israel's bombing of Osiraq in 1981. Although various leaders might have been privately relieved that Israel thwarted Iraq's nuclear weapons ambitions, at least temporarily, public reactions to the strike were generally quite negative. Both the International Atomic Energy Agency director general and the UN Security Council characterized the raid as an attack on IAEA safeguards and as a threat to the foundation of the NPT. See "Peaceful Nuclear Development Must Continue," *IAEA Bulletin*, vol. 23, no. 3 (September 1981), p. 3. In a particularly public demonstration of its disapproval, the United States joined Iraq in drafting a UN Security Council resolution condemning the bombing. See Michael J. Berlin, "U.S., Iraqis Agree on U.N. Resolution Condemning Israel," *Washington Post*, June 19, 1981. There was, however, scattered praise for this preventive strike. A June 9, 1981, editorial in the *Wall Street Journal*, for example, praised the Israeli action as "effective anti-proliferation policy."

29. Whether Patriot actually reduced damage on the ground has been hotly debated. See, for example, Theodore A. Postol, "Lessons of the Gulf War Experience With Patriot," *International Security*, vol. 16, no. 3 (Winter 1991/92), pp. 119–71; Reuven Pedatzur and Theodore Postol, "The Patriot Is No Success Story," *Defense News*, December 2, 1991, p. 24; Charles Zraket, "Patriot Gave Stellar Gulf Performance," *Defense News*, December 9, 1991, p. 31; Reuven Pedatzur and Theodore Postol, "Patriot Article Fails," *Defense News*, January 13, 1992, p. 18; Charles Zraket, "Patriot Defense," *Defense News*, January 20, 1992; and Robert M. Stein and Theodore A. Postol, "Correspondence," *International Security*, vol. 17, no. 1 (Summer 1992), pp. 199–240.

30. This theme runs throughout former Secretary of Defense Cheney's *Report of the Secretary of Defense to the President and the Congress*, February 1992, and is one of the foundations on which the congressional consensus in support of GPALs was built.

31. Editorial, "Don't Rush to Deploy ABM's," *New York Times*, February 27, 1992, p. A24.

32. The crucial question of how the United States can help establish and fortify these norms before a military confrontation arises is addressed by Joseph S. Nye, Jr., in chapter 4 on diplomatic measures.

CHAPTER SEVEN

Offensive Military Options

PHILIP ZELIKOW

Suppose that in 1991 we had known all we now know about Iraq's nuclear program, but that Saddam Hussein had not invaded Kuwait. Iraq's preparations to wage nuclear war would have alarmed the United States and other governments, but no ready *casus belli* would have been at hand. Iraq would have appeared to be formidably defended. The world and Baghdad's Arab neighbors would have been deeply divided on the advisability of trying to eliminate the Iraqi threat with massive military action.

The United States and other countries could have chosen to live with the new reality and adapt to Saddam's nuclear striking power, or chosen to say: "No. We just cannot accept this development. It is too dangerous." The example is hypothetical; the problem is not. My premise is that there are some states, in some circumstances, whose development, acquisition, or deployment of nuclear weapons could endanger the vital interests of the United States. This chapter analyzes options for military disarmament of such states.

To determine whether the dangers from weapons of mass destruction justify recourse to military action, the political and military leaders of the United States would need to make at least six key judgments:

1. Are we confident that, in the given circumstances, country X can be deterred from using its nuclear weapons against America or America's allies?

2. Are we confident that country X will not transfer or can be prevented from transferring its nuclear weapons capability to other countries or groups that might be more likely to use nuclear weapons?

3. If we acquiesce in the development, acquisition, or deployment of nuclear weapons by country X, will the resulting state of affairs significantly increase the danger of conventional war—with the possibility of nuclear escalation—that would threaten American vital interests?

4. If the answers to *any* of the three preceding questions is yes, are we confident that the dangers can be sufficiently contained by diplomatic countermeasures, including possible military enforcement of economic sanctions?

5. Do the actions and behavior of country X, in preparing to wage an aggressive war of mass destruction, ethically and legally justify offensive military action by the United States which could cost many lives, both Americans and others?

6. Can military action by the United States and/or its allies contain or eliminate the danger without risking retaliation that would pose an even greater risk to U.S. interests?

This chapter addresses primarily the last of these questions. All of them, however, require highly subjective judgments about the feasibility of preventive or preemptive military action.[1] Preventive military measures are currently being suggested by some analysts in order to prevent the acquisition of nuclear weapons by either Iraq or North Korea. But as Lewis Dunn concluded, "little has been done to identify the prerequisites of successful deterrence or preemption, let alone planning to try to meet them."[2]

This chapter examines a fundamental concept: the inverse relationship between the threat posed by nuclear proliferators and their vulnerability to military countermeasures. It describes three sets of variables that can set the parameters for military planning, and notes specific operational requirements for military action (illustrated by a hypothetical attack plan). Several key strategic and diplomatic issues raised by the contemplation of offensive military options are also considered.

The chapter concludes that offensive military options can conceivably disrupt efforts to acquire nuclear arms. The options are, however, much less likely to succeed and are far less attractive once the target country has already built a number of nuclear weapons.

A successful attack against an advanced nuclear weapons program, even one that has not yet built a nuclear explosive device, is likely to require a considerable exertion of political and military power. The operation would probably involve hundreds of American aircraft as well as other components of the U.S. armed forces, and close cooperation with U.S. allies in the region.

The sheer scale of the operation is likely to create its own escalatory momentum and dictate very high standards for measuring ultimate success. Yet a successful example of forcible disarmament can strengthen deterrence of other would-be nuclear proliferators, and there is tentative evidence that the Gulf War may have already had this effect.

The analysis demonstrates the value of amending international norms to legitimize action against nuclear outlaws while their weapons programs are still immature. And it illustrates the possible yield from force restructuring to increase the long-range striking power of American aircraft.

THREAT GOES UP; VULNERABILITY GOES DOWN

As a state's nuclear (or other weapons of mass destruction) capability becomes more threatening, it becomes less vulnerable to military action by an outside power. This inverse relationship affects all strategic planning against new proliferators.

At one end of the continuum is an immature nuclear program that possesses a source of uranium, possibly its own uranium mines. Both Iraq and North Korea, for example, have indigenous uranium ore, although Iraq also imported enriched (90 percent plus) uranium reactor fuel from the Soviet Union under International Atomic Energy Agency safeguards (the fuel is to be returned to Russia by the IAEA).

An immature program has a nuclear research reactor, almost certainly acquired and built with foreign help, which can produce a little plutonium. The reactor may even be under the nominal supervision of the IAEA. The program also has a scientific installation with laboratories, including a radioisotope lab where chemical separation of tiny amounts of fissionable material could occur, using fuel irradiated in the reactor. Experiments with uranium enrichment may also be underway.

An immature nuclear program is vulnerable to relatively small military attacks, as the Iraqi program was in 1981. Most vulnerable is the reactor itself. Bombs or cruise missiles in a single strike could crack the reactor containment vessel or bring down the cooling tower or other heat exchangers. This damage could turn the fuel core into radioactive slag or even cause a meltdown that would kill the reactor's operators and release deadly radiation into the surrounding area. But even without a meltdown, reactor repairs might be difficult, if not impossible, without substantial foreign help.

Other countries will probably be aware of the existence of these programs since concealment of the construction and operation of even a small nuclear reactor would be difficult. Any evidence of a clandestine effort would inflame suspicions, not deflect them.

Yet immature nuclear programs, their purpose ostensibly in doubt, are not likely to be attacked. After Iraq lost its French-built nuclear reactor to Israeli bombing in 1981, Baghdad deemphasized its overt nuclear activities. Iraq's purpose was ambiguous, it had accepted IAEA safeguards, and the international community took little notice. Meanwhile, Iraq's air defenses also improved. Intelligence limitations as well as the political and military environment kept Israel from being able to attack the new Iraqi program, just as it now lives with the more distant nuclear reactors (being built or operating) in countries like Iran or Algeria.

Further along the threat-vulnerability continuum is the immature nuclear weapons program that has not been disrupted or, having suffered a setback, has recovered. The mature program is then very different. Uranium ore or other raw materials have been stockpiled, so interruptions in supply will make less difference than they would to an immature program. Instead of one reactor, there are at least two or three.

The reactors may no longer be indispensable to the weapons program. Even if they are destroyed, they may have already produced a stockpile of irradiated fuel that can separately be reprocessed into the fissionable material required for a small nuclear arsenal. And these stockpiles might be dispersed. In Iraq, some stockpiles of radioactive material were hidden in open fields near the nuclear installations, with no buildings or other obvious indicators to give away their location.

The radioisotope separation lab may still exist, but its function will have been eclipsed by much larger reprocessing or uranium enrichment facilities. In Iraq, a cascade of gas centrifuges was scheduled to begin production in 1991. According to some reports, it was scheduled to expand to a 100-machine cascade by 1993, and 500 machines by 1996. By the mid-1990s the centrifuge enrichment effort would have been producing enough fissionable material to manufacture a small arsenal. Unknown to the West, Iraq had also built, at vast cost, a facility for electromagnetic enrichment of uranium which might have been able to produce enough fissionable material to build weapons within eighteen months. A mature program's uranium enrichment facilities could be dispersed, and they are easier to conceal than a nuclear reactor.

Even if the location of enrichment facilities were known, such facilities are more difficult to destroy than reactors, since they can consist of numerous redundant machines, built with less sophisticated engineering, in which there are no nuclear chain reactions and less risk of system catastrophe from a disruption. The enrichment/reprocessing facilities may be easier to rebuild than reactors. They are also easier to hide. Iraq did not have indigenous ability to build reactors, but it had used reverse engineering and a large industrial base to figure out how to build enrichment facilities, produce maraging steel and centrifuges, and utilize (even if not construct) precision machine tools.

A mature nuclear program might also have one or more weapons fabrication facilities and sites for the production and assembly of special explosives. These sites can be destroyed, but they can also be rebuilt.

Some facilities, including storage sites for nuclear materials, may be located in deep underground structures that might be unsuitable for a nuclear reactor. While one or two such structures might be spotted, blocked, or destroyed with concentrated effort, it would be very difficult to give intensive attention to each well-concealed and well-protected site in a more advanced program with its much more diverse set of activities.

An advanced weapons program has another critical asset that is harder to replace but also much harder to eliminate: a large and diversified community of scientists and engineers. This community, and the technological base built up as the nuclear program reaches maturity, are what gives the mature program its resilience.

If the mature nuclear weapons program continues its work, it approaches the far end of the threat-vulnerability continuum by producing a nuclear arsenal. A country with a nuclear weapons arsenal is clearly much harder to attack than a state that has only a nuclear weapons program. The most immediate problem for a military planner considering a preemptive strike is the possible dispersal of these nuclear weapons to a number of locations, some of which may not be known.

While an immature nuclear program is rarely a major source of international tension, it is most vulnerable to military attack. A mature, resilient nuclear program is, in turn, more vulnerable than a program that has built up an arsenal of nuclear weapons and is more likely to be the target of heightened international scrutiny. At this point the country will be more sensitive to the danger of military attack and is likely to have developed responsive political and military strategies to limit its program's vulnerability.

There is a precedent for striking a nuclear weapons program while it is still in its infancy: the successful Israeli raid in 1981 against the Iraqi nuclear facilities at Al-Tuweitha, outside Baghdad. In that case Israel attacked a program that was still small enough to be hurt badly by a single small-scale air strike. Because the program was small, and was monitored under IAEA safeguards, the world considered Iraqi intentions uncertain and widely condemned the Israeli action (at least in public).

The 1981 raid against Iraq does not, however, offer a precedent that can be emulated by a country such as the United States. Israel acted as it did because of its weakness, not because of its strength. Lacking any serious diplomatic options and doubtful of its military capacity to deal with a more mature and far-flung Iraqi nuclear program, Israel did what it could, while it could, against a country with which it had long been in a formal state of war.[3]

What Israel could do was to set back Iraqi plans for years. But Israel could not fully thwart these plans. As Iraq rebuilt its program, this time on a larger scale and with much more deception, Israel had to stand by, unable to do anything but further prepare its own nuclear arsenal. Even if Jerusalem had possessed full and accurate intelligence on the extent of the danger, it would, on its own, have been unable to repeat its 1981 success. Alone, it had no viable option by which it could safely neutralize the far more elaborate Iraqi nuclear program (and air defense network) that existed by the end of 1990.

So, the more threatening a nuclear program becomes, the less vulnerable it is to military attack. The political implications of this are clear enough: there is a major incentive to develop a political basis for decisive diplomatic or military action against a nuclear weapons program as early as possible in the program's development. If the program appears too innocuous or ambiguous to support such a strategy, it can be adopted later, but with greater difficulty. There is likely to be a limited period (several months, perhaps even a year or two), when the threat posed by a nuclear proliferator is acute enough to justify contemplation of military action, but where the risks associated with the use of force are still manageable. Once this period ends, conventional military action to eliminate the threat will probably be too risky.[4]

Unfortunately, as in the Iraq case, military intelligence is likely to indicate only possibilities, not certainties. Uncertainty can be ameliorated through an extensive diplomatic regime of outside inspections, or by assuming the worst and attacking sooner rather than later. International political norms tend to deal with uncertainty by allowing questionable behavior to be considered ambiguous, rather than by equating ambiguity with hostility.[5]

Countries suspected of developing nuclear weapons also have a strong incentive to manipulate international perceptions of where they are along the threat-vulnerability continuum. For as long as possible, they would probably want to downplay (at least to outsiders) the importance of nuclear weapons to their national defense. Yet after a few weapons are ready, they might acknowledge and even exaggerate their weapons capability in order to deter a preemptive strike. In both cases the main goal is to avert initiation of preventive or preemptive war by an outside power, keeping the window of vulnerability as small as possible. The Soviet Union's behavior between 1945 and 1962 bears some resemblance to this model, as does the behavior of China between 1950 and 1970.

CONTINGENCIES FOR PLANNING: THREE SETS OF VARIABLES

Military planning for the use of force to limit or eliminate the danger of nuclear proliferation will be defined by three parameters: the timing and political context for military action; the nature of the adversary; and the kind of targets to be attacked. Political judgments about these parameters will vitally affect the prospects for military success.

1. Timing and Context for Offensive Action

The least likely scenario for U.S. military action against a proliferator would be a bolt from the blue. America has never initiated major military action without a prior gathering of political storm-clouds, and Washington would be unable to rally strong support for military action unless the threat posed by a nuclear weapons program was acute. Indeed there is no evidence that military action is currently being contemplated against any of the several countries, such as Iran, that appear to have embarked on a nuclear weapons program but are believed to be years away from producing or acquiring sufficient fissionable material to construct a bomb.

The United States would be unlikely to consider a bolt from the blue attack as Israel did in 1981 when it attacked the Iraqi nuclear facilities outside Baghdad. Washington would see an entirely different menu of diplomatic opportunities and ultimate military possibilities. It would be making national security decisions in a more open and more questioning domestic environment. It also would probably be considering an attack on countries with which we are at least formally at peace. So the 1981 precedent of

Israel's preventive strike against Iraq does not disturb the conclusion that, for America, a military bolt from the blue is not a serious contingency for defense planning.

A more likely contingency would be offensive action arising from a prolonged period of political crisis. The suspect nuclear program would for some time have received sustained domestic and international attention. The target country, fearing military action, would already have adopted diplomatic measures to dampen or deflect international suspicion while intensifying military preparations to defend against an attack, such as concealment and dispersal of critical strategic assets and placing defense forces in a higher state of readiness.

The political crisis that provides the occasion for offensive military action need not arise from the weapons of mass destruction (WMD) program. The United States might have decided to prepare for military conflict for entirely separate reasons, as in the decision to retaliate against Libya in 1986 for Tripoli's direction of terrorist operations against Americans. The United States also marshaled, but did not use, military power against North Korea in 1976 after North Korean soldiers murdered two American servicemen in the Demilitarized Zone (DMZ).

If a decision to use military power had been made on other grounds, the United States could decide to include, among the targets for the attack, other programs to produce weapons of mass destruction. This scenario is one of the only circumstances in which the United States might attack potential WMD facilities before they are threatening enough to justify an assault and while they are still immature enough to be most vulnerable to military action.

An entirely different contingency for military action against an outlaw nuclear program would be as part of the opening phase of general war. If the United States goes to war against a country, it will treat any enemy WMD facilities as high-priority targets. This was true in both the Second World War and during the Gulf War against Iraq.

Finally, the United States could find itself targeting the nuclear program of another country because of the escalation of an ongoing limited war. The United States could be involved in a war in which it had previously refrained from attacking an opponent's most important military assets in its homeland, in an effort to keep the scope of conflict limited to a particular country or theater of military operations.[6] If the conflict expands, the nuclear program would no longer be off-limits.

One conclusion stands out. The United States is only likely to use force against a proliferator in a climate of heightened political tension that will have put a potential adversary on notice of the possibility of an American attack. From a purely military standpoint, this means that the target country will have received strategic warning, will have concealed and dispersed its most important targets to the extent possible, and will have enhanced the readiness of its general defenses.

2. The Nature of the Adversary

For purposes of planning offensive military options, four intelligence issues are likely to be most important.

Does the adversary possess deliverable weapons of mass destruction? There is a fundamental distinction between planning to attack a nuclear program and planning to attack a nuclear arsenal. If the target country already has nuclear, chemical, or biological weapons at hand, this danger will powerfully influence U.S. planning in several ways.

The United States will seek to avoid deploying large concentrations of men or materiel within range of effective WMD retaliation because the consequences would be too great. Retaliation could kill thousands of Americans, block the achievement of military objectives, inflame domestic political opposition to U.S. military action, and threaten a counterproductive escalation of the conflict.[7] In addition, American allies, also vulnerable to retaliation, will be less likely to support U.S. action or allow U.S. forces to deploy to forward bases on their territory.

Any U.S. planning to attack a country equipped with nuclear, biological, or chemical weapons must take account of the possible use of these weapons. These American plans would probably therefore need to include carefully developed options for the retaliatory employment of U.S. nuclear weapons.

In the fall of 1990, the United States assumed that Iraq possessed substantial stocks of chemical weapons and possibly some biological toxin weapons as well. Washington further believed that Baghdad could deliver at least the chemical weapons with aircraft, artillery, and possibly missiles. This danger did not stop the deployment of coalition forces, which prepared frantically to survive a chemical or even biological attack. But America tried to deter such attacks by hinting to Iraq that use of chemical weapons risked retaliation by American nuclear weapons.[8]

Countries near Iraq that supported the coalition, especially Saudi Arabia, Turkey, and Israel, were deeply concerned about the possibility that Iraq might attack them with chemical or biological weapons. Yet the United States was able to assuage these fears and obtain both political support and basing rights by offering strong assurances at the highest political levels of American readiness, in the event of war, to remove Iraq's strategic military potential.

These assurances might not have been adequate if the neighboring countries feared nuclear retaliation. Countries may be reluctant to grant basing rights, for example, unless the United States could promise that the nuclear weapons capability would be destroyed first, before substantial U.S. forces arrived on their territory. Washington, too, may have its worries about deploying units into areas where they could be vulnerable to an initial nuclear strike.

Faced with an enemy nuclear arsenal, the United States would attempt to neutralize this danger, by operating from bases well out of range of retaliation. With the enemy nuclear striking power disabled or momentarily paralyzed, both the United States and the basing country would be better able to go ahead with forward deployments of the forces needed for follow-up strikes.

What is the general condition of the adversary's defenses? Special attention would be given to the air defense network and the degree to which critical targets have been hardened against air attack. Iraq, for example, possessed an extraordinarily elaborate and sophisticated air defense system. The North Korean air defense system is smaller and less advanced, but the terrain makes targets easier to conceal and harder to destroy. Many key facilities in North Korea have long been buried well underground or are dug into mountains, accessible only through cave entrances.

What is the conventional offensive power of the adversary? Like weapons of mass destruction, conventional armed forces also permit retaliation—sometimes months or even years later—against neighbors who support U.S. military action. Washington will therefore be pressured for assurances that its action will deal definitively not only with the WMD capability, but also with this capacity for retaliation by the enemy government.

How distant is the adversary from U.S. forces and bases? Geography is important. It shows which countries are most in danger because they are within range of the adversary's forces. Yet an American military planner will also be looking hard at another factor—seemingly obvious but often overlooked: How far away is the country from U.S. forces and their bases?

American B-52H and B-1B bombers can, with refueling and overflight rights, fly almost anywhere, but these aircraft are not currently armed or equipped to carry the main weight of a sustained conventional strategic air campaign. The B-2 bomber will be more capable when it enters the force in the mid-1990s, but it is not likely to be available in significant numbers anytime in this century.

U.S. Navy carriers and submarines can attack targets within several hundred miles of any of the world's oceans, but these forces, too, may not be able to provide the sustained striking power needed for a major conflict. The naval units may also require at least several days in order to reach their combat stations.

U.S. special operations forces other than those involved in small clandestine activities are likely to operate successfully only within the radius of air and naval protection.

Therefore, unless the threatening nuclear activity is quite vulnerable to small-scale military attack, it must be within range, or be placed within range, of substantial U.S. air and naval power. Even if the necessary forward bases exist or can be constructed, and are politically available for use by American forces, there must be time to deploy appropriate ships, aircraft, fuel, and ammunition to the right spots. For example, the United States is fortunate already to have excellent bases in South Korea and Japan within combat range of North Korea. Yet, even if the host countries agreed that the danger warranted extraordinary action, neither the right kinds nor the right numbers of U.S. ships and aircraft are routinely stationed in these countries. The necessary deployments would take time, and they would probably be noticed.

3. The Targeting Objectives

The third fundamental parameter for military planning is to determine the kinds of targets to be attacked. As Thomas Schelling explained: "In addition to seizing and holding, disarming and confining, penetrating and obstructing . . . military force can be used *to hurt*. In addition to taking and protecting things of value, it can *destroy* value."[9] Options which "destroy value" are likely to be used against a state with a threatening nuclear program or new nuclear arsenal. Four kinds of targets need to be considered: Those associated with weapons of mass destruction; with air superiority; with political leadership; and with fielded military forces.

Targets associated with weapons of mass destruction. Even if the nuclear program is the greatest source of concern, any chemical or biological weapons programs would almost certainly be attacked at the same time. Targets could include: 1) nuclear reactors, chemical extraction or enrichment plants, engineering labs, fuel fabrication, weapon design centers, ammunition depots stockpiling special explosives, other research and development facilities, and local power sources;[10] 2) biological weapons laboratories, facilities for producing toxins, and storage bunkers for these weapons; and 3) chemical weapons research, production, and storage facilities. If nuclear weapons have been fielded, the military must also attack the delivery systems, such as short- or intermediate-range ballistic missiles; the research, production, and storage facilities for the missiles; any aircraft or aircraft support activities associated with nuclear weapons; and any identifiable links in the command and control over the nuclear weapons.

The United States will need retaliatory options if the adversary's nuclear weapons have been fielded. Preemptive use against an outlaw state might be an option if intelligence shows that a devastating nuclear or other WMD attack against the United States is imminent and if the United States concludes that the attack can only be averted by using nuclear weapons first. There is no publicly available evidence, however, to show that current U.S. nuclear weapons employment policy includes an option for preemption that is distinct from the counterforce options developed for the contingency of war with the former Soviet Union.[11]

Before the war against Iraq, the last systematic Western efforts to destroy enemy weapons of mass destruction were against Nazi Germany. This experience sheds some light on appropriate targeting objectives. In the case of the German atom bomb program, there was little to attack because the atom bomb's potential was not adequately recognized or developed by Hitler or Speer. Nonetheless, to slow Nazi atomic research, the allies prevented German achievement of an experimental chain reaction by bombing and sabotaging the needed supply of heavy water from southern Norway.

The German V-1 pilotless aircraft and V-2 rocket, which each carried a ton of explosives, were more difficult to preempt. Allied intelligence on these systems was good, but the U.S. effort to stop their use largely failed because bombing of the key research facility (at Peenemünde in 1943) came too late. The weapons had already been developed for large-scale production, and repeated bombing of major production facilities was ineffective because production was in only a small area of the plant, the factory was hardened against blast, and most V-1 and all V-2 production was moved deep underground to the miles of factory tunnels 140–200 feet beneath the earth at Nordhausen. The United States also lacked information on the vulnerability of some key components (electrical power and two chemicals), and showed an understandable unwillingness to attack the nearby labor force—the tens of thousands of slave laborers in the Nordhausen concentration camp.[12]

Targets associated with achievement of air superiority. The United States must plan on overcoming air defenses to clear the way for air attacks on an adversary. This can be done by using Stealth aircraft to defeat radar and evade enemy air defenses; by direct attacks on the enemy air defense network, including early warning and air surveillance radars, command and control facilities such as sector operation centers, communications and computer links, and the supporting electrical power; by strikes against the enemy surface-to-air missile systems or antiaircraft artillery (perhaps using missiles which home in on enemy air defense radars); by electronic countermeasures to jam or interfere with enemy radar and defensive measures; and by raids aimed at the enemy air operations, to disable main operating bases or dispersal airfields, destroy aircraft in the air or in their ground shelters, or destroy critical fuel production or storage centers.

Targeting decisions will be driven by how long air superiority must be maintained, and over what area. In the most likely scenarios, one or two waves of strikes will probably not be enough. The Gulf War experience, and certainly World War II precedents, indicate that bomb damage assessments will reveal the need for targets to be attacked again, even as new targets are identified. Selection will be cued in part by the way the enemy government and agencies react to the initial strikes on their facilities. So military planners are likely to seek thorough targeting of enemy air defenses. They will at a minimum insist on complete disruption of the air defense command and control network.

The organization of state leadership and government authority. The idea of targeting political and military leadership as part of a strategic air attack is not new. There has been ample discussion of these issues with respect to nuclear targeting, but the current conception of strategic conventional targeting is not an offspring of nuclear doctrine. It is more a revival and refinement of the earlier conceptions of strategic air power dating from before the Second World War. The most influential strategic thinkers in the U.S. Air Force, some of whom played key roles in designing the air campaign against Iraq, believe that technology has finally caught up with doctrine to allow air power, practically alone, to decide the outcome of war. It does so not by the volume of destruction, but by the precise selection of targets.

Episodes from World War II, Vietnam (Linebacker II), and the Gulf War support the hypothesis of Air Force strategists that, if critical areas of vulnerability are properly identified, a relatively small number of air attacks can paralyze warmaking capacity. During the Gulf War, precision attacks on leadership and command control, and communications targets clearly disrupted and dislocated the functioning of the Iraqi government. Electrical power in central and southern Iraq was shut down and almost all of Iraqi oil refining was also eliminated without inflicting lasting damage on either of these vital parts of Iraqi society.

Technology has allowed crucial "centers of gravity" to be identified and located with increasing precision, to include command headquarters, bunkers, and key government ministries; facilities used by the secret police, ruling political party, and the agencies which control and shape public information; civil and military intelligence organizations; communications networks including satellite links, radio and TV transmission facilities, and telephone centers; key parts of the national transportation system such as certain bridges and railway centers; oil refining (avoiding needless damage to crude oil production); and electrical power.

Traditional strategic targeting has usually included an extensive list of economic and industrial targets associated with a country's capacity to make war. Current doctrine is evolving away from the need for mass strikes against enemy industry. If the power supply can be completely interrupted, and the transport system degraded, the goals of an ambitious strategic campaign can be accomplished—at least for a while—with fewer air attacks and with significantly reduced danger to urban populations.

The main issue, though, will be whether to include strategic targeting objectives at all, to decide whether to attack the political leadership or paralyze state authority. If the objectives of attacking WMD capability and winning the necessary degree of air superiority are narrow and "military," then attacks on the leadership of the country are broad and "political." Going beyond limited anti-WMD strikes thus seems to approach the initiation of all-out conventional war.

Yet there are at least four reasons to consider political targets in plans to disarm a potential nuclear power:

- The attacks will yield direct military advantages by increasing chances for tactical surprise, weakening the air defense network, and crippling military reaction to the air strikes.

- They might block or slow damaging retaliation.

- They go to the heart of the problem that caused the crisis—the "outlaw" political leadership.

- They could compel the enemy government to accept terms for settlement of the dispute.[13]

The escalation represented by turning a military attack on WMD potential into a truly strategic air campaign with political objectives widens the scope of the conflict. U.S. leaders must decide if such escalation is consistent with the country's overall interests and objectives.

Fielded military forces. Fielded military forces may be the least important consideration in a military action against a state posing new nuclear dangers, or—if a nuclear program has produced a nuclear arsenal—they can be the most important of all. If nuclear weapons are not in the field, attacks on military units are relatively inefficient—one weapon to neutralize one weapon system, while diverting efforts to destroy the strategic targets that could cripple the capacity to use force at all. If, however, nuclear, chemical, or biological weapons have actually been deployed with units, or if the enemy's ballistic missiles threaten friendly cities, then attacks on fielded forces become unavoidable. They will also be necessary if the proliferator threatens to invade or fire missiles against allies of the United States.

Further, if there is a general war, the enemy's entire army, navy, and remaining air forces must eventually be contained or defeated. Finally, as in the Gulf War, the United States and its allies may use the outbreak of fighting, whatever the cause, as an opportunity to get rid of the most destabilizing elements in the enemy's military establishment.

OPERATIONAL REQUIREMENTS

To see how these military considerations affect actual operational plans, let us plan for action against a fictional country, "Alberich." Alberich has some resemblance to Iraq in 1990 or North Korea in 1992.

The first requirement will be for very detailed intelligence on the targets in Alberich: What are the key WMD facilities, air defense centers, military command headquarters, and other points of special interest? An intensive effort will already have assessed the status of its nuclear weapons program.

Characteristics of each target are needed to determine specific aimpoints where a bomb should actually hit. An extensive nuclear research facility can have dozens of different buildings spread over a large area. A military planner might locate twenty or more aimpoints in one target area. After the initial strikes, further intelligence will determine whether the target must be hit again, and is also likely to reveal new targets. Therefore, in practically every category, the target list can be expected to expand by 50 percent or more as the attacks continue.

Alberich is a medium-sized state with an advanced nuclear weapons program that has both enriched a substantial quantity of uranium and operates reactors that can produce plutonium. The United States doubts that any nuclear explosive devices have been completed but cannot be sure. Alberich also has significant conventional forces, a growing chemical arsenal, and a possible but unconfirmed biological weapon program. A possible target list for Alberich is depicted in table 1.

Table 1

Target List for Nuclear Disarmament of Alberich

Target	Number of Targets	Number of Aimpoints
WMD potential	25	200
Air superiority (no individual aircraft)	100	400
Strategic (command, control, telecom)	75	150
Strategic (energy, transport)	70	200
Strategic (selected military production)	20	100
Military forces (but only missiles)	50	100
TOTAL:	340	1150

Some readers will consider this target list too extensive, even though it excludes almost all fielded military forces. Leslie Gelb, for example, argued that renewed attacks against Iraq to enforce UN-imposed ceasefire terms were being impeded because "the pro-force group" is "hung up on thinking too big." General Powell, he alleged, "has dutifully prepared for them a strike plan with too many targets, too many aircraft, too many allied approvals to ask for and too many risks." Surely, he argued, the risks could be minimized by using "a single, pinpointed strike."[14]

In October 1962 President Kennedy and his advisors asked the U.S. Air Force to develop a plan for neutralizing Soviet nuclear missiles being deployed in Cuba. They were surprised and annoyed to find that the Air Force came up with a plan that included at least 500 sorties and would attack the missile facilities, Cuban air force bases, other large airfields, and many other targets. General Sweeney also said this strike could not guarantee elimination of more than 90 percent of the missiles. Some analysts believed the plan was unduly cumbersome because it was simply grafted onto an existing plan for the contingency of comprehensive military action against Castro. There is no doubt that the size of the contemplated air strike helped dissuade President Kennedy from electing the military option during the last week of October.[15]

The understandable longing for that "single, pinpointed strike" is likely to continue to be frustrated in the future. In the fortunate event that the nuclear program is indeed critically vulnerable to a single strike, military planners are probably still going to need to prepare for a more comprehensive air campaign in order to preempt Alberich's retaliatory moves or respond to such retaliation. In either case planners must be ready to execute a comprehensive plan.

In planning an operation against Alberich, military planners will want to hit as many targets as they can, as quickly as they can. The initial strikes in a comprehensive campaign must be decisive, disrupting all air defense and command networks, smashing Alberich's ability to adapt to the new situation, and keeping it from being able to recover military coherence and organize counterattacks. So the plan is to be able to attack every target on the initial list at least once in the first two or three days of fighting. By the end of one week, all of them, plus the most important new targets identified after the initial strikes, would have been attacked and destroyed.

To achieve these goals, substantial military forces are needed within combat range of the targets. The main striking forces will be ground-based or sea-based aircraft.

Special operations forces (SOF) can destroy certain kinds of targets. For the United States, SOF include the Delta Force, Special Forces and Ranger Army units, special Air Force helicopters and aircraft, and Navy SEAL teams. The Department of Defense's official position is that, in helping to deal with the "ongoing proliferation of weapons of mass destruction and the means to deliver them," SOF "special reconaissance and direct action capabilities can help to locate and destroy storage facilities, control nodes, and other strategic assets." Such forces are advertised as "one of the few instruments available to precisely apply measured force to deal with an adversary's nuclear, biological, or chemical weapons capabilities."[16]

Special operations forces played an important role in the Gulf War, including efforts to locate and target mobile Scud missiles. They tend to operate in small units, seldom larger than platoon strength, relying on clandestine movement behind enemy lines in order to avoid detection by major combat units. While they may complement the work of other branches of the armed forces, they cannot be expected to be inserted as large combat units to attack installations which may employ thousands of people in close proximity to heavy enemy forces. Therefore, while SOF units may provide indispensable help, they are not substitutes for the air or naval forces that would carry out the principal strikes on heavily defended targets.

The most critical components of air power in an attack upon Alberich are likely to be jet aircraft which can both laser-designate their targets and carry large laser-guided or inertially guided bombs, and have the potential range to deliver the heavy bombloads—unrefueled—against targets at ranges at least several hundred miles from their base. Only some U.S. strategic or tactical aircraft currently meet these criteria. The B-2 bomber is not yet in the force. The B-52H can deliver conventionally armed cruise missiles, once air superiority has been established in its operating area and altitude. The B-1B bomber was not able to carry out conventional missions in the

Gulf War, although it may be equipped to carry standoff air-to-ground missiles in the future.

Cruise missiles such as those launched from heavy bombers or the sea-launched Tomahawk missile (TLAM) can be accurate and highly effective, especially since they can attack the most heavily defended targets in daylight. It might be several days before the necessary ships and submarines to launch TLAMs could be moved into position. But the presence of these vessels can be more easily concealed from an enemy, and they avoid the high political profile associated with the use of ground bases. Unfortunately, such cruise missiles are only suitable at present for attacking fixed targets with coordinates known in advance that can be programmed into the missile's navigational system. Current conventional cruise missiles also do not carry enough explosive punch to destroy the most hardened targets.

The F-117A Stealth aircraft can deliver weapons with exceptional accuracy and consistency. They can also attack the most heavily defended targets. But there are only about forty of these aircraft available and, since they fly only at night, each can usually fly just one sortie a day.

The F-15E Strike Eagle, F-111F, and the carrier-based A-6E/TRAM would be likely to carry the main load in operations against a country like Alberich. But depending on the number of carriers on station, probably no more than 150 to 200 such aircraft could be massed at any given place in the foreseeable future, especially if notice is short or basing options are constrained. The number of available aircraft may increase, as single-seat F-16s or F/A-18s are modified to carry LANTIRN pods that can make it easier for the pilot alone to operate laser-guided bombs effectively and if longer-range F-16 or F/A-18 variants become more widely available.

Table 2 illustrates the size of the forces that might be needed to attack every target on the initial list (table 1) in no more than two or three days of massive strikes. It is assumed that aircraft used in the operations against Alberich can carry their heavy bomb loads, unrefueled, against targets at least 400 miles away, and that they can operate in any weather, or at night, to allow maximum flexibility in timing and planning.

The method I have used is simple and transparent. But readers who choose to substitute their figures for mine will find that if they

Table 2
Force Plan for Alberich Conflict

Aircraft Type	Number of Aircraft	Bombs	Probability of Success*	Sorties Per Day†	Aimpoints Destroyed Per Day‡
F-117A	35	2	.7	1.0	50
F-111F	30	4	.6	1.5	110
F-15E	70	8	.6	1.5	450
A-6E	60	2	.6	1.2	85
TLAM		150	1.0	.65	100
B-52H	60	8 ALCM	.6	.5	140
ECM/ARM[17]	80				
Escort	120+				
Refuelers	40				
C³I aircraft[18]	10				
TOTAL	505+				835

*Author's estimate for probability of success, factoring probability of arrival over target and probability of kill for weapon delivery.
†Author's estimate for average sorties flown per day.
‡Aimpoints destroyed per day, approximate and rounded off.
Note: Table assumes three aircraft carriers on station within range of A-6E targets and sufficient other warships to fire 150 TLAMs per day. Table also assumes some targets are at shorter ranges or are "soft," allowing for substantial employment of cruise missiles and shorter-range attack aircraft.[19]

try to cover the number and kind of targets postulated here (including many hardened and well-defended targets) from a range of 500–1,000 kilometers, they can change the mix of forces. But hundreds of aircrafts and dozens of warships delivering strikes over a period of days are still likely to be needed in order to cover just the initial list of targets. In fact, this scenario against the hypothetical country of Alberich requires far fewer aircraft than were used in the 1991 air campaign against Iraq. In addition, several of the assumptions here are actually quite optimistic. For example:

- Since aircraft and their weapons will not be evenly distributed over an optimum number of targets, the actual number of aimpoints probably destroyed would be somewhat lower than shown in the figure.

- There is no allowance for attrition of U.S. forces.

- There are no forces set aside to deter or defeat attacks by Alberich's conventional forces or WMD. Nor was allowance made for aircraft to fly thousands of sorties chasing mobile ballistic missile launchers.

- The power and accuracy of properly utilized laser-guided bombs (perhaps supplemented in a few years by bombs with inertial guidance and separate terminal seekers)[20] are assumed to hold up against almost all available defensive countermeasures.

The key point is that the military forces involved in these operations will be large. Not all of the forces would have to be provided by the United States; help from allies could be valuable politically as well as militarily. Yet America has a near monopoly on the most sophisticated aircraft and weapon systems, and on the personnel trained to use them. And only the United States has the intelligence resources to support such a substantial but discriminating military effort.

What if Alberich launched a nuclear, chemical, or biological attack against American forces or their allies, or indeed against America itself? To supplement conventional force plans, the United States would need an option for the retaliatory use of nuclear weapons. If Alberich has nuclear weapons, an option for preemptive use of nuclear forces might be needed too.

To be more specific, U.S. nuclear forces could be used to retaliate in response to the use of nuclear weapons, or possibly other weapons of mass destruction, against America or her allies. They could be needed for preemption if the nuclear arms being readied for use against American or allied targets cannot be destroyed quickly enough by conventional means to avert the danger of imminent enemy nuclear attack. The absolute size of nuclear forces needed for such contingencies is likely to be quite small when compared to the overall size of the current U.S. nuclear arsenal. Yet the large current arsenal may not be configured for options involving the delivery of extremely accurate but very low-yield nuclear weapons from aircraft, ICBMs, or SLBMs. If U.S. planning includes readying missiles for delivery of nuclear weapons in such a scenario, and since new intelligence might invalidate the basis for the original launch decision, Washington may also wish to consider development of technology to neutralize a nuclear-armed reentry vehicle in flight as a corollary to development of a preemptive option.

OTHER STRATEGIC ISSUES

Implications of the Size of the Air Operations

An action against a proliferator involving several hundred top combat aircraft, several aircraft carriers, and the necessary support units, fuel, and munition supplies is a massive undertaking. Such an operation bears almost no resemblance to the Israeli strike against Iraq in 1981, and eclipses the scale of the American punitive raid against Libya in 1986.

The number of targets could certainly be reduced if a country is struck much earlier on the threat-vulnerability continuum than seems politically possible. They could also be reduced if the United States is willing to accept lower levels of confidence in the success of its operations or more limited air superiority, or if it ignored strategic targets that would weaken the enemy's stability or ability to resist. Yet it seems highly likely that the military will urge that the more ambitious objectives be pursued, or that preparations are ready to follow a limited strike with a more comprehensive campaign—with political support for such readiness to carry forward large-scale hostilities as needed.

Clearly a U.S. president authorizing such action will need a supportive domestic political base. He will have to alert the Congress and key opinion leaders repeatedly to the depth of U.S. concern—even if not to the specific consideration of military action—to increase the lead time between the threat and the decision to act. He will have committed substantial American prestige to the success of the operation, which means that he will need to be especially careful in formulating the initial public definition of success.

Relations with regional allies will also be of the utmost importance. The United States and these allies will probably be dependent on each other: the allies are likely to be dependent on U.S. military aid in the event of conflict against a renegade neighbor. The ally's fear of the outlaw state will lead the ally to ask the United States for the strongest possible assurance of military success if the ally is to join in the gamble of military action. America, if it offers such assurances, will then face pressure to adopt more ambitious operational objectives—including a forced regime change—than our government might otherwise have chosen on its own.

Yet the United States, in the event of a conflict, depends on having a reliable partner in the region who can provide bases and other logistical support for military operations. These forward bases, well stocked with the fuel and munitions the forces will need, may be indispensable. This requirement alone would oblige the United States to participate in coalition political and military planning, accepting the added layer of consultations and the reckoning with the judgments of others that are the difficult but necessary adjuncts of a coalition process.

Even if suitable forward bases are available, U.S. military planners may not wish to use them if they are within accurate striking range of the enemy's own missiles and if these missiles might be armed with nuclear or effective biological weapons. Even if U.S. missile defenses become more advanced, the risks of a catastrophe that could inflict thousands of casualties and immobilize a substantial fraction of the aircraft may be deemed unacceptably high.

For all these reasons, American defense planners might seek to improve their long-range striking power. To illustrate the effects of possible improvements, one can construct another sample force plan for a conflict with Alberich (table 3). The time is 1999. The United States has five B-2 bombers, and it has enhanced the capabilities of the B-52H and, in particular, the B-1B. All these aircraft now carry inertially guided 2,000-pound bombs, perhaps rocket boosted to be launched as stand-off weapons as much as 50 miles away from the targets. Operating ranges are assumed to be at least 2000 miles each way, unrefueled. The bombers would be pushed hard to generate an average of nearly one sortie a day for their intercontinental range missions during the first few days of the conflict.

Table 3
Alternative Force Plan for Alberich Conflict

Aircraft Type	Number of Aircraft	Bombs	Probability of Success	Sorties	Aimpoints Destroyed Per Day
B-2	5	16	.7	.8	45
B-1B	70	24	.65	.8	875
B-52H	60	8 ALCM	.6	.6	175
TLAM (subs only)		100	.65		65
Refuelers	100				
C³I aircraft	5				
TOTAL	240+				1160

Turning the B-1B into a more useful aircraft (a process now scheduled to be completed by 1999) can make a big difference in long-range American conventional striking power. This plan would cover many more targets than the one offered earlier, using fewer than half the number of aircraft, all of which would be operating from bases thousands of miles away from the enemy country (or from underwater).

However, even if the long-range bombers have the capability and munitions to carry out the mission, this plan will not be feasible unless enemy air defenses can be suppressed or evaded without the assistance of a lot of forward-based aircraft. The plan assumes that B-2s and TLAMs can get at the most heavily defended targets and key air defense centers, and that B-1Bs and B-52H ALCM carriers can, on their own, penetrate the weakened enemy air defenses enough to use their precision standoff weapons. These assumptions were tested successfully in the Gulf War.[21]

Even if better solutions are developed to reduce reliance on forward bases and advanced forward deployments, air operations against a country like Alberich would still be massive and could escalate into a more general regional conflict. The air campaign may only be part of ongoing fighting by ground or naval forces. The initiation of ground warfare could even be triggered by the air attack itself.

Military planners may need to allocate a reserve of air power (possibly deployed forward) to support U.S. or allied ground forces in such fighting. Or they could decide that the available air power is not sufficient both to support the ground troops and to cover the strategic targets in the enemy homeland. A choice would then have to be made whether the strategic targets are too vital to permit a substantial diversion of aircraft away from the air campaign to deal with the crisis on the ground.

The Problems of Completeness and Irreversibility

Even with a substantial air campaign that goes as planned, perfection will be elusive. The Iraqi example has shown just how much can remain undone, even after a well-planned and very successful campaign. In the Cuban missile crisis the air strike plans could not assure elimination of more than 90 percent of Soviet missiles on the island, thereby prompting plans for a follow-up invasion. Those considering a military operation must therefore decide, before they go forward, just how much imperfection they are prepared to tolerate. How much destruction is enough?

The military objectives must be expressed with some precision, as a function of time and mass. What proportion of certain kinds of targets must be destroyed within how many days, or hours? How confident do we need to be that the destruction has actually occurred? How long will the operation need to continue?

The purpose of the military action—to head off the danger of nuclear attack—implies an extremely high standard for completion. Once a conflict has begun the chances that any surviving weapon would be used against the United States (or its allies) are much higher. Disruption of the adversary's nuclear program must be so severe as to seem irreversible.

The military is likely to develop plans to meet this objective in two ways. First, the planners may seek a comprehensive list of the full range of strategic targets, enough forces to do the job, and authorization to continue follow-up operations for weeks or even months. Second, it will seek to obtain a change in the governing regime.

Another path toward greater confidence would be for civilian and military advisers to conclude that the ultimate objectives of the campaign should include either regime change or the regime's surrender to long-term, intrusive disarmament controls analogous to those imposed on Iraq. If this path is chosen, these more ambitious political objectives will reinforce pressure to turn a campaign conceived for the narrow purpose of erasing a nuclear threat into an air (and even combined arms) offensive that can compel broader submission to the political will of the United States and its allies.

When plans for an air strike were developed for President Kennedy during the Cuban missile crisis, both of these conditions prevailed: the target list was expanded to guard against uncertainty and, because the uncertainty could not be eliminated even then, plans were made for a subsequent invasion to ensure that the Soviet missiles were neutralized and, in the process, to overthrow the Castro regime.

Risks of Military Operations

Any use of armed force is risky. Some of the risks are self-evident: loss of life among American or allied servicemen and women; damage to the structures and public services that support local communities. In any large air attack, inevitably some innocent noncombatants will be killed and injured—by secondary explosions, the dispersal of radiation by debris.

Innocent civilians can also be killed if they are in a place that was wrongly identified as a military target, by weapons that do not work properly, or as an indirect consequence of the catastrophic damage to local institutions and facilities. These collateral casualties can be minimized; in the Gulf War they were orders of magnitude lower than in any other modern war. But they cannot be eliminated.

Other risks are also apparent, including the danger of WMD or other conventional military retaliation against the United States or its friends in the region. If the United States takes action against North Korea's nuclear program,[22] South Korea could readily imagine immediate ground, air, and missile attacks on Seoul, located so close to the DMZ. U.S. military action could also heighten the danger of terrorist retaliation against the United States, or government retaliation if a country that might have used nuclear weapons against America decides, under attack, that it will definitely use them before they are irretrievably lost.

U.S. lives may be lost; U.S. military personnel may be captured. Iraq was unsuccessful in its attempt to capitalize on the precedent of Syria and Vietnam's exploitation of captured American airmen, but no U.S. political leader can ignore the fate of American citizens in hostile hands.

Finally, of course, military operations on the scale described here cost billions of dollars. The United States absorbed these costs during the Gulf War by receiving substantial contributions from other leading economic powers. If this pattern is not repeated, the monetary costs underscore the president's reliance on a base of domestic support, principally in the Congress.

CONCLUSION

The proliferation of nuclear weapons could pose a grave threat to the most vital interests of the United States. The United States will do everything in its power to avert such a threat. But if deterrence fails, and if Washington concludes that nuclear weapons are simply too dangerous to be possessed by some governments or some leaders, exhaustion of diplomatic remedies could compel the United States to consider direct military action.

Such offensive action is likely to require a very considerable exertion of political and military power involving hundreds of highly capable aircraft, other major components of the armed forces, and close cooperative relationships with allies in the region. It is an investment that clearly implies a determination to succeed. The readiness of such options, and an adversary's fear of certain defeat, can significantly strengthen U.S. and multilateral diplomacy. Outlaw governments should come to understand that their nuclear weapons programs absolutely will not survive to fruition, so a peaceful compromise is the least bad way out.

The success of offensive military action against an outlaw proliferator can have a major international impact. Some developing countries are likely to protest the violent enforcement of a nonproliferation regime that preserves a hierarchy of power headed by the United States. But when they calculate the pros and cons of adherence to the regime, these countries will nonetheless need to adjust their arithmetic. Deterrence against the development of nuclear weapons, not just their use, would be strengthened.

Countries may also work hard to manipulate Western perceptions of their place on the continuum of threat and vulnerability. They will try to use diplomatic maneuvers to downplay their progress as they survive the period of greatest hazard, the period before they can credibly threaten that weapons are ready for use.

The most immediate task for the United States, then, is to help shape an international environment and a set of normative principles that will interpret ambiguity as hostility and nuclear evasion as potential nuclear aggression. Political norms should support the use of force to contain the danger presented by those countries which have been branded as nuclear outlaws by the international community.[23] Working with the United Nations, the United States should help to develop common standards of behavior that affirm the urgent concerns about suspect nuclear weapon programs and send out a global assurance that such concerns must and will be addressed, one way or another.

Notes

1. I define "preventive" military action as measures taken to prevent another country from acquiring a threatening military capability. I distinguish it from "preemptive" action which attempts to neutralize with a first strike a danger that already exists.

   On consideration of preventive and preemptive war in the nuclear age, see NSC 5440 in Department of State, *Foreign Relations of the United States 1952–1954*, vol. 2, p. 815; Russell Buhite and William Christopher Hamel, "War for Peace: The Question of an American Preventive War Against the Soviet Union, 1945–1955," *Diplomatic History*, vol. 14 (Summer 1990): pp. 367–84; David Alan Rosenberg, "The Origins of Overkill: Nuclear Weapons and American Strategy, 1945–1960," *International Security*, vol. 7 (Spring 1983): pp. 3, 17, 25, 31–35; Marc Trachtenberg, "A 'Wasting Asset': American Strategy and the Shifting Nuclear Balance, 1949–1954," *International Security*, vol. 13 (Winter 1988/89): p. 5; Raymond L. Garthoff, *Assessing the Adversary: Estimates by the Eisenhower Administration of Soviet Intentions and Capabilities* (Washington, D.C.: The Brookings Institution, 1991), pp. 14–23; Henry Kissinger, *The White House Years* (Boston: Little, Brown,

1979), pp. 171–86; William G. Hyland, *Mortal Rivals: Superpower Relations From Nixon to Reagan* (New York: Random House, 1987), pp. 24–26.
2. Lewis A. Dunn, *Containing Nuclear Proliferation*, Adelphi Paper No. 263 (London: International Institute for Strategic Studies, 1991), p. 60.
3. On the Israeli raid against Iraq, see Shlomo Nakdimon, *First Strike: The Exclusive Story of How Israel Foiled Iraq's Attempt to Get the Bomb*, Peretz Kidron, trans. (New York: Simon and Schuster, 1987); Shai Feldman, "The Bombing of Osiraq—Revisited," *International Security*, vol. 7 (Fall 1982): pp. 114–42.
4. This analysis is limited to conventional military action to avert the deployment of atomic weapons that could be used against America or her allies. It is possible that the United States could be alarmed by the efforts of a nuclear-armed country to replace its atomic arms with thermonuclear weapons having ten or a hundred times the yield of the first-generation devices. A preventive war to avert such a danger would probably not be solely initiated with conventional forces—which could not promptly destroy enough targets with high enough levels of confidence. A more likely option would involve a preemptive nuclear strike by the United States (as was considered in the early 1950s). These scenarios are so unlikely, and already so familiar to nuclear strategists and targeters, that I see no need to analyze them further in this chapter.
5. Since Israel has not openly admitted the possession of a nuclear arsenal, it is well to add that the *current* Israeli posture is not one of uncertainty about whether the arms are there—but to acknowledge the fact reluctantly and give it international status. Formal declaration of the fact would require formal reactions which, at this time, neither Israel nor the United States find to be in their interest.
6. In the Korean War, for example, the United States did not launch attacks against strategic military targets in China or in the USSR, although the People's Republic of China (and, to a far lesser extent, the Soviet Union) had sent soldiers and airmen to fight the UN forces led by the United States. Yet if China had threatened the use of weapons of mass destruction, like poison gas, it is quite possible that the U.S. would have retaliated with air attacks against strategic targets in the Chinese homeland. The United States might also conceivably escalate an ongoing limited war if Washington saw the need to intervene in ongoing fighting between other countries in order to disarm the nuclear weapons being readied for use by one side or the other.
7. A damaging WMD attack on U.S. forces could also place the president under very great pressure to authorize a response with U.S. nuclear forces, even if such a response might turn out to be considered counterproductive or excessive.
8. President Bush, in his January 5, 1991, letter to Saddam Hussein, warned that "unconscionable acts" like "the use of chemical or biological weapons" would cause the American people to "demand the strongest possible response," and "you and your country will pay a terrible price." This carefully drafted letter was backed by further public statements, as on February 5, when the president deliberately declined to rule out a nuclear response to Iraqi use of chemical weapons. The United States government, in its private and public diplomacy, consistently sought to keep Saddam uncertain about the possibility of U.S. nuclear retaliation for Iraqi chemical or biological attack.

Nuclear-capable weapon systems were deployed within range of Baghdad, and Saddam's advisors could readily have called their leader's attention to this fact. See also McGeorge Bundy, "Nuclear Weapons and the Gulf," *Foreign Affairs*, vol. 70 (Fall 1991): pp. 83, 84–85.

9. Thomas C. Schelling, *Arms and Influence* (New Haven, Conn.: Yale University Press, 1966), p. 2.

10. Perhaps the most irreplaceable elements in a nuclear program are the scientists and engineers who make it possible. Deliberately targeting these individuals is possible, either through the remote instruments of air power or through kidnapping or assassination operations (such as the one in which Gerald Bull, designer of the Iraqi supergun, was killed in Brussels). The possibility raises difficult ethical and legal questions that are beyond the scope of this paper. U.S. intelligence agencies are legally forbidden to plan or engage in assassinations of foreign citizens. But whatever may be the practice in peacetime, in wartime the United States has deliberately targeted senior military commanders or military scientists involved in directing or devising forces that would kill large numbers of Americans.

11. If complete preemption *is* feasible with nuclear weapons (which is more likely to be the case now than ever during the U.S.–Soviet rivalry), then withholding U.S. forces until a potentially unstoppable enemy nuclear attack is confirmed to have occurred, or until the weapons have actually detonated, could saddle the U.S. president with the responsibility for the deaths of thousands of his countrymen, and earn for him a large and unenviable place in American history. On the other hand, if the intelligence is wrong, the president would be responsible for the consequences of the U.S. nuclear attack, which could be severe even after trying to discriminate in the choice of targets and weapons. The counterforce options developed in the East–West context simply do not go very far in addressing this dilemma.

12. United States Strategic Bombing Survey (U.S.SBS), *Aircraft Division Industry Report*, European Report No. 4 (Washington, D.C.: U.S.SBS, 2d ed., 1947), pp. 112–23; U.S.SBS, *Over-all Report (European War)*, European Report No. 2 (Washington, D.C.: U.S.SBS, 1945), pp. 87–89. V-1 attacks against England were delayed for two months by an enormous number of sorties against their launching sites on the French coast (9 percent of all allied bomb tonnage dropped between August 1943 and September 1944) but were stopped only when ground forces occupied the launch sites. The Germans then launched strikes from Germany against continental targets, mainly Antwerp, until Germany itself was overrun in March 1945.

13. Following the original surrender of Iraq's leaders to UN demands in February and March 1991, in July 1991 U.S. officials leaked, perhaps deliberately, their professed readiness to focus on at least twenty Iraqi national command and control targets if Baghdad refused to comply with the cease-fire agreements concluded with the UN. Eric Schmitt, "U.S. Tries to Intimidate Iraq With Military Targets List," *New York Times*, July 12, 1991, p. A3.

14. Leslie Gelb, "Target Al-Atheer," *New York Times*, March 23, 1992, p. A17.

15. See Graham Allison, *Essence of Decision: Explaining the Cuban Missile Crisis* (Boston: Little, Brown, 1971), pp. 124–26.

16. Secretary of Defense Dick Cheney, *Annual Report to the President and the Congress* (Washington, D.C.: U.S. Government Printing Office, 1992), p. 100.

17. These are aircraft designed to suppress enemy air defenses using electronic countermeasures (ECM), anti-radiation missiles (ARM), or other direct attacks. F-16C LANTIRN and F/A-18C attack aircraft and specialized ECM and ARM aircraft can be used against these targets. The F-16C and F/A-18C attack aircraft could also be used against other targets that are not so distant, for example, within about a 300-mile radius of their bases.

18. This category would include AWACS, JSTARS, and other intelligence-gathering and airborne command and control aircraft.

19. I make no allowance for U.S. attrition. Estimates for such attrition typically run at about 2 to 4 percent per sortie or per day; actual Gulf War experience was far lower. The force sizing changes introduced by factoring in attrition were not enough to affect the argument, so I do not ask readers to put up with the extra complication. It is one of several factors, however, that make my model a bit optimistic for the U.S. side in extrapolating the number of aircraft that will be needed.

    This is a very simple planning model. There are no firepower scores or Lanchester-derivative equations (which have even less validity for air power than they do for ground forces). Nor does my model have the scale and elaboration to be found in some alternative air power models, such as the one offered to answer much more ambitious questions about the old Soviet air force in Joshua Epstein, *Measuring Military Power: The Soviet Air Threat to Europe* (Princeton N.J.: Princeton University Press, 1984). I can only claim that the model presented here bears some resemblance to the planning done by air force officers under pressure to develop mission force requirements and begin structuring air tasking orders.

    I have calculated the air superiority problem quite differently than Barry Posen did with his useful SEAD model in Appendix 1 of *Inadvertent Escalation: Conventional War and Nuclear Risks* (Ithaca, N.Y.: Cornell University Press, 1991). In part this is because Posen is asking different questions about one aspect of a longer campaign against a much bigger adversary. The biggest difference, however, is that he defines the target set as the thousands of individual enemy air defense radars. I defined the air superiority target set (listed in table 1 and described earlier) mainly around the network's command, control, and communications nodes in order to cripple overall capability from the center or sector operation centers, with some effort dedicated to interrupting airfield operations, and some assigned to SAM fields, while allocating a good number of ECM and Wild Weasel aircraft to jam or kill individual radars. If the central network is destroyed and there is a constant radar suppression underway to encourage operators to keep them turned off, there may be no need to spend thousands of weapons on trying to kill all the individual radars. So I do not bother to assess detailed target numbers or PS for the ECM/ARM aircraft, and I measure overall success in relation to a smaller target set (though one likely to be more hardened against attack and more distant from the likely U.S. bases).

20. For a short summary of these munitions developments, see David Fulghum, "USAF to Increase Bombers' Precision, Procure Powered Radar Decoys," *Aviation Week & Space Technology*, February 17, 1992, p. 60.

21. Substantial long-range striking power could, in theory, also be provided by aircraft launched from well-positioned aircraft carriers (in addition to the TLAMs already mentioned). At least for the next five years, though, the U.S. Navy does not appear to be planning to deploy new aircraft or reconfigure current air wings in order to be able to use its carriers as bases for much more powerful long-range strike forces.

22. For this reason, as well as an understanding of the size of possible military operations, some commentators have strongly cautioned against any consideration of military options against North Korea. See, for example, William J. Taylor and Michael Mazarr, "Defusing North Korea's Nuclear Notions," *New York Times*, April 13, 1992, p. A19. The Taylor/Mazarr argument depends vitally on their contention that "U.S. and South Korean diplomacy has nudged the North well down that path" toward agreeing to nuclear inspections and, presumably, denuclearization. But in speculating about the various North Korean motives for such progress, the authors do not mention the possibility that North Koreans might be fearful that diplomatic failure could lead to American military action. Nor do they acknowledge that the Gulf War experience may have made such a deterrent to outlaw nuclear weapons development more plausible. Military power and diplomatic strategy cannot be understood in isolation from each other. See, for example, Jim Hoagland, "Will Kim Blink?" *Washington Post National Weekly Edition*, April 27–May 3, 1992, p. 29.

23. Mikhail Gorbachev has similarly called for "rigid controls" on nuclear and chemical weapons "to prevent their dissemination, including measures of compulsion in cases of violation." "Gorbachev's Talk: Building on the Past," *New York Times*, May 7, 1992, p. A14.

CHAPTER EIGHT

Defenses Against New Nuclear Threats

ALBERT CARNESALE

Defense is the last potential barrier against nuclear weapons. The goal of eliminating the nuclear vulnerability of our society, our military forces, our friends, and our vital assets is hardly new; its achievement, however, has been and remains elusive.

The earliest nuclear threats to U.S. interests were posed by Soviet bombers capable of attacking America's forces and allies in Europe and Asia and, by the late 1950s, the continental United States. Air defenses, including interceptor aircraft and surface-to-air missiles (SAMs), constituted part of the U.S. response, but greater emphasis was placed on offensive nuclear forces intended to deter Soviet nuclear (and conventional) aggression.

As long-range ballistic missiles entered the Soviet arsenal, substantial rhetoric, but relatively little funding, was devoted to ballistic missile defense (BMD).[1] By the mid-1960s, the United States recognized that key sensors and command and control nodes in its air defense network had become vulnerable to preemptive attack by Soviet intercontinental ballistic missiles (ICBMs), and that technologies then available were incapable of providing effective protection against missile attack. As a result, much of the U.S. air defense system was subsequently dismantled.

In response to Soviet construction of a BMD system around Moscow, the Johnson administration in 1967 announced its intention to deploy the Sentinel ABM system designed to provide a "thin" nationwide defense against light attacks. This would be especially effective against small, unsophisticated strikes of the kind that China might eventually be able to launch. The Nixon administration transformed Sentinel into "Safeguard," a system based on the same hardware but whose primary purpose was the protection of American strategic bombers and ICBMs. Only one site of the Safeguard system was completed, and it was shut down after two years. The Moscow system, however, was modernized in the 1980s and remains functional.

Two decades have passed since the United States and the Soviet Union signed and ratified the ABM Treaty. Under the terms of the 1972 accord, each side undertakes "not to deploy ABM systems for a defense of the territory of its country and not to provide a base for such a defense." The ABM deployments permitted under the Treaty are severely constrained geographically, quantitatively, and qualitatively.

On March 23, 1983, President Ronald Reagan directed "a comprehensive and intensive effort to define a long-term research and development program to begin to achieve our ultimate goal of eliminating the threat posed by strategic ballistic missiles." This announcement marked the birth of the Strategic Defense Initiative (SDI) which, despite the protests of its proponents, instantly acquired the popular appellation "Star Wars." As the Soviet nuclear threat diminished, the focus of the SDI shifted from the highly ambitious objective of "rendering nuclear weapons impotent and obsolete" to the far more modest goal of limiting damage against small-scale attacks of the kind that might be launched accidentally, or without the authorization of a national leader, or deliberately by a nation with only a small number of long-range ballistic missiles.

The performance of the Patriot air defense system against Iraq's Scud missiles, widely perceived as a success in the immediate aftermath of the Gulf War, gave a political boost to all forms of BMD, and especially to theater missile defenses (TMD). While official estimates of the success rate of Patriot in intercepting Scuds have declined over time, many still believe BMD to be a promising response to ballistic missile threats.[2]

At present, the United States homeland is unprotected against ballistic missile attack and has only very limited protection against bombers. Our allies suffer the same degree of nuclear vulnerability. American military forces abroad enjoy substantially better defenses against aircraft and limited (but slowly expanding) defenses against theater ballistic missiles. In short, our democratic societies remain totally vulnerable to nuclear attack by long-range missiles and highly vulnerable to attack by bombers; our military forces are only somewhat less vulnerable.

Nuclear weapons can, of course, be delivered by means other than ballistic missiles and bombers. For example, nuclear-armed artillery shells, land mines, torpedoes, and cruise missiles long had places in superpower nuclear arsenals, and could be used by others as well. Even the most primitive nuclear explosive device could also be delivered by truck, trawler, passenger aircraft, or other unconventional means. Moreover, a nuclear device could be assembled covertly at the location at which it was to be detonated (e.g., somewhere within a large city). Defense against such unconventional means of delivery received little attention during the Cold War, but these may be the more likely threats posed by newly nuclear-armed pariah states and by nations that either do not have or choose not to use more conventional nuclear delivery systems.

CENTRAL QUESTIONS

The prospect of eliminating or significantly reducing our vulnerabilities to nuclear weapons surely has strong emotional, ethical, political, and military appeal. Yet the subject of defense remains controversial. The central questions to be addressed by the United States in deciding on the role to be played by defensive systems in meeting new nuclear threats are these: What are the current and potential nuclear threats to U.S. interests? What kinds of defenses might be deployed to deal with them? How effective and how costly would the defenses be? How would they affect the risks of war, the prospects for arms control, and U.S. relations with allies and others?[3]

Nuclear Threats to U.S. Interests

Highest on any nation's ranking of vital assets is its people, closely followed by the homes, businesses, and infrastructure of a functioning society. Next come the strategic offensive forces and associated command and control network upon which nuclear deterrence relies. Further down the list are U.S. power-projection forces—land, sea, and air—and the facilities and equipment to support them. Included on the list, but harder to rank, are the homelands and military assets of U.S. allies and friends, U.S.-owned facilities abroad, sources of natural resources and products required for the smooth functioning of our industrial economy, and installations such as nuclear power reactors whose destruction could cause widespread environmental contamination.

America's interests are thus truly global. Defending all of them against all plausible nuclear threats is technically and economically infeasible. Nor can we simply work our way down the priority ranking. Our population centers are both the most precious and the most fragile of our assets, making this highest priority for defense the most difficult to defend. An assessment of the potential utility of defenses must take into account not only the value of the asset, but also the nature of the nuclear threats it faces and the prospects for defending against them.[4]

The declared nuclear weapons states—those nations that have confirmed their possession of nuclear arsenals—are the United States, the United Kingdom, France, and China; prior to its disintegration, the list would have concluded with the Soviet Union. But it is insufficient merely to insert the word "former" before "Soviet Union" to update this list, for the former Soviet Union now encompasses more than one nation. Of these, Russia is a declared nuclear weapons state. Ukraine, Kazakhstan, and Belarus have substantial numbers of strategic nuclear missiles deployed on their territories, but the weapons are not under their independent national control. All three of these new states profess their intention never to take control of these weapons, and are committed to having them removed from the territory within the seven-year implementation period of the Strategic Arms Reduction Treaty (START). In these countries more than most, however, the leadership and their security policies are subject to change.

While Israel, India, and Pakistan have not declared their nuclear status, they are generally recognized as being "beyond the nuclear threshold." Israel is presumed to have an arsenal on the order of a hundred weapons; India conducted a "peaceful" nuclear explosion in 1974; and Pakistan either has joined or is very close to joining the nuclear club. Each of these countries is expected to enter the twenty-first century with hundreds (or at least tens) of nuclear warheads in its possession.

Apart from these states, it becomes very difficult to identify those countries that will have nuclear forces by the turn of the century. The "usual suspects" include Algeria, Egypt, Iran, Iraq, Libya, North Korea, and Syria—each of which might acquire an arsenal (of one to ten weapons) over the next decade.[5] This list could be much longer, since any industrialized country that chooses to produce nuclear weapons in the next decade could do so. The exclusion of Japan, Germany, Sweden, Hungary, the Czech Republic, and a host of other advanced nations from the list of likely proliferators reflects an assessment of their intentions rather than of their ability to manufacture nuclear explosive devices. Finally, it should be noted that nuclear weapons might be acquired by entities other than national governments, such as terrorist organizations, ethnic groups, or religious factions.

Nuclear powers can threaten U.S. interests in several ways. Consider first the potential threats to American population centers. Russia is likely to maintain nuclear-armed land- and sea-based missiles and bombers capable of reaching any American city, and China probably will have a small force of nuclear-armed ICBMs. Ukraine, Kazakhstan, and Belarus might retain ICBM threats to the U.S. homeland. (The United Kingdom and France, with large nuclear arsenals, are not even remotely viewed as threats to the United States.)

None of the new nuclear nations is expected to have missiles or bombers of ranges sufficient to deliver nuclear warheads from its homeland to the United States, although India and Israel have space launch vehicles that could conceivably be converted into crude ICBMs capable of delivering nuclear weapons to intercontinental distances. All of the nuclear nations, of course, would have at their disposal unconventional means of nuclear delivery—means limited more by imagination than by technology—that would be more than adequate to destroy a city.

American strategic forces and the associated command and control network are likely to remain sufficiently survivable against nuclear attack. Only Russia conceivably could launch a strategic counterforce attack of the kind that preoccupied U.S. defense planners throughout the Cold War; the arsenals of the new proliferators will be far too small to pose a comparable threat.

U.S. projection forces and support facilities overseas, as well as the territory and forces of American allies and friends, will in some instances be within range of nuclear-capable ballistic missiles and bombers of new nuclear nations. Israel and India are expected to have intermediate-range ballistic missiles in the next decade; the other new nuclear nations are likely to have only short-range weapons. In theory, military assets, like cities, are also vulnerable to unconventional delivery means, but in wartime or when on alert they could probably achieve sufficient security to make such delivery unreliable.

Kinds of Defenses

What kinds of defenses might be deployed to deal with the new nuclear threats to America's interests? Defenses can be described as active or passive. Active defenses are intended to prevent weapons from reaching and detonating at their intended targets; passive defenses are designed to minimize damage from such detonations should they occur. The focus here is on active defenses, but passive measures—hardened shelters for aircraft and missiles, dispersal of ground and naval forces, plans for sheltering and evacuation of urban populations, and so on—have played and can continue to play useful roles.

Defenses may also be categorized in terms of the kinds of delivery vehicles they are intended to counter: against ballistic missiles, against air-breathing vehicles, or against unconventional means of delivery.

Ballistic missile defense (BMD). Ballistic missiles defense systems can be configured to provide "global," "area," or "point" defense. A global defense is intended to protect targets everywhere; an area defense would provide coverage for a large section of territory, such as a metropolitan area, or even an entire country; and a point defense would shield discrete targets such as missile launchers, airfields, ships, and command and control installations.[6]

In his 1991 state of the union address, President Bush announced that the SDI program was being "refocused on providing protection from limited ballistic missile strikes, whatever their source," and that such protection was intended to "deal with any future threat to the United States, to our forces overseas, and to our friends and allies."[7] In response to this directive, the Strategic Defense Initiative Organization (SDIO) proposed a System for Global Protection Against Limited Strikes (GPALS), designed to provide worldwide protection against attacks consisting of up to about 100 warheads.

The GPALS system is a layered defense that would be deployed in stages. The first increment would be for theater missile defense (TMD), initially by means of near-term upgrades to the Patriot air defense system, followed by area defense systems employing longer-range ground-based interceptor missiles, such as the Israeli ARROW system or the United States' THAAD (Theater High Altitude Area Defense) system.

The second stage of GPALS is intended to protect the United States. Mobile radars and about 750 ground-based interceptor missiles would be deployed at six sites: one in Alaska, one in Hawaii, and four in the continental United States. In addition, a large number of small space-based sensors, known as Brilliant Eyes, would be deployed to improve the effectiveness of both the national missile defense and the TMD systems.

The third GPALS increment would consist of about 1,000 Brilliant Pebbles, space-based hit-to-kill interceptors, each equipped with its own autonomous sensors. While the performance of such devices would be highest against long-range ballistic missiles, SDIO claimed that Brilliant Pebbles could also defend effectively against ballistic missiles with ranges as low as 600 kilometers.[8]

In the Missile Defense Act of 1991, Congress supported the Bush administration's aim of deploying BMD systems to deal with limited attacks. The act declared that, "It is the goal of the United States to . . . deploy an anti-ballistic missile system . . . capable of providing a highly effective defense of the United States against limited attacks . . . [and to] provide highly effective theater missiles defenses (TMDs) to forward-deployed and expeditionary elements of the United States and to our friends and allies."

Defense of the United States would be provided initially by a system at a single site, compliant with the ABM treaty, to be deployed by 1996 or as soon as possible within the constraints of technology. The ABM treaty limits deployment at the single site (at Grand Forks, North Dakota, or, if that site is dismantled, either at another ICBM field or at Washington, D.C.) to no more than 100 interceptor missiles and specified fixed ground-based radars, and would preclude deployment of mobile ground-based sensors and space-based interceptors, including Brilliant Pebbles. The Missile Defense Act does, however, urge the president to negotiate possible modifications in the ABM treaty with the nations of the former Soviet Union.

Currently, the only ballistic missile defenses deployed by the United States are a small number of upgraded Patriot air defense systems. All U.S. BMD options plausibly achievable by the year 2010 lie somewhere between this very modest deployment and the SDIO's most ambitious aspiration for GPALS.

Air Defense. Air defense refers to active defense against vehicles that rely upon the atmosphere for flight, particularly aircraft and cruise missiles (which are essentially small unmanned jet aircraft).[9] The earliest nuclear threats to American interests, including the U.S. homeland, were posed by Soviet bombers. In response to this, the United States and Canada deployed scores of early warning radars across Alaska, Canada, and Greenland, over 3,000 interceptor aircraft, and thousands of surface-to-air missiles (SAMs). Widespread deployment of Soviet ICBMs and submarine-launched ballistic missiles (SLBMs), in combination with the ABM treaty, undermined support for these strategic air defenses. By the early 1980s, the United States no longer deployed SAMs to protect the homeland, and the number of interceptor aircraft had shrunk by a factor of ten. The Reagan administration's Air Defense Initiative, announced some time after the Strategic Defense Initiative, resulted in little new funding, and focused on aircraft surveillance and tracking rather than on increasing interception capabilities.[10]

Defending an area as large as the United States to ensure that virtually no nuclear weapons-bearing aircraft could reach any of our cities is a daunting task. Defending military forces is less difficult, although still formidable, and U.S. forces abroad and at sea are generally accompanied by air defense units. The most advanced air defense system, Patriot, initially was provided with sufficient anti-missile capability to defend itself, and is now being upgraded to provide wider area coverage.

Cruise missiles exacerbate the air defense problem. Because they are unmanned and are used on one-way missions, they can be much smaller than combat aircraft, rendering them more difficult to detect, track, and intercept. While this may not place much excess burden on point defenses, it surely would stress any area defenses against air-breathing vehicles.

Defense against unconventional means of delivery. What is the defense against a nuclear weapon being transported to its intended target by an unconventional delivery system such as a truck, a trawler, or a passenger aircraft? If intelligence reports or terrorist threats indicated that a nuclear explosive device was in an American city, what could be done to prevent its detonation? The principal barrier to dealing with such threats is not knowing the location of the device. Once its location is known, options include disarming, destroying, or removing it.

In response to two incidents involving accidental "losses" of bomber-borne nuclear weapons (at Palomares, Spain, in 1966, and Thule, Greenland, in 1968) and an extortionist's threat to explode a nuclear bomb in Boston (in 1974), in 1975 the United States established a Nuclear Emergency Search Team (NEST). NEST personnel and equipment in Las Vegas, Nevada, and at Andrews Air Force Base outside of Washington, D.C., stand ready to be transported on short notice to locations around the world. With sophisticated radiation monitoring equipment designed for use from planes, helicopters, ships, vans, and on foot, these teams can survey an area to search for the nuclear materials at the heart of an explosive device. Having located the device, the team can identify and neutralize booby traps or other mechanisms intended to restrict access; it can take measures to disarm, destroy, or remove the device; it can minimize damage from any explosion; and it can clean up any radioactive debris.[11]

Little information about NEST procedures or capabilities is available in the unclassified literature. The original organizer of NEST, Mahlon E. Gates, in 1987 wrote that it is able "to respond rapidly to threats and discover devices." He went on, however, to note the limitations to NEST's capabilities: "If an improvised nuclear device were hidden in a large metropolitan city such as New York or Chicago, with no further information on its location, it would be next to impossible for NEST to find it within a limited period."[12] To improve its search capabilities, NEST continues to increase the sensitivity of its radiation monitoring equipment, and to measure and record the levels of background radiation in several U.S. cities and federal buildings, so that any increase in radiation caused by the introduction of a nuclear device could more readily be recognized.

Detection of a well-shielded nuclear device is difficult in any event, but far less so if the area to be searched is no larger than a building, a truck, a trawler, or a plane. The barriers to applying surveillance equipment and procedures to buildings, highways, ports, and airports are not so much technical as economic and political.

Feasibility and Costs of Defenses

Until very recently, debates over defenses against nuclear weapons were held in the context of the Cold War. The technical feasibility, design specifications, performance characteristics, costs, and political and diplomatic repercussions of defensive systems were assessed in terms of the threat posed by a hostile Soviet Union possessing tens of thousands of nuclear weapons. The world has changed, and so too must the objectives and measures of effectiveness of our investments in national security.

Because we have little recent experience in developing, producing, deploying, and operating systems for defense against nuclear weapons, estimates of their performance and costs are notoriously speculative and volatile. Nowhere is this more apparent than in the case of ballistic missile defense.

Ballistic missile defense (BMD). The Sentinel system of the late 1960s, and the Safeguard of the early 1970s, were both designed to deal only with "limited strikes." Yet Americans engaged in intensive debates over the feasibility and costs of both systems and ultimately decided to deploy neither of them. Early goals for SDI were much more grandiose, claiming a system that would render "nuclear weapons impotent and obsolete"[13] and promoting it as "thoroughly reliable and total."[14] This, however, soon gave way to the more modest rhetoric of enhancing deterrence and fostering offensive arms reductions. Despite five years of intensive effort by the Reagan administration, doubts about technical feasibility, concerns about costs, and other uncertainties led Congress to prohibit any SDI experiments that might violate the ABM Treaty, and the nation made no commitment to SDI deployment. The already dim prospects for SDI were just about extinguished in May 1993, when U.S. Secretary of Defense Les Aspin replaced the SDIO with a New Ballistic Missile Defense Organization (BMDO), and directed it to focus on ground-based systems.

Congressional suspicions of BMD did not extend to theater missile defenses, and for the past several years Congress has fully supported administration requests for TMD funding. The televised images of Scud ballistic missiles arriving in Israel and Saudi Arabia during the Gulf War provided convincing evidence of the threat posed by theater ballistic missiles; the pictures of Patriot missiles soaring toward the incoming Scuds, and exploding close to (and, we believed, destroying) the attackers were sufficient to convince most observers that TMD would be effective. Subsequent downward revisions in estimates of Patriot performance do not seem to have dampened this enthusiasm for TMD; rather, they appear to have reinforced support for developing more advanced TMD systems.

It has been estimated that fourteen nations now have ballistic missiles in their arsenals, and that another six could join the group over the next decade.[15] Many of the missiles could be within range of U.S. forces and allies overseas; hence, support for TMD continues. Not all of the missile-equipped Third World countries, however, are seen as emerging nuclear powers. The seven that might acquire nuclear-armed ballistic missiles of short or medium range are India, Pakistan, Egypt, Iran, Libya, North Korea, and Syria—a small though significant group—and only India might have missiles capable of reaching the United States.

Estimates of the costs of ballistic missile defenses vary widely. In May 1991, SDIO Director Henry F. Cooper estimated the overall acquisition cost of GPALS to be about $46 billion: $10 billion for TMD; $25 billion for the six ground-based national missile defense sites and the accompanying space-based sensors; and $11 billion for about 1,000 Brilliant Pebbles.[16] The Congressional Budget Office (CBO), in a report issued in 1992, estimated $85 billion to be the "total expense of developing and deploying GPALS, coupled with the costs of other research under the SDI program . . . between 1993 and 2005 [plus] additional costs to operate and support the systems that are deployed."[17] The difference in these estimates is attributable to what is included: CBO's higher figure includes SDIO's estimates of the costs of the various associated programs.

Far less costly is the program to upgrade the Patriot system to enhance its TMD capabilities. Modifications in the radar, the homing sensor, and the missile warhead would extend the area covered by the system and would also improve the chances that intercept would result in the destruction of an incoming missile warhead. Although Patriot cannot be made to have capabilities comparable to those prescribed for THAAD, upgraded Patriots are much more likely to be deployed in this era of declining U.S. defense budgets. Thousands of Patriot missiles are on order by the U.S. Army and by a number of U.S. allies for its primary air defense purpose; the incremental cost of upgrading those Patriot batteries is estimated to be quite small—certainly far smaller than would be the cost of deploying THAAD. And, because THAAD would have no air defense capability, Patriot still would be needed to perform that role.

Air defenses. U.S. forces overseas have been within range of military aircraft of active and potential adversaries for more than half a century, and air defenses have been and will continue to be an integral element of any U.S. force projection activities. The effectiveness of these theater defenses traditionally has been assessed in terms of the attrition rate they impose on enemy aircraft; they have not been expected to intercept and destroy each and every attacking plane before it reaches its target. If, however, only a small number of aircraft were attacking simultaneously, U.S. air defenses might well destroy them all. In the case of a new nuclear power, the number of attack aircraft bearing nuclear weapons would be small; thus, if the defenses could distinguish nuclear-armed from other aircraft, current and projected theater air defenses should be effective in defending our forces against new proliferators.

Cruise missiles would be harder to counter. It is unlikely, however, that any of the new nuclear nations will acquire both nuclear weapons sufficiently small to be borne by cruise missiles, and cruise missiles accurate and reliable enough to be preferred to aircraft and ballistic missiles as means to attack forces in the field. Here too, current and projected theater defenses should be able to stay ahead of the potential threat.

The central question with regard to air defense is whether the United States should reverse a pattern of more than two decades and attempt to build up the air defenses of the U.S. homeland. At this time, only Russia poses a strategic bomber threat to the United States. But Russia also possesses large numbers of strategic ballistic missiles. Thus, the logic that for decades persuaded Americans that it made little sense to maintain an expensive nationwide air defense network in the absence of effective ballistic missile defense remains applicable.

The United States does not now plan to deploy a full nationwide defense against large air-breathing threats. If it decided to do so, the cost of the air defense system could be as high as $100–$200 billion.[18]

Defenses against unconventional means of delivery. Given that every new nuclear power will have access to unconventional means of delivery and that few, if any, of them will possess nuclear-armed missiles or bombers of intercontinental range, optimal responses to those threats should focus more on dealing with the unconventional threats (such as the bomb-laden truck parked under New York's World Trade Center) and less on the traditional delivery vehicles characteristic of the strategic arsenal of the former Soviet Union. It is difficult to estimate how effectively the United States could monitor its borders to detect and foil any attempts by hostile powers to introduce nuclear explosive devices or the components essential to assembling them. The United States is a large country, with thousands of miles of relatively unguarded borders. Our notable lack of success in cutting off the supply of drugs to our cities is hardly encouraging on this point.

Risk of War and Arms Control

How would widespread defenses affect the risk of war? In the context of the Cold War, it was argued persuasively that widespread BMD would undermine "crisis stability"; that is, it would increase the incentive to risk striking first.[19] This followed from the belief that a massive, well-coordinated preemptive strike would be better able to counter defenses than would a ragged retaliatory attack employing the smaller number of weapons that had survived the preemptive attack. However, only Russia now has a strategic arsenal even approaching the capability necessary for a massive, well-coordinated preemptive strike against the United States, and the chances of such an event seem more remote than ever. Given Russia's dismal economic condition, it is extremely unlikely that its response to a U.S. BMD deployment costing on the order of $50–100 billion would be to deploy a Russia-wide BMD system that would threaten America's nuclear retaliatory capability. More likely would be for Russia to maintain its own retaliatory capability by not reducing its offensive arsenal and withdrawing from any agreements calling for such reductions; it might also build up its offensive arsenal. Moreover, should the United States simply withdraw from the ABM treaty and proceed to deploy an extensive BMD system, Russia would no longer be bound by the treaty or any related arms control accords.

In short, any BMD deployment consistent with the ABM treaty—either in its current form or as modified through negotiations with Russia—is unlikely to have much effect either on the risk of war or on existing and potential arms control agreements between them. Deployment beyond the constraints of the treaty almost surely would undermine prospects for further arms control and, depending on the magnitude of the deployment and the Russian responses, could increase the likelihood of nuclear conflict. Such a deployment would also adversely affect the nonproliferation atmosphere the United States seeks to impose on other states.

New U.S. air defense deployments would have less effect than BMD on the likelihood of war and on arms control. Unlike the

United States, the Soviet Union maintained an extensive nation-wide air defense network, the elements of which remain deployed throughout the former republics. Thus, a U.S. air defense deployment could be seen as merely redressing an asymmetric advantage enjoyed by Russia and other republics of the former Soviet Union. And, because Russia relies far more heavily on strategic missiles than on bombers for deterrence, increased air defenses in the United States would provide little incentive for increases in the Russian bomber force.

However, modern air defenses, especially if designed to deal with stealthy aircraft and cruise missiles, are likely to be seen as also possessing substantial BMD capability. To the extent that any new U.S. air defense network might appear to the Russians as threatening the ability of their ballistic missiles to penetrate to targets in the United States, it could stimulate Russian reactions similar to those that would be expected in response to American BMD. Like upgraded Patriot, THAAD, and Arrow, the TMD systems now being marketed aggressively by Russia have some capability to intercept intercontinental-range ballistic missiles, albeit within a very restricted area and then only under very favorable conditions. There is no "bright line" distinguishing a capability for theater missile defense from that for strategic missile defense. Therefore, deployments and transfers of TMD systems by either of the parties to the ABM treaty should be made only after reasonable efforts to satisfy the other party that the TMD deployments would not create true strategic defense capabilities of any significance.

Allies and Others

The United States has long sought participation by allies in research and development on space-based BMD, with only limited success. Most of them are more interested in theater missile defenses than in global defenses since, unlike the United States, most are within range of theater ballistic missiles. The spectacle of Scud attacks in the Gulf War only heightened their interests in TMD, and several have placed orders to purchase Patriots from the United States.

The United Kingdom, Germany, Israel, Italy, and Japan have been willing to sign formal memoranda of understanding on participation in SDI research, but mainly they have registered skepticism as to its technical feasibility, cost effectiveness, technological spin-off potential, and effects on stability and arms control. The British and French, in particular, have long been concerned about the impact of widespread defenses on the effectiveness of their ballistic missile forces as independent deterrents.

The Russian reaction to SDI has been far less negative than had been the reaction of the Soviet Union, and is even seen as positive by some American proponents of GPALS. In a televised speech early in 1992, Russian president Boris Yeltsin said:

> Russia confirms its adherence to the ABM treaty. It is an important factor in maintaining strategic stability in the world. We are ready to continue discussion without prejudice of the U.S. proposal for limiting non-nuclear ABM systems. . . . We are ready jointly to work out and subsequently to create and operate a global system of defense in place of SDI.[20]

Indications are that the Russian interest in joint U.S.–Russian efforts in the BMD domain is motivated less by a perceived need to cope with new ballistic missile threats than by desires to provide gainful employment for Russians in the relevant defense institutes and enterprises, to obtain access to U.S. technology, and to forestall any unilateral U.S. surge to deploy GPALS.

A decision on the extent to which the United States should help other nations bolster their defensive capabilities will have to take into account all of the factors that the United States has traditionally considered in assessing potential transfers of offensive weapons. Transfer of defensive systems may seem more humanitarian and less dangerous, but changes in regional defensive capabilities, just as in offensive capabilities, can enhance or undermine stability, dampen or stimulate arms races, and increase or decrease U.S. influence and freedom of action. Depending upon the circumstances, transferring U.S. defensive technologies and hardware may or may not serve U.S. interests; in this regard, defense is no different from offense.

CONCLUSION

Russia, China, and (depending upon who has control of the nuclear-armed ICBMs on their territories) possibly Belarus, Kazakhstan, and Ukraine may presently pose nuclear threats to the U.S. homeland.[21] Over the next ten to fifteen years, the list of nuclear powers might lengthen to include Algeria, Egypt, Iran, Iraq, Libya, North Korea, and Syria—none of which is expected to have missiles or bombers of range sufficient to reach the United States.[22] Most of the new nuclear powers will, however, have missiles and bombers capable of reaching U.S. allies and assets overseas.

The observations offered below provide some indication of the contributions that defensive systems might make to the U.S. response to new nuclear threats:

- U.S. plans for theater missile defense should proceed along the lines indicated in the Missile Defense Act of 1991 and the Bush administration's proposal for the first increment of GPALS. Careful consideration should be given to any proposed transfer of theater missile defense technology or systems, recognizing that alterations in a regional balance of defensive arms can lead to virtually all of the consequences—for good and for ill—that would attend changes in the offensive balance. It is also important that U.S. TMD systems be consistent with the ABM treaty, which, unless and until it is revised, requires that such systems not be capable of countering strategic ballistic missiles, specifically ICBMs and SLBMs.

- A nationwide BMD system of the kind called for in the Missile Defense Act of 1991 or proposed as the second increment of GPALS would not constitute a meaningful response to nuclear proliferation in the next two decades, since none of the potential new nuclear states is expected to have ICBMs or SLBMs available as nuclear delivery vehicles. It is only with respect to nuclear threats posed by China and the nuclear-armed nations of the former Soviet Union—which could include a Russian state reverted to authoritarian rule and hostile to the United States—that the national missile defense has relevance. Scarce defense resources devoted to early nationwide BMD deployment would better be spent on other capabilities to enhance our national security. However, while such a deployment is likely to be wasteful, it is unlikely to be dangerous.

- Research on space-based BMD components should continue, but no commitment to deployment should be made. For some time to come, it is likely that theater ballistic missiles will be intercepted more effectively by defenses in the theater than by defenses in space. And, as indicated, no anticipated nuclear threats to the U.S. homeland would justify deployment of a space-based defense.

- Consideration of potential new nuclear forces reveals no requirements for air defenses beyond those already incorporated in U.S. defense plans. Only if a decision were made to deploy a nationwide system to defend against ballistic missiles would it appear worthwhile to deploy a corresponding air defense system (and vice versa).

- Because every new nuclear nation will have access to unconventional means for delivering nuclear weapons to the U.S. homeland and other areas of vital interest to us, greater emphasis should be given to hedging against this potential threat. Little unclassified information is available about the capabilities of the Nuclear Emergency Search Team and associated activities, hence it is difficult to prescribe just where this increased emphasis should be placed. In light of the growing importance of these efforts, however, it is likely that additional resources could productively and effectively be applied to them.

This exploration of defensive systems indicates that they could make a modest but useful contribution to dealing with new nuclear threats and that near-term emphasis should be given to deployments of theater missile defenses and to improvements in our capabilities for dealing with unconventional means of nuclear delivery.

Notes

1. "Ballistic missile defense" has largely replaced "anti-ballistic missile" (ABM) in national security jargon. Both refer to systems for countering ballistic missiles in flight.
2. For a heated and informative discussion of Patriot's performance in the Persian Gulf War, see Theodore A. Postol, "Lessons of the Gulf War Patriot Experience," *International Security*, vol. 16, no. 3 (Winter 1991/92), pp. 119–71, and the subsequent exchange between Robert M. Stein and Postol in "Correspondence: Patriot Experience in the Gulf War," *International Security*, vol. 17, no. 1 (Summer 1992), pp. 199–240.
3. These questions are similar (though not identical) to those formulated by Michèle A. Flournoy in chapter 6.
4. The capabilities of current and potential nuclear powers are examined in some detail by Lewis A. Dunn in chapter 2 of this volume.
5. See chapter 2, table 1.
6. An excellent analysis of U.S. defenses is provided by Mark W. Goodman, "Defenses Against Nuclear Weapons," in Michèle Flournoy, ed., *Nuclear Weapons After the Cold War: Guidelines for U.S. Policy* (New York: HarperCollins, 1992).
7. "Address Before a Joint Session of the Congress on the State of the Union" (January 20, 1991), in *Public Papers of the President of the United States: George Bush, 1991* (Washington D.C.: U.S. Government Printing Office [USGPO], 1992), pp. 74–80.
8. Strategic Defense Initiative Organization, *1991 Report to Congress on the Strategic Defense Initiative* (Washington, D.C.: U.S. Department of Defense, May 1991), pp. 2–5.
9. For an analysis of strategic air defenses, see Arthur Charo, *Continental Air Defense: A Neglected Dimension of Strategic Defense*, CSIA Occasional Paper No. 7 (Lanham, Md.: University Press of America and Center for Science and International Affairs, 1990).
10. See Goodman, "Defenses Against Nuclear Weapons," p. 229.
11. For an informed description of NEST, see Mahlon E. Gates, "The Nuclear Emergency Search Team," in Paul Leventhal and Yonah Alexander, eds., *Preventing Nuclear Terrorism* (New York: Lexington Books, 1987), pp. 397–402.
12. Gates, "The Nuclear Emergency Search Team," p. 401.
13. President Ronald Reagan, televised address, March 23, 1983.
14. Secretary of Defense Caspar Weinberger, appearance on "Meet the Press," NBC-TV, March 27, 1983.
15. Henry F. Cooper, testimony before the Subcommittee on Legislation and National Security, Committee on Government Operations, U.S. House of Representatives, May 16, 1991, in *Strategic Defense Initiative: What Are the Costs, What Are the Threats* (Washington, D.C.: USGPO, 1991).
16. Cooper, testimony.
17. *Cost of Alternative Approaches to SDI* (Washington, D.C.: Congressional Budget Office, May 1992).

18. Charo, *Continental Air Defense*, p. 131.
19. For an assessment of strategic defenses in the context of the Cold War, see Albert Carnesale, "The Strategic Defense Initiative," in George E. Hudson and Joseph Kruzel, eds., *American Defense Annual, 1985–1986* (Lexington, Mass.: Lexington Books, 1986), pp. 187–205.
20. Boris Yeltsin, televised speech of January 29, 1992, FBIS–SOV–92–019.
21. Britain and France have nuclear weapons, Israel probably has them, and India and Pakistan either have or are very close to having them, but none of these nations are perceived as posing plausible threats to the United States.
22. Belarus, Kazakhstan, and Ukraine are committed to the removal of all nuclear weapons from their territories within a decade. If this happens, the list of nuclear powers might actually shorten.

CHAPTER NINE

The Role of Intelligence

ROBERT D. BLACKWILL and ASHTON B. CARTER

This chapter seeks to answer two questions: First, what implications do the capabilities and limitations of U.S. intelligence have for managing the emergence of new nuclear weapons states? Second, does nuclear proliferation require new and distinct intelligence collection or analytical approaches?

Intelligence is in many ways the long pole in the tent of coping with nuclear proliferation. The success or failure of alternative policy approaches discussed in this book turns crucially on whether U.S. decisionmakers can form an accurate picture of a proliferator's intentions and capabilities at that moment in time when action can make a difference. Unfortunately, this sensitivity of policy success is not likely to be well served by the large gaps and uncertainties that will probably exist in the intelligence picture.

The first section of this analysis surveys the problem of monitoring a proliferator close to the threshold of attaining nuclear weapons capability, and of penetrating its program after it has produced a weapon. A number of intelligence problems are common to preventing or slowing proliferation as well as to dealing with it once it has occurred. Recent experiences with Iraq and North Korea are illustrative in this regard.

Next, there is an analysis of the critical respects in which the intelligence challenge of managing U.S. security policy toward new nuclear states differs from the traditional postwar preoccupations of the American intelligence community: of assessing the nuclear threat posed by the USSR and monitoring potential nuclear weapons programs around the world. Unlike the large and overt nuclear arsenal of the former Soviet Union, the nuclear weapons program of a new nuclear state is likely to be small, detached from the regular military establishment and its chain of command and control, and difficult to illuminate solely through national technical means.

Another challenge concerns the difficulty of pinning down the moment a proliferating nation crosses the threshold from having a "nuclear program" to having a "nuclear arsenal." Intelligence operations for states with a nuclear weapons capability differ in several respects from maintaining surveillance of potential proliferators. The new task of tracking nuclear status entails a global reach to encompass all likely suspects, and an intensified focus on individual nations when critical U.S. policy moves, including even military action, depend on detailed intelligence information. U.S. intelligence will rely more on cooperation with the intelligence services of other nations, because they may possess valuable complementary information, and because their support of U.S. policy will be enhanced if they have access to the same intelligence data base.

The next section looks at the three intelligence problems that present themselves only after the threshold to nuclear weapons possession has been decisively crossed and a target nation is known to possess one or more nuclear weapons. The first is unlocking the "strategic personality" of the new proliferator: what purposes does it see for its nuclear weapons, when and how might it use them, and in what way are its answers to these questions influenced by its culture and politics? The second problem is to conduct traditional "threat assessments" of the new proliferator, analyzing the number and types of nuclear weapons systems it acquires and the doctrine and practices of the military organizations that operate them. (This also addresses the prospect of unconventional, paramilitary, or terrorist use of nuclear weapons.) The third potential challenge to U.S. intelligence may be to offensive military operations aimed at retarding a nuclear program. Such operations would likely require fairly large forces acting under tight political constraints with a demand for clear and definitive results in a brief strike—a recipe for information-intensive warfare of the type conducted by the United States in Desert Storm, but conceivably under entirely different politico-military conditions.

Finally, conclusions are presented concerning the relationship between the intelligence challenge posed by new nuclear weapons states and U.S. policymakers.

MONITORING PROLIFERATORS NEAR THE THRESHOLD: IRAQ AND NORTH KOREA

Intelligence monitoring of a proliferator near the threshold can help determine the magnitude, pace, and capabilities of its nuclear programs: its acquisition of parts and equipment; scientific resources; reactors; reprocessing; uranium ore, conversion, or enrichment; weaponization; and delivery systems. It can gather data on a nation's financial reserves available for a nuclear program; on its existing industrial capacity, natural resources, and scientific base; and on its international economic and scientific contacts.

Monitoring can also track a proliferator's political and military intentions; provide relevant threat assessments to the United States, its allies, and other friendly states; and produce evidence to persuade U.S. politicians and the public that a serious danger to the United States has emerged and that appropriate steps need to be taken to deal with it. It can form the basis of a U.S. diplomatic effort to organize the international community to contain new nuclear weapons states. And intelligence information can, *in extremis*, guide efforts through targeting data to destroy a proliferator's nuclear weapons capability by U.S. military action, alone or with the help of allies.

There are two recent cases against which to test current American intelligence capabilities and future requirements, and about which there is abundant public information. Iraq was the object of a significant if not successful U.S. intelligence effort before, during, and after the Gulf War. There is similar recent, though more limited, experience from the disclosures of North Korea's developing nuclear program. Using the Iraqi and North Korean cases, it is possible to illustrate the variety of intelligence targets and methods involved in assessing the status of a proliferator's nuclear program, or of its fledgling arsenal.[1] It identifies areas where intelligence is likely to be ambiguous, particularly with regard to the critical question of how close the nation is to weaponization. Iraq and North Korea admittedly pose hard cases for foreign intelligence since both are rigidly controlled, closed societies. Nations like India, Pakistan, or Ukraine are somewhat "softer" intelligence targets. But the "outlaw" states that isolate themselves from the international community are precisely those that are most likely to pose the problems discussed in this book.

Procurement of Nuclear Parts and Equipment

There are three broad avenues for acquisition of parts and equipment for a nuclear program: through legal purchases, seeking dual-use items that have applications in a civil nuclear program or other industries; covertly, either through illegal sales or theft; or by developing the indigenous capability to produce, upgrade or alter the foreign technology. Iraq used all these avenues, and indications are that North Korea has similarly cast a wide international procurement net while also attempting to develop its own indigenous manufacturing abilities.[2]

Learning from International Inspections, Institutions, and Contacts

UN/International Atomic Energy Agency inspectors and the public alike were stunned as the Iraqi nuclear program was revealed.[3] The inspectors compiled a list of suppliers and of materials already delivered[4] and made their names available to other governments, with the aim of checking their future activities. Washington also pressed successfully for some of the names to be released to the press. As one proliferation expert advised, "That network is at the disposal of Iran, Libya, Pakistan and India still. The best way to close it off is to make it public."[5]

Inspections also provided a view of the role of Iraq's manufacturing infrastructure in its nuclear program. There were production plants for parts and equipment to enrich uranium, including vacuum chambers and specialized magnets for electromagnetic isotope separation.[6] Seized documents showed Iraqi awareness that extensive foreign purchasing would raise suspicions abroad. This led Baghdad to use locally produced materials as much as possible in the civilian sector, saving imported parts for the nuclear weapons program.[7] Inspectors were able to reconstruct a picture of Iraq's strategy for acquiring needed nuclear parts and equipment.

But there are serious problems with dependence on outside inspectors to detect and classify the programs and capabilities of new nuclear weapons states. Even though Iraq had suffered a crushing military defeat, and faced a powerful U.S. military presence in the region and solid UN backing for inspections, it frustrated inspection efforts through a determined attempt to cover its import trail and disguise its intended use. The vast majority of procurement-related information had been destroyed or hidden.[8] Since IAEA inspections began, millions of dollars worth of nuclear technologies believed to be in Iraq are still unaccounted for.[9]

New nuclear weapons states are not likely to allow international inspectors access anything like the freedom enjoyed by the UN in Iraq. (North Korea's dramatic March 1993 announcement that it intended to withdraw from the Nonproliferation Treaty rather than accede to IAEA inspections underscores the danger of relying on the international inspection regime for information on new nuclear weapons programs.[10] Though North Korea subsequently made some conciliatory gestures towards ending the NPT crisis, the problem at this writing remains unresolved.) Nevertheless, the Iraqi experience provides lessons that can be used to improve U.S. intelligence collection and analysis on new proliferators.

Intelligence agencies should continue to seek information from the shadowy Western commercial network of suppliers, intermediaries, and front companies.[11] We now know that nearly 500 Western companies were involved in supplying or installing sensitive nuclear-related materials to the Iraqi program.[12] The names—and methods—of Iraqi front companies have also been exposed.[13] This data provides the intelligence community with a crucial running start.[14]

Intelligence agencies can take advantage of the willingness of some members of the international scientific community to use their professional networks to gain information about equipment sought or obtained by nuclear proliferators. Particular benefit attaches to receiving such information from sources who are versed in the technological language of nuclear parts and can recognize efforts to provide misleading information, and who can more readily approach a fellow scientist from a proliferating nation.[15]

International banking institutions are also vital to the procurement process. In Iraq's case, many of the arrangements that involved banks were legal, since the materials were ostensibly intended for use in its civil nuclear power program.[16] In addition, banks are not subject to any legal requirement to inquire into the exact details of the trade.[17] The use of banks by proliferators for covering up the procurement path, particularly with regard to illegal single-use sales, hinders detection efforts since it allows suppliers and purchasers to disguise the ultimate destination of sensitive materials.[18] But the dependence by proliferators on financial institutions—to finance sales or issue letters of credit—furnishes a fruitful source of intelligence information. For example, documents seized in Iraq and declassified in the United States indicate that the Bank of Commerce and Credit International (BCCI), several European banks, and the Atlanta branch of the Italian Lavaro Bank may have been intimately involved in expediting nuclear transactions.[19]

Law enforcement and intelligence agencies can work with banks to follow the activities of suppliers and intermediaries to proliferating nations. For this kind of cooperation to be effective, banks will have to exercise greater scrutiny over the deals they facilitate, especially those involving dual-use technology. If they are unwilling to cooperate, and to police themselves and their clients, however, intelligence efforts should focus on penetrating the financial institutions, both to cut off an acquisition route and perhaps more importantly, to gather clues about a proliferator's procurement strategy. Human intelligence also plays an important part in this process. Wire-tapping and signal intercepts are critical.[20]

Customs information remains an essential component of intelligence efforts to track acquisition of nuclear parts and equipment. In the five years preceding the Gulf War, the U.S. government alone authorized the sale of $1.5 billion worth of electronic equipment, computers, and machine tools that were relevant to Iraq's nuclear and ballistic missile programs.[21] While the vast majority of the sales appear to have been legal, U.S. companies exported extensive shipments of highly sensitive dual-use materials, either through Iraqi front companies or directly to Iraq.[22] Disclosures that the Energy and State departments may have stifled warnings in 1989 about U.S. sales of sensitive technologies to Iraq highlights the need to better monitor external as well as internal customs activities.[23]

What a new nuclear weapons state does not pursue on world markets may provide as much information about its indigenous capabilities as what it does purchase. Iraq claimed that it was undaunted by a 1990 sting operation at London's Heathrow Airport that seized technologies for krytrons because the Ministry of Industry and Military Industrialization had succeeded in its indigenous production. While the claim could not be fully verified, Western intelligence was able to confirm that Iraq had bought a lower-quality version of the same technology and was believed to be capable of upgrading it.[24]

The challenges of gathering data on a new nuclear weapons state's procurement of parts and equipment are, therefore, considerable. Among the many hurdles are the wide range of dual-use materials that can be purchased legally and the ability of a new nuclear weapons state to convert technologies that were not originally intended for use in a nuclear program. One encouraging point, however, is that a large portion of this detection activity can occur without direct penetration of a police state.

While efforts to discover the size, capabilities, and activities of a proliferating nation's scientific community might appear relatively straightforward, Western attempts to assess the level of Iraqi scientific expertise demonstrate the serious problems with such an objective. As a part of its broader effort to initiate a nuclear weapons program, Iraq aggressively began in 1974 to recruit scientists, technicians, and engineers from the Arab world. With promises of large salaries and the distinction of working on an all-Arab nuclear project, over 4,000 experts arrived in Iraq to work on high-tech programs. It appears that Washington underestimated the consequences of this recruiting effort.[25] It came as a surprise to Western analysts to learn that Iraq's nuclear program included as many as 10,000 technical employees. Few had suspected that the region's largest scientific base existed in Iraq.[26]

Numerous avenues exist for gaining intelligence about a new

nuclear weapons state's commitment to human scientific capital. Critical details can be obtained through monitoring Western scientific conferences and foreign recruitment efforts. Intelligence agencies can seek out foreigners who have been involved in the proliferator's nuclear efforts and who might provide insights into the size of the program and the investment being made in scientists as well as giving indications of dependence on foreign technical contributions. Determination that a proliferating nation is successfully able to convert imported materials should also provide insights into its human resources. Finally, the intelligence community can seek the voluntary cooperation of professional scientific networks to gather information and perhaps even preempt potential defectors.[27]

Even if the proliferator is an authoritarian state,[28] it is possible, but difficult, to follow the development of scientific human capital. A robust nuclear community is unaffected by inspections or destruction of equipment.[29] Former Director of Central Intelligence (DCI) Robert Gates warned in the aftermath of the Desert Storm bombing that "the cadre of scientists and engineers trained for these programs will be able to reconstitute any dormant program rapidly."[30] The same will be true for other new nuclear weapons nations.

It is possible that the abrupt changes occurring in the nuclear weapons establishment of the former USSR will put on the international market a large number of unemployed and disaffected scientists, engineers, and technicians with experience in nuclear materials production and handling, bomb design and fabrication, and maintenance and handling of weapons systems. One to two thousand former Soviet scientists reportedly have nuclear weapon design skills, while over one million individuals may have been engaged in some activity of the nuclear program.[31] Whether many of them can be wooed by hard currency remains uncertain; there is not yet any evidence of significant scientific migrations or sale of technical know-how.[32] Western efforts to initiate joint civil programs to occupy nuclear experts from the former republics can mitigate but not resolve the problem. Nuclear "brain drain" thus represents a substantial potential resource-in-waiting for a proliferator's long-term efforts. Since the Soviets reportedly supplied North Korea with substantial nuclear assistance, and in conjunction with China, began training their North Korean counterparts in the 1950s,[33] former Defense Secretary Richard Cheney has expressed his fear that unemployed nuclear scientists from the former Soviet Union could make their way to Pyongyang.[34]

Information concerning nuclear facilities and personnel in the former Soviet Union, made relatively more available now by the end of communist rule, should assist in keeping tabs on who is heading where. U.S. intelligence agencies should expand their base of contacts and informants within the former Soviet scientific community.[35] Scientists are most likely to be approached by nations with which they have had scientific exchanges in the past. Robert Gates indicated that "Cuba, India, Syria, Egypt and Algeria are most likely to have the contacts and resident scientists to assist emigrating Soviets."[36] In this connection, U.S. intelligence agencies should try to work closely with the intelligence communities of the former Soviet Union to join forces against this common threat.

Monitoring Technological and Resource Assets

Different types of reactors require different technological assets and specifications and lead to distinct intelligence challenges. Research reactors can generally be built with relatively little outside help and can be small enough that detection by satellite is difficult. Since the hardware for this type of reactor can be obtained domestically, a proliferator can avoid international safeguards and constraints. Small production research reactors are also not technologically complicated. In both cases, intelligence can best be acquired through human sources—defectors, scientific contacts, and employees at the facilities when possible. As of April 1993, inspectors were searching for an underground reactor which experts believed was still hidden somewhere in Iraq. Reconnaissance satellites have provided no assistance in this effort.[37]

Large production research reactors lead to greater plutonium generation rates, thus facilitating bomb fabrication, but also increasing the chances of satellite detection.[38] Power reactors have significantly greater technological requirements and are much larger still, thus making information gathering on them somewhat easier. Intelligence efforts should focus especially on their technical aspects—modification of design restrictions, alteration of use, and so on. Early

Iraqi efforts to expand beyond its five-megawatt research reactor provided by the Soviet Union, and to acquire a French-made power reactor, were closely monitored by Israeli Mossad agents who uncovered procurement information and shipment details.[39] As a result, a team of three Israeli agents blew up critical reactor cores shortly before their delivery from France to Iraq in 1979.[40]

Satellites alone cannot always provide all the necessary information. Reconnaissance imagery, however, can make substantial contributions to detection of reactors and their capabilities, especially if the proliferator has decided to pursue speed over secrecy.[41] It can be supplemented by human intelligence, such as details on the rate of reactor production and the intended use and location of the produced nuclear material. A North Korean diplomat who defected in September 1991 disclosed that Pyongyang had built a secret underground research reactor north of the capital.[42]

Reprocessing facilities separate plutonium out of spent nuclear fuel from reactors, providing material that can be used in nuclear weapons. Detailed information about reprocessing has been in the public domain for years, partly because similar processes are used in civilian applications. Thus, a proliferating nation may quickly and cheaply produce a small reprocessing plant, often with minimal foreign technological assistance.[43]

Western efforts to track North Korea's production of plutonium have relied on satellite imagery and on-site inspections. Beginning in 1988, U.S. intelligence officials began monitoring the development of a large facility in the vicinity of other North Korean nuclear sites at Yongbyon. Intelligence officials believed that the new facility was a reprocessing plant.[44] Since 1989, the United States has reportedly felt confident, through reconnaissance imagery, that North Korea was indeed separating plutonium at the site.[45] The small size of North Korea's civil nuclear power program suggested that the relatively large facility was intended for the nation's nuclear weapons program.[46] Satellites detected intensive North Korean efforts to camouflage the plant and nearby nuclear waste storage areas.[47] Sophisticated on-site inspections confirmed that plutonium production had indeed occurred since 1989.[48] North Korea's possible withdrawal from the NPT, after being confronted with the incriminating evidence, now intensifies the intelligence task.

With the possible end of IAEA inspections in North Korea, that nation could decide to divert large amounts of spent fuel from its once monitored reactors and reprocess it into enough weapons-grade plutonium for two to three bombs.[49] Greater pressure will likely be on satellites and on-site human intelligence to manage this development.

If a proliferator decides to use highly enriched uranium rather than plutonium as a nuclear weapons material, the first stage towards indigenous production is procurement of uranium ore. Ore is also needed to construct a reactor, even if it will eventually use plutonium as the chosen fissile material.[50] A new nuclear weapons state with an active nuclear weapons program would need a steady supply of uranium.

Acquisition of ore can occur either through legal import or through exploitation of indigenous resources. Reserves are sufficiently extensive worldwide that nations seeking the ore can readily obtain it, which makes implementation of international constraints particularly difficult.[51] Where constraints do exist, they can lead to unanticipated results. North Korea received technical assistance from the IAEA in order to locate and mine its uranium deposits, which may later have been used in its independently produced reactors.[52]

Most Iraqi ore is believed to have been purchased abroad, but efforts were also reportedly made to mine indigenous supplies in northwestern sections of the country.[53] Inspections revealed information on an Iraqi mining network that included a facility capable of extracting nearly 200 tons of uranium ore a year. (The facility was undamaged in allied bombing; another mine that extracted small amounts of uranium phosphate was successfully bombed.)[54] Satellite information can provide some information, but the process is not foolproof.[55]

Yellowcake, a uranium oxide that has been refined or concentrated from uranium ore, can be converted into uranium hexafluoride, the material generally used to produce highly enriched uranium. Yellowcake can be bought on world markets or produced indigenously. Nations are free to buy and sell the material for a declared peaceful purpose, such as a civilian nuclear program.[56] Iraq's 100-ton purchase of yellowcake from Brazil in 1979 was part of a larger agreement to share peaceful nuclear technology.[57] Over the past decade, it bought additional yellowcake from Niger, Portugal, Brazil, and Italy, and legally obtained a plant capable of conversion that was built by a group of European firms ostensibly for processing phosphate ore.[58] Other sites subsequently discovered may have had similar conversion capabilities.[59] A useful focus for any intelligence monitoring effort, including customs regulation, should therefore be the detection of the rate of acquisition of yellowcake, as well as the intended use of the material, even if procurement is legal.

A variety of technical routes exist for a nation to produce bombs based on highly enriched uranium as a nuclear material. Gaseous diffusion, the process by which the United States, Britain, France, China, and the former Soviet Union first enriched uranium, generally demands extensive financial and technical resources. It also requires a large facility and substantial sources of electrical power. Given these constraints, and the fact that such a plant would be easy to detect, nations covertly attempting to maintain a nuclear weapons program are unlikely to choose this route.[60]

A second method for acquiring highly enriched uranium for making nuclear weapons is centrifuge enrichment. Western efforts to determine whether Iraq was developing a centrifuge enrichment program illustrate the dimensions of this problem. The United States remained relatively confident throughout the Gulf War that Iraq did not have a centrifuge enrichment capability, based on estimates that a plant able to supply enough enriched uranium for one or two bombs a year would require up to one thousand centrifuges and would therefore be an easy target for satellite detection.[61] Dissenters argued that a centrifuge enrichment facility could in fact be constructed cheaply, based on readily available literature, and that it could be easily hidden.[62]

After months of inspections, it was discovered that Iraq had developed the capacity to construct two thousand centrifuges a year.[63] (One German company alone had provided components for production of 10,000 centrifuges.)[64] These enrichment facilities had not been identified as nuclear-related and thus were not targeted by allied bombing.[65] As late as April 1993 inspections had failed to discover any Iraqi facility in which the centrifuges could be assembled, or even a pilot plant to test use, which indicates either that such sites do not exist, or more troubling, that they have been successfully hidden.[66]

Discovery of Iraq's electromagnetic isotope separation (calutron) facilities reflected particularly worrying challenges to intelligence efforts. As early as September 1990, the United States received information from Polish workers departing Iraq about the possible existence of an enrichment facility near Mosul.[67] After the Gulf War an Iraqi defector told UN officials of an untouched underground enrichment site using the antiquated electromagnetic isotope separation technique.[68] Inspections revealed multibillion-dollar facilities devoted to electromagnetic separation, including a substantial capability to produce equipment indigenously.[69] The facility was undamaged in bombing raids, probably because it was successfully disguised as a civil industrial site.[70] Limiting access to the most modern and efficient enrichment methods, or monitoring export licenses for high-tech equipment, is therefore, not enough to deter a determined proliferator.[71]

Regardless of whether a proliferating nation chooses to use high- or low-tech methods, it is now indisputable that a new nuclear weapons state has much greater opportunity to conceal enrichment facilities than was earlier believed. Iraq's multipronged effort to proceed covertly with its uranium enrichment effort illustrates a need to reassess means for detecting such programs. Western intelligence officials have suggested the possibility that North Korea may have built and hidden uranium enrichment facilities, though no specific details of sources or types of processes have been disclosed.[72]

Theft or diversion might be the avenue of choice for nations unwilling or unable to gather the technological information and materials necessary for an indigenous enrichment production program.[73] Plutonium or highly enriched uranium could be stolen or diverted from the large inventories at reactors worldwide,[74] or even from its own safeguarded supply, if it has one. Such strategies, while limiting the need for extensive procurement efforts or scientific recruitment, would probably only be useful for nations interested in one or a few bombs for their possible terrorist or limited deterrent value.

It is difficult to assess the potential for diversion from the numerous international civil stocks of fissile material.[75] Keeping track of large stores of plutonium in the former Soviet Union or Japan, for instance, poses particular challenges.[76]

Inspections in Iraq yielded evidence that Baghdad had proceeded with plans for an implosion-type nuclear weapon, as well as with research on linking weaponization developments with surface-to-surface missile improvements.[77] Several thousand Iraqi scientists and technicians were involved in the weaponization program alone.[78] A site was also found for high explosive testing that had apparently gone undetected before the war.[79]

Determining the extent of a new nuclear nation's weaponization development will depend on observation of a range of activities, including procurement and scientific expertise. The intended means of delivery will also affect the type of weaponization decided upon. Making a bomb that will be transported by aircraft, ground vehicle, or ship is obviously considerably easier than fitting a missile warhead.[80] Consequently, efforts to determine a proliferator's weaponization activities or intentions will rest on a broader knowledge of its nuclear program capabilities and goals.

Delivery Systems

While the United States located many fixed Iraqi Scud launching sites, and reportedly identified every liftoff by satellite, mobile launchers proved much more difficult to pinpoint. After the war, inspectors found Scud sites that were either untargeted or had been repaired after being damaged.[81] Before the war, Washington knew of Iraqi missile testing in Mauritania[82] and had closely followed technological transactions between Iraq and known missile-producer Brazil,[83] but it was apparently unaware of the advanced stage of the program.

The imperfection of means of keeping track of missile proliferation has also been illustrated in U.S. efforts to monitor North Korean shipments of advanced Scud missiles, which Robert Gates indicated could soon have a 1,000-kilometer range.[84] In May 1991, U.S. satellites followed the Iranian launch of a North Korean delivered Scud-C missile;[85] in February 1992 Israeli intelligence officials indicated that a shipment of Scud-Cs was being delivered to Syria.[86] The shipment was tracked for over a week until the North Korean vessel "dropped off the radar"; it was not detected again until reconnaissance imagery showed it docked in Iran.[87]

Intelligence efforts would be aided by stricter Missile Technology Control Regime (MTCR) guidelines,[88] especially considering that as many as fifteen developing nations will be producing their own ballistic missiles by the end of the decade.[89] Similarly, technical improvements in reconnaissance imagery will be critical for detecting missile proliferation,[90] especially since satellite imagery is increasingly available to aid deliberate deception. Iraq may have used American intelligence information it received during its war with Iran to learn techniques of disguising its missile sites, as well as other military and industrial installations.[91] Washington now faces the problem of more and more countries with the satellite technology to hide installations from reconnaissance imagery.[92]

PROBLEMS OF INTELLIGENCE ASSESSMENT

Differences From Cold War "Threat Assessment" of the Soviet Union

During the Cold War public debate over arms control led to a belief in the ability of the U.S. intelligence community to provide accurate characterizations of the numbers and types of nuclear weapons systems of the former Soviet Union. Intelligence uncertainties remained, however, over the question of whether the Backfire bomber had intercontinental capability, or whether the Soviets had conducted underground nuclear tests exceeding the 150-kiloton limit prescribed by the Threshold Test Ban Treaty. To be sure, "verification" was a key point of argument for those opposed to various arms control treaties. But directors of Central Intelligence testified frequently to their confidence in the intelligence community's general understanding of Soviet nuclear deployments and even development programs.

This confidence seemed all the more remarkable because the Soviet Union was for most of the period a rigid and closed police state that kept foreigners from having contact with its people. With some exceptions, U.S. intelligence evidently did not derive from human contact inside the country but from national technical means—on the outside looking in.

New nuclear nations that are the focus of this book present a very different intelligence objective from the old Soviet Union.

Moscow's nuclear program was enormous, and it was overt. Indeed, Soviet leaders touted it as a symbol of their country's technological prowess. Vitally important from the intelligence point of view, nuclear weapons were fully integrated into the Soviet Union's military forces and command and control structure. Tens of thousands of personnel were trained to maintain and use the Soviet arsenal, and some of them emigrated or defected to the West. Exercises and maneuvers were held which could be monitored by Western intelligence. Officers wrote about nuclear doctrine in professional journals, which were either unclassified or could occasionally be obtained by outside intelligence services. Missiles were test launched year after year along the same missile ranges. Model after model of cruise missile and long-range aircraft were flown from the same air development centers, and generation after generation of ships and submarines were launched from the same shipyards. The highly bureaucratized Soviet system followed standard operating procedures at every step, establishing patterns that were easily discernible over time by intelligence analysts.

Compare the level of detectable activity of the large and overt nuclear establishment of the Soviet Union with the corresponding signatures a new proliferator would carry out. The latter is likely to conduct its nuclear activities in deep secrecy, by a small and elite organization. It will be accompanied by a determined effort not only to conceal information from foreign intelligence services but to deceive them with a deliberate strategy of disinformation. It is likely to be run outside of the normal military establishment and chain of command. There will probably be no exercises, no chatter over the radio during training, no regular development and test sites, no standard patterns of activity. Monitoring such a program bears more resemblance to the intelligence problems posed by counterterrorism than by superpower arms control verification.

Even the Soviet Union, it is now clear, successfully concealed some types of nuclear activity despite more than four decades of intense focus and massive investment by the U.S. intelligence community. In the course of describing the fate of the nuclear arsenal at the time of the breakup of the USSR, Robert Gates observed that the

United States did not know the number of nuclear weapons possessed by the Soviet Union within a very large margin of error. It has similarly been revealed that Washington did not always know the number of intercontinental missiles (in contrast to silos) possessed by the Soviets. Intelligence could follow large and overt deployments; it could not discover small covert ones, or pin down the whereabouts of nuclear weapons in ones and twos. Yet such tasks as these are exactly the ones that will assume great importance if the United States faces new nuclear weapons states.

In addition, the national technical means from which much intelligence was derived resulted from forty years of massive investment in collection resources directed geographically and technically at a single nation. The same intensity of effort will not be possible with respect to each country near or past the nuclear threshold. Since it was well known, moreover, that the United States regarded the Soviet Union as an important intelligence target, much of the infrastructure that supported intelligence collection against the Soviet Union was, despite its formal security classification, equally well known, at least to the nations that hosted it. Thus the large U.S. intelligence installations in West Germany and West Berlin, South Korea, and in many other nations less overtly aligned with the United States in the Cold War made the intensive collection effort against the USSR possible.

When facing new proliferators, U.S. intelligence will often be unable (for political reasons) even to acknowledge which nation it is collecting against. Technical intelligence efforts will frequently have to be conducted covertly, and the inefficiency and cost that attend clandestine collection—especially when combined with the number and geographic spread of target nations and reductions in the budget of the U.S. intelligence community—will make it unlikely that any new nuclear weapons state will face anything like the intensity of the intelligence directed at the former Soviet Union.

Program or Arsenal? Critical Uncertainties at the Threshold

For a variety of reasons, U.S. intelligence assessments of exactly where nuclear programs actually stand—just below, at, or just above the threshold—are likely to be quite uncertain. Well before the threshold, programs can be characterized by the thermal output of potential plutonium production reactors, the likely throughput of reprocessing or enrichment facilities, and other parameters that, if they can be known, tell how far the program is from producing enough fissile material for one bomb. Well after the threshold, if the state has a well-developed though perhaps small arsenal that is at least partially integrated into its military and command and control structure, then it should be possible to characterize the basing, delivery systems, strategic purpose, and likely operational characteristics of this nuclear capability. The threshold itself, however, at which a program becomes a small arsenal of one or two bombs, is characterized by subtle and easily hidden parameters—exactly how many kilograms of fissile material have been acquired, whether its experts have full confidence in the design, whether a workable device has actually been assembled, and what delivery system (possibly makeshift or covert) has been selected. It is generally taken for granted that a full scale nuclear test is not a necessary step for attaining confidence that a device works. Such a test is therefore not likely to occur and conveniently provide a clear signal that the threshold has been passed.

Yet it is precisely at the threshold, if it could be defined and recognized, that many of the policy measures discussed in this book would most effectively apply. It is at that juncture that proliferators make critical decisions about whether and how to breach the threshold, and it is then that U.S. policy can best influence those decisions. The fact that the point of highest leverage coincides with the time when intelligence uncertainty is likely to be greatest means that the theoretical appeal of various policy actions must be tempered by the likely difficulty in supporting them with precise intelligence.

Breadth and Focus: The Multiplying Tasks of Intelligence

Dealing with new nuclear weapons states is not one national security problem, but a complex of them, and the variety of intelligence needed by U.S. military and diplomatic leaders is correspondingly great. Consider, for instance, how these intelligence requirements evolve as a target nation passes through the stages from establishment of a nuclear weapons program, to completion of a first bomb, to deployment of a small arsenal; and as U.S. responses shift from

234 ◆ NEW NUCLEAR NATIONS

surveillance and program assessment, to threat assessment, and perhaps to offensive and defensive military action.

As noted, critical information about the early stages of a nuclear program can be obtained from such sources as analysis of international financial transactions, intelligence-sharing liaison with other nations, telltale residue taken by an international inspector with an adhesive glove, or a single defector revealing the outline of a secret program.

Planning an air strike on the nuclear facilities of a nation approaching construction of a first bomb, by contrast, requires entirely different types of collection and analysis. Military planners need to study the buildings the raid is supposed to destroy. The aircraft delivering the bombs will require information about the location, radar frequencies and signal structures, and command and control of air defenses surrounding the target. If cruise missiles and other "smart weapons" are to be used, terrain contour maps, terminal area images, global positioning coordinates, and other precision guidance information will have to be assembled. Analysis will be sensitive to the possibility that the raid will disperse harmful substances associated with nuclear, chemical, or biological warfare. If special forces are used to destroy proliferation targets, different intelligence questions will be posed: Which way do the doors on a building open, outward or inward? Where are the light switches or electric generators?

When a target nation has acquired a small arsenal of nuclear weapons, the questions posed to intelligence multiply again: Where are the weapons stored? What signs are there that they are being readied for use? What are the target country's alerting practices and operational procedures? What is its command and control? Can weapons or mobile launchers be tracked when they change location?

These intelligence challenges are characteristic of coping with new nuclear weapons states. Individually, none of the tasks is distinctly different from those pursued during the Cold War. They do not call for specific new collection technologies or analytical techniques. They do, however, invite a style of intelligence operation that relies not on a standing data base of the kind maintained on Soviet forces, but rather on a geographic breadth of coverage combined with an ability to focus flexibly on particular intelligence problems in particular target nations.

One consequence of this change is that Washington decision-makers will have to take account of the time needed to prepare the target adequately from the intelligence point of view. It would take months to collect and process the kinds of intelligence upon which, for example, the safety and success of U.S. military forces operating against a new proliferator would depend. Many postmortems of the Gulf War attest to the importance of the five-month period between Iraq's invasion of Kuwait and the initiation of coalition combat operations. During this time a vast cadre of U.S. specialists in various intelligence disciplines were hard at work—learning how to identify and target nuclear weapons-related installations, how to disrupt telephone and power networks, how to recognize various military formations and types of equipment, and so on. It is unrealistic to expect all such information to be on the shelf when it is needed, but timely policy guidance from the top can help.

Finally, an important role will be played by intelligence liaisons and sharing agreements. Even with an aggressive strategy of flexible focus, the United States will not be able to cover all proliferation targets in adequate depth, and will profit from local help. Nations in the same region as the target will frequently share U.S. proliferation concerns, and by virtue of shared language and culture, intimate regional knowledge, and standing effort will have information that complements that collected by U.S. intelligence. The United States can trade its unique strengths, such as satellite photography, for information turned up by others. As this book makes clear, U.S. policies for managing proliferation after it occurs will frequently depend on persuading other countries of the need for action, and getting them to cooperate in taking it. The United States must therefore be prepared to share intelligence with other countries and international institutions.

INTELLIGENCE AND NEW NUCLEAR ARSENALS

Beyond the threshold of production of one weapon there are three critical problems: unlocking the strategic personality of a new proliferator; military "threat assessment" of new nuclear arsenals; and intelligence support for a U.S.-led attack on a fledgling arsenal.

Understanding the Strategic Personality of a New Proliferator

Having obtained the bomb, a new proliferator must adopt a position on its possession and use. Does it view nuclear weapons as a last-ditch deterrent to protect the homeland? Or does it see nuclear weapons as battlefield systems, ready to compensate for any tactical disadvantage that arises? What conditions will trigger use? What countries are targeted in its war plans? The answers to questions like these define what might be called the "strategic personality" of the new nuclear weapons state. Understanding it will be critical to U.S. policymaking.

A wider variety of proliferator personalities is possible than is sometimes acknowledged in writings about nuclear strategy, and there is little guidance in the public domain for intelligence assessment. The strategic personality of the Soviet Union was the subject of analysis for nearly half a century. But one case does not make much of a comparative reference, and analysis of other nuclear nations—France, say, or China or India—is much less well developed. Moreover, in Western approaches to divining the Soviet strategic nuclear personality, one can observe a tendency to minimize the importance of historical, cultural, and leadership attitudes. Westerners, influenced by economist-strategists like Thomas Schelling, tended to conceive of nuclear strategy as reducible to a cost-benefit calculus which, if performed rationally by all nuclear nations, would be universal. Arms control tended to reinforce this tendency toward symmetry, since its whole purpose was to damp down tensions between "us" and "them" by emphasizing common security dilemmas shared by both sides. The nature of nuclear weapons themselves also suggests universality: any force so elemental must elicit a common, fundamental human reaction. Ignoring culturally or politically derived attitudes toward nuclear weapons was made easier by the closed nature of Soviet society, which gave little evidence of its nuclear personality beyond glimpses at the hardware. As a result, those in the West who spoke of a distinctly "Soviet" approach to nuclear weapons were often dismissed as mindless hawks bent on demonizing the Soviet Union.

A proliferated world will give scope for variety and complexity in how nations view nuclear weapons. Clues will come from the public statements of political and military leaders, although these may be veiled and even deliberately misleading. These leaders might also have contending views, and the internal politics might be sufficiently unstable that it cannot be predicted which opinions will prevail. Inferences might be drawn from the character of the fledgling arsenal and its command and control system: whether it is closely associated with air, naval, or ground forces; whether long-range delivery is an aspiration; whether weapons storage is dispersed or hardened; whether commands pass through normal military or special channels; and how political and military control is exercised. To the extent that training and exercises with nuclear-capable forces occur, these can be observed for what they reveal about alerting, operational procedures, and employment doctrine. Finally, engagement of the new proliferator in open dialogue as part of a program of technical assistance, can reveal or even influence the nuclear doctrine of a new proliferator. Indeed, such engagement might usefully be initiated for its intelligence value alone.

Threat Assessment

If U.S. forces face the prospect of operating against or in the presence of the nuclear forces of a new proliferator, they will wish to know a great deal about the nature of the opposing force and of its operational doctrine.

It is now clear that despite the large and sustained investment made in collecting intelligence on Soviet nuclear forces, the U.S. intelligence community never knew how many nuclear warheads the Soviet Union possessed. The United States was able to count and characterize the delivery systems for those warheads; it knew the number and locations of strategic missiles, bombers, and submarines, and how many warheads they were capable of carrying. It was also able to identify the many types of nonstrategic nuclear-capable delivery systems, ranging from artillery to naval torpedoes. But the existence and location, let alone the yield, of every Soviet nuclear weapon remained unknown outside of the Soviet nuclear establishment. Similarly, the general characteristics of delivery systems of a new nuclear weapons state will probably be discernible, but not the precise number of completed weapons.

Even information on delivery systems will be hard to come by. A new proliferator will probably plan to deliver its arsenal in one of three ways: by aircraft, by missile, or by unconventional means. The various ways of monitoring the flight tests of ballistic missiles have been widely discussed: preparations for the test are detected from photography and radio traffic, and the flight trajectory can be followed by space-based sensors, ground-based radars, and telemetry monitoring. A variety of methods are available and have been used in monitoring Soviet missile flight tests. But these methods are expensive, requiring satellites in the right place at the right time and radars located within a country very near the target. They presuppose a cadre of analysts familiar with the peculiarities of the target nation's test procedures. Even if the new proliferator buys its missiles from another country (rather than develop them indigenously), that fact only shifts the focus of the intelligence problem from the buyer to the seller, who might not be willing to share technical information about its export missiles with the United States and who might be unaware of modifications made by the buyer after sale.

The characteristics of nuclear explosions are well known and unalterable. They vary little in their essential features within a relatively wide range above and below the Hiroshima-level yield likely with a new proliferator's weapon. From this point of view, the task of a designer of passive defenses against nuclear attack—dispersal of tanks and armored vehicles, protection of structures from the blast and thermal pulse of relatively distant detonations (it is usually impractical to protect tactical equipment from nearby bursts), shielding from prompt radiation and delayed fallout—does not depend on detailed intelligence. But this is not so with the design of active defense systems—air defenses and theater missile defenses. Missile defenses, for example, require a relatively extensive and detailed information about missile range (reentry velocity), radar cross section, and penetration aids. In many cases the footprint of the defense can be expanded by having some approximate advance knowledge of likely launch locations.

Operational Military Doctrine

U.S. forces would wish to have a wealth of accurate intelligence information about the operational as well as technical characteristics of a new nuclear force. This information is just as formidable and costly in terms of collection resources and analysis effort as threat assessment. Specifically, U.S. commanders would want information on the following features of the proliferator's operational doctrine:

- the military doctrine for use, including likely target types;

- command and control procedures;

- U.S. statements or behavior that might trigger an enemy's nuclear use;

- alerting procedures that would warn of possible intention to initiate use of nuclear weapons;

- strategic warning indicators, denoting that a nuclear attack by the proliferator was imminent;

- tactical warning indicators, signifying that nuclear attack against U.S. forces was underway, e.g., that a nuclear-armed missile or aircraft was in flight to its intended target; and

- attack assessment, giving U.S. commanders information about targets struck and the amount of damage.

A final problem concerns unconventional delivery means and terrorist use of new nuclear weapons, since most would be small and compact enough to be carried unobtrusively by truck or small ship. The nuclear materials in the weapon would emit gamma rays and neutrons, but these are detectable only at short range and can be shielded by a casing of heavy material. Thus there is likely to be no purely technical solution to the intelligence objective of detecting unconventional delivery.

Attacking a Fledgling Program or Arsenal

Intelligence on a nuclear program dependent on large facilities for making fissile materials is likely to be much better than intelligence on an arsenal consisting of a few completed bombs hidden in some austere location or buried deep underground. In the event of an offensive U.S. attack, expectations of success in attacking the program will be much greater than in striking the arsenal.

Target Development

Precise attack requires detailed intelligence. Target structures such as buildings, bunkers, and power stations must be intensely studied for their structural weak points, to emulate the success of the much-publicized ventilation-shaft bombings of the Gulf War. Such analysis might be based on photographs taken during the building's construction (when its structural components were exposed), or by contacting architects and construction engineers involved in the project, who in many cases might be foreign contractors. Heavily fortified bunkers and caves dug into mountains, which have been used in North Korea, present special problems.

If an arsenal rather than a program is to be struck, then the intelligence problems become truly daunting. A few nuclear weapons could easily be concealed, and even if it were known that they were stored in a building, one or a few bombs dropped on the building may not suffice to make all the devices unusable.

Precision Weapons Planning

Once targets are selected and exact aimpoints designated, intelligence is required to program the guidance system on the precision weapons being used. If the Global Positioning System (GPS) or so-called differential GPS is used for guidance, the GPS coordinates of the aimpoint or of a landmark nearby must be determined. If the weapon guides itself to the target using a radar map, as some types of cruise missiles do, then routes and waypoints to the target areas of interest must be mapped. If some form of terminal guidance is contemplated, in which the weapon compares a picture it takes (visible, infrared, or radar) of the target area to an image programmed into its guidance computer before launch, then photos of the target areas from the appropriate angle must be taken in advance. All of these preparations take time and considerable intelligence resources.

Defense Penetration

It is natural that pilots want to minimize risk. They will want to know the locations of surveillance and engagement radars in the target country, to avoid or suppress them; the frequencies and signal structures of radars, so they can tune their electronic countermeasures; the command and control system of the target's air defense, to learn its vulnerabilities to disruption or intelligence exploitation; the characteristics and current locations of surface-to-air missile systems and antiaircraft artillery; the status of the enemy air force and of any fighter interceptors that might be launched to engage the attacking U.S. aircraft; and the rescue sites for search-and-rescue teams. Here, too, a substantial amount of up-to-the-minute detailed intelligence must be collected prior to conducting such an operation.

Damage Assessment and Re-strike

The Gulf War pointed out the difficulty of assessing the damage done in air attacks. Paradoxically, precision weapons pose particular problems in this regard, since the only visible sign that a building was struck by one of these systems might be a hole in the roof. Planners of an air strike on the program or arsenal of a new proliferator would put a premium on rapid assessment and re-strike, since—unlike in the Gulf War, where a target could be attacked again the next day if there was doubt that it had been destroyed—the political circumstances of the strike could well dictate a single strike, or two in rapid succession.

The Problem of Relocatable Targets

The lack of success in the "Scud hunt" during the Gulf War demonstrates that the problem of tracking mobile missiles and other relocatable targets is far from solved. Various technical approaches have been devised for this task, which has been thoroughly studied by the intelligence community during its preoccupation with targeting Soviet mobile missiles. These techniques include space-based infrared sensors for determining launch point, airborne radars like the JSTARS with its moving target indicator and synthetic-aperture radar modes, space-based cameras and radars, and surveillance by special forces. Several judgments seem to apply: first, any technical approach that involves continuous wide-area coverage will be very expensive; second, the degree of success will probably depend more on the operational practices of the target force than on the technical intelligence approach. If the United States can determine systematic deployment practices or patrol patterns, it might have some success; but if the target force randomizes its activities and employs concealment, decoy missiles (as used by Iraq) and other forms of deception, the problem will be exceedingly difficult. Finally, finding a missile is no use unless it can be attacked before it moves. The requirement for simultaneous detection and positioning for prompt attack adds yet another layer of difficulty. For all these reasons, one doubts whether it will be possible to strike relocatable targets with confidence.

CONCLUSION

Supporting the new types of policy action discussed in this book will entail substantial innovations in the way intelligence is collected and analyzed. Dealing with new nuclear weapons states will create intelligence requirements different from preventing proliferation, and from managing the Soviet nuclear threat. This innovation will not occur without the active guidance of the intelligence community by policymakers. It will require tight, policy-oriented tasking from the top to help dislodge intelligence collectors and analysts from their normal tasks; to preempt other pressing intelligence needs; and to immerse them in a particular application of their skills that might be unfamiliar to them. In addition to commanding the intelligence community's attention and resources, decisionmakers will need to pose sharply the questions whose answers are most critical for their policy actions and successful execution. Indeed, it is not too much to say that the intelligence concerning new nuclear weapons states that is required will not be available when the president and his chief advisors need it unless the policy level has given the intelligence community guidance much earlier.

Notes

1. The authors are grateful to Michael Wigotsky for his research assistance in developing this section.
2. David E. Sanger, "Data Raise Fears of Nuclear Moves by North Koreans," *New York Times*, November 10, 1991, p. 1.
3. David A. Kay, deputy director of the International Atomic Energy Agency (IAEA), pronounced that there was "no region in the world that you will find that did not contribute to that program." Thomas W. Lippman, "International Banks Said to Be Financial Supporters of Iraqi Nuclear Program," *Washington Post*, October 18, 1991, p. A3. See also statements by Robert Gallucci, the deputy chairman of the Special Commission established by the United Nations to oversee the inspections, in "Report on the Eighth IAEA On-Site Inspection in Iraq Under Security Council Resolution 687 (1991), November 11–18, 1991," United Nations, December 12, 1991, p. 10; and Paul Lewis, "UN Suspects Iraq Has a 4th A-Plant," *New York Times*, October 3, 1991, p. 3.
4. R. Jeffrey Smith, "13 Firms Named as Sources of Nuclear Items for Iraq," *Washington Post*, December 12, 1991, p. A43.
5. Michael Wines, "Documents Said to Name Iraq Suppliers," *New York Times*, September 30, 1991, p. A3. See also Michael Wines, "U.S. Is Building Up a Picture of Vast Iraqi Atom Program," *New York Times*, September 27, 1991, p. A8; and Gary Milhollin and Diana Edensword, "Iraq's Bomb, Chip by Chip," *New York Times*, April 24, 1992, p. A35.
6. "Report on the Seventh IAEA On-Site Inspection in Iraq Under UNSC Res. 687 (1991), October 11–22, 1991," United Nations, November 14, 1991, p. 5. See "Consolidated Report on the First Two IAEA Inspections Under UNSC Res 687 (1991) of Iraqi Nuclear Capabilities," IAEA, July 11, 1991, p. 13. The Al-Dijla and Al-Rabee sites were used to manufacture parts for use in uranium enrichment using the electromagnetic isotope separation technique. See "Report on the Fourth IAEA On-Site Inspection in Iraq Under UNSC Res 687 (1991), July 27–August 10, 1991," United Nations, August 28, 1991, pp. 1, 6.
7. "First Report on the Sixth IAEA On-Site Inspection in Iraq Under UNSC Res. 687 (1991), September 22–30, 1991," United Nations, October 8, 1991, p. 5.
8. R. Jeffrey Smith and Glenn Frankel, "In 45,000 Pages, How Iraq Fooled World on Nuclear Aims," *International Herald Tribune*, October 14, 1991, p. 1.
9. Diana Edensword and Gary Milhollin, "Iraq's Bomb: An Update," *New York Times*, April 26, 1993, p. A17.
10. Douglas Jehl, "US Seeking UN Pressure to Compel North Korea to Honor Treaty," *New York Times*, March 13, 1993, p. 3; David E. Sanger, "The Nonproliferation Treaty Bares Its Toothlessness," *New York Times*, March 14, 1993, p. 18.
11. American information about German chemical weapons plant sales to Libya was the result of tapped phone lines and intercepted fax messages. *World Press Review*, March 1992, p. 9. See also John J. Fialka, "North Korean Nuclear Effort Tests U.S.," *Wall Street Journal*, November 14, 1991, p. A10.

12. Kenneth Timmerman, "Surprise, We Gave Iraq the Bomb," *New York Times*, October 25, 1991, p. A33.
13. James Brooke, "Iraq's Nuclear Quest: Tentacles in Four Continents," *New York Times*, December 23, 1990, p. 1.
14. Extreme challenges are also faced in attempting to monitor sales of parts from the former Soviet Union. The well-publicized creation of International Chetek Corp., a private Russian company with close ties to former Soviet atomic energy officials that has been advertising the sale of underground nuclear detonations for ostensibly peaceful purposes, highlights what one Yeltsin aide called the "Wild West capitalism" evolving in the former Soviet Union. Carla Anne Robbins, "The Nuclear Epidemic," *U.S. News and World Report*, March 16, 1992, p. 49. See also Kurt Campbell, Ashton B. Carter, Steven E. Miller, and Charles A. Zraket, *Soviet Nuclear Fission: Control of the Nuclear Arsenal in a Disintegrating Soviet Union* (Cambridge, Mass.: Center for Science and International Affairs, November 1991), pp. 41–42.
15. Roy Godson, ed., *Intelligence Requirements for the 1990s: Collection, Analysis, Counterintelligence and Covert Action* (Lexington, Mass.: Lexington Books, 1989), pp. 42–43.
16. "Iraq Tested Missiles to Carry A-Bomb, a U.N. Report Says," *New York Times*, October 5, 1991, p. 2.
17. Lippman, "International Banks Said to Be Financial Supporters of Iraqi Nuclear Program," p. A3.
18. Jonathan Bealy and S. C. Gwynne, "Not Just a Bank," *Time*, September 2, 1991, pp. 56–57.
19. Lippman, "International Banks Said to Be Financial Supporters of Iraqi Nuclear Program," p. A3; William Safire, "Baker's Guilty Knowledge," *New York Times*, June 22, 1992, p. A17; Dean Baquet, "Documents Charge Iraqis Made Swap: U.S. Food for Arms," *New York Times*, April 27, 1992, p. A1.
20. Gerald W. Hopple and Bruce W. Watson, eds., *The Military Intelligence Community* (Boulder, Colo.: Westview Press, 1986), pp. 39–53, discusses the primarily military uses of signal intelligence. Such practices also have applications in corporate monitoring.
21. See William J. Broad, "Warnings on Iraq Published by U.S. Energy Department Reveals Documents About Dispute Over Nuclear Program," *New York Times*, April 23, 1993, p. A7.
22. Mark Hosenball, "Blind Eye: Ignoring the Iraqi Bomb," *New Republic*, November 25, 1991, pp. 20–24; David Albright and Mark Hibbs, "Iraq and the Bomb: Were They Even Close?" *Bulletin of the Atomic Scientists* (March 1991), p. 20; "Bombs Away at Heathrow," *The Economist*, March 31, 1990, p. 38; Malcolm W. Browne, "Iraq Could Have Atomic Arsenal by 2000, Intelligence Experts Say," *New York Times*, November 18, 1990, p. 14; Milhollin and Edensword, "Iraq's Bomb, Chip by Chip," p. A35; Neil A. Lewis, "New Jersey Concern Is Tied to Iraq Arms Network," *New York Times*, February 19, 1993, p. A18.
23. William J. Broad, "Warnings on Iraq and Bomb Bid Silenced in '89," *New York Times*, April 20, 1992, p. A1; Broad, "Data on Nuclear Warnings Released by

U.S.," *New York Times*, April 23, 1992, p. A7; "U.S. Accused of Punishing Monitors on Iraq," *New York Times*, April 25, 1992, p. A4; Safire, "Baker's Guilty Knowledge," p. A17.

24. Albright and Hibbs, "Iraq and the Bomb"; Paul Lewis, "Iraq Says It Made an Atomic 'Trigger,'" *New York Times*, May 9, 1990, p. A5.

25. Smith and Frankel, "In 45,000 Pages, How Iraq Fooled the World on Nuclear Aims," p. 5.

26. Ahmed Hashim, an expert on the Iraqi military, asserted, "What we've found is that Iraq now has the largest technical and scientific base in the Middle East. I'd say that Israel is qualitatively better, but in terms of numbers, Iraq is the largest." Wines, "U.S. Is Building Up a Picture of Vast Iraqi Atom Program," p. 8. See also Paul Lewis, "UN Officials Seek Mastermind in Charge of Iraq's Nuclear Effort," *New York Times*, October 1, 1991, p. A11.

27. Some have suggested, however, that the intelligence community has yet to establish a mutually satisfactory relationship between itself and the academic world. Allan Goodman, "Dateline Langley: Fixing the Intelligence Mess," *Foreign Policy*, no. 57 (Winter 1984–85), pp. 160–79, asserts that the CIA consistently dragged its feet in establishing contacts with the academic world. In a letter of response, George Lauder, then director of public affairs at the CIA countered that the CIA had stepped up its communication with universities and private sector think tanks. Former Director of Central Intelligence Robert Gates frequently stressed his intention to improve contacts between academic experts and intelligence analysts. Lauder, "Correspondence," *Foreign Policy*, no. 58 (Spring 1985), p. 172.

28. Cooperation of the international scientific community to glean facts through contacts has worked in the least amenable of situations, including preglasnost Soviet Union. Godson, *Intelligence Requirements for the 1990s* (Lexington, Mass.: Lexington Books, 1989), p. 17.

29. Wines, "U.S. Is Building Up a Picture of Vast Iraqi Atom Program," p. 8.

30. *Proliferation Testimony for Senator John Glenn's Governmental Affairs Committee by Director of Central Intelligence Robert Gates* (Washington, D.C.: January 15, 1992), p. 8.

31. In testimony before the Senate Committee on Governmental Affairs, Gates stressed that the status of scientists in the former republics was the area that caused the greatest concern in trying to determine the impact of the Soviet Union's collapse on world proliferation. Many nuclear technicians, he remarked, have skills that have no civilian application. Other administration officials have questioned the accuracy of Gates's estimate that there were one to two thousand nuclear weapons designers in the former Soviet Union, suggesting that the number refers to all those with intimate and sophisticated—but incomplete—knowledge of bomb fabrication rather than the much smaller group of actual device designers.

32. Reports have surfaced of former Soviet technicians working in Libya and Algeria. Carla Anne Robbins, "The Nuclear Epidemic," *U.S. News and World Report*, March 16, 1992, pp. 41, 49.

33. Leonard S. Spector and Jacqueline R. Smith, "North Korea: The Next Nuclear Nightmare?" *Arms Control Today* (March 1991), p. 9. See also James L. Tyson, "Chinese Nuclear Sales Flout European Embargoes," *Chris-*

tian Science Monitor, March 10, 1992, p. 1. See also Paul Lewis, "U.N.'s Nuclear Inquiry Exposes Treaties' Flaws," *New York Times*, November 10, 1991, p. 10.

34. "Spreading the New World Order," *The Economist*, November 16, 1991, p. 39.

35. Clinton O'Brien, "Russian Nuclear Scientists Offered Positions in Libya, Co-workers Say," *Boston Globe*, January 9, 1992, p. 2.

36. *Proliferation Testimony for Senator John Glenn's Governmental Affairs Committee by Director of Central Intelligence Robert Gates*, p. 6. See also Jonathan Dean and Kurt Gottfried, *A Program for World Security* (Cambridge, Mass.: Union of Concerned Scientists, February 1992), p. 11.

37. Paul Lewis, "Iraq Trying to Make Plutonium, Too, UN Aide Says," *New York Times*, February 13, 1992, p. A16; Edensword and Milhollin, "Iraq's Bomb: An Update," p. A17.

38. *Nuclear Power and Nuclear Weapons Proliferation*, vol. 1: *Report of the Atlantic Council's Nuclear Fuels Policy Working Group* (Boulder, Colo.: Westview Press, 1977), pp. 18–19.

39. The French company that sold the reactor to Iraq made several design modifications that, according to numerous nuclear experts, made plutonium production impossible. Israel believed otherwise. Richard Wilson, "Nuclear Proliferation and the Case of Iraq," *Journal of Palestine Studies*, vol. 20, no. 3 (Spring 1991), pp. 9–11.

40. Ronald Payne, *Mossad: Israel's Most Secret Service* (London: Bantam Press, 1990), p. 173. See also, Brooke, "Iraq's Nuclear Quest: Tentacles in Four Continents," p. 1. On intelligence regarding North Korea's reactors, see Ben Sanders, "North Korea, South Africa Ready to Tell All?" *Bulletin of the Atomic Scientists* (September 1991), p. 8; "North Korea May Be Developing Ability to Build Nuclear Weapons," *Wall Street Journal*, July 19, 1989, p. A16; Spector and Smith, "North Korea: The Next Nuclear Nightmare?" p. 9; Don Oberdorfer, "Korea Seen Closer to A-Bomb," *Washington Post*, February 23, 1992, p. A1; David E. Sanger, "Nuclear Activity by N. Korea Worries U.S.," *New York Times*, November 10, 1991, p. 1; Jim Hoagland, "Stopping N. Korea's Bomb," *Washington Post*, October 24, 1991, p. A23; Leonard S. Spector and Jacqueline R. Smith, *Nuclear Ambitions: The Spread of Nuclear Weapons 1989–1990* (Boulder, Colo.: Westview Press, 1990), p. 128; Sanger, "Data Raise Fears of Nuclear Moves by North Koreans," p. 1. See also Charles Lane, et al., "A Knock on the Nuclear Door?" *Newsweek*, April 29, 1991, p. 38; T. R. Reid, "North Korea Building an Atomic Fuel Plant," *Herald Tribune*, May 18, 1992, p. 6; "Something's Ticking," *The Economist*, September 21, 1991, p. 50; and Paul Lewis, "Iraq Admits Buying German Material to Build A-Bombs," *New York Times*, January 15, 1992, p. A12.

41. Failure on the part of the new nuclear weapons state to submit to inspections will also provide a critical acid test to confirm what satellites suggest.

42. While acknowledging that he knew few details about the facility, the diplomat claimed that North Korea's use of the various facilities put it within one to three years of making nuclear weapons. "North Korea Reported Near Nuclear Ability," *New York Times*, September 14, 1991, p. 2. Some intelligence offi-

cials question whether the defector would have been able to gain access to North Korea's nuclear capabilities given his diplomatic duties abroad the last few years. Paul Shin, "Defector Says N. Korea Building Atom Bomb," *Washington Post*, September 14, 1991, p. A20. See also Sanger, "Nuclear Activity by North Korea Worries U.S.," p. 1. Reports have also surfaced that Iraq may have a secret underground research reactor; see "Losing Patience," *The Economist*, February 15, 1992, p. 46.

43. *Nuclear Power and Nuclear Weapons Proliferation*, vol. 2: *Report of the Atlantic Council's Nuclear Fuels Policy Working Group* (Boulder, Colo.: Westview Press, 1977), p. 18. See also Robbins, "The Nuclear Epidemic," p. 43.

44. Don Oberdorfer, "N. Korea Seen Closer to A-Bomb," p. A26.

45. David E. Sanger, "West Knew of North Korea Nuclear Development," *New York Times*, March 13, 1993, p. 3.

46. Spector and Smith, *Nuclear Ambitions*, p. 126. See also Spector and Smith, "North Korea: The Next Nuclear Nightmare?" p. 9.

47. U.S. satellites have reportedly detected recent North Korean efforts to camouflage their nuclear facilities. Jack Anderson and Michael Binstein, "North Korea: Loose Nuclear Cannon," *Washington Post*, March 29, 1992, p. C7; Sanger, "West Knew of North Korean Nuclear Development," p. 3; Jeff Smith, "North Korea and the Bomb: A High-Tech Game of Hide and Seek," *Washington Post*, April 27, 1993, p. A11; Spurgeon M. Keeny, Jr., David Albright, and Michael Mazarr, "North Korea at the Crossroads: Nuclear Renegade or Regional Partner," *Arms Control Today*, May 1993, p. 4.

48. Smith, "North Korea and the Bomb," p. A11; David Albright, "North Korean Drops Out," *Bulletin of the Atomic Scientists* (May 1993), pp. 9–11.

49. David E. Sanger, "North Korea Stirs New A-Arms Fears," *New York Times*, May 6, 1993, p. A7.

50. John J. Fialka, "North Korea May Be Developing Ability to Build Nuclear Weapons," *Wall Street Journal*, July 10, 1989, p. 16. See also Robbins, "The Nuclear Epidemic," p. 42.

51. *Nuclear Power and Nuclear Weapons Proliferation*, vol. 2, pp. 14–15.

52. Because North Korea has two safeguarded research reactors, it is entitled to IAEA mining assistance for its civil program. Fialka, "North Korea May Be Developing Ability to Build Nuclear Weapons," p. 16. "It would be sadly ironic, however, if the uranium that the IAEA helped Pyongyang mine turned up as fuel in the unsafeguarded reactor at Yongbyon, providing fissile material for nuclear weapons." Andrew Mack, "North Korea and the Bomb," *Foreign Policy*, no. 85 (Summer 1991), p. 88.

53. Malcolm W. Browne, "Iraq Could Have Atomic Arsenal by 2000, Intelligence Experts Say," *New York Times*, November 18, 1990, p. 14.

54. Elaine Sciolino, "Word of Iraqi Nuclear Effort Is a Mixed Blessing for Bush," *New York Times*, July 10, 1991, p. A9.

55. As late as March 1991, U.S. intelligence officials reportedly had "looked in vain" for any Iraqi mining operations. Albright and Hibbs, "Iraq and the Bomb," p. 20.

56. Possession of yellowcake is not subject to international safeguards.

57. Brooke, "Iraq's Nuclear Quest: Tentacles in Four Continents," p. 1.

58. "The Nukes: How Quickly Can Iraq Get the Bomb?" *U.S. News and World Report*, June 4, 1990, pp. 49–51.
59. Disclosures from Iraq indicated that there was "a complicated network of intermediate installations to prepare large amounts of uranium ore for use in [enrichment] processes." Sciolino, "Word of Iraqi Nuclear Effort Is a Mixed Blessing for Bush," p. A9.
60. *Nuclear Power and Nuclear Weapons Proliferation*, vol. 1, pp. 38–39. See also ibid., vol. 2, p. 15.
61. Tom Wicker, "Gambling on the Bomb," *New York Times*, December 5, 1990, p. A27.
62. *U.S. News and World Report*, June 4, 1990, p. 50. See also *Nuclear Power and Nuclear Weapons Proliferation*, vol. 1, p. 15.
63. Debate has persisted on the effectiveness of Iraq's centrifuge design and on whether the plants would have been able to yield significant amounts of enriched uranium in the near future. Paul Lewis, "U.N. Experts Now Say That Baghdad Was Far From Making an A-Bomb Before Gulf War," *New York Times*, May 20, 1992, p. A6.
64. Stephen J. Hedges, "How Iraq Plays Nuclear Chicken," *U.S. News and World Report*, January 20, 1992, p. 45. See also "Report on the Seventh IAEA On-Site Inspection in Iraq," p. 19.
65. "Report on the Fourth IAEA On-Site Inspection in Iraq," p. 3.
66. Lewis, "Iraq Admits Buying German Materials to Make A-Bombs," p. A12. See also "UN Suspects Iraq Has a 4th A-Plant," *New York Times*, October 3, 1991, p. 3, and "Report on the Seventh IAEA On-Site Inspection in Iraq," p. 19; Edensword and Milhollin, "Iraq's Bomb: An Update," p. A17.
67. Malcolm W. Browne, "Iraqi Chemical Arms: Difficult Target," *New York Times*, September 5, 1990, p. A15.
68. Paul Lewis, "UN Aides Say Iraq May Be Concealing Nuclear Material," *New York Times*, June 15, 1991, p. A1.
69. "Consolidated Report on the First Two IAEA Inspections . . . of Iraqi Nuclear Capabilities," pp. 11–14. Some nuclear experts have asserted that Iraq required several more years to make its calutron system operational. Lewis, "UN Experts Now Say That Baghdad Was Far From Making an A-Bomb Before Gulf War," p. A6.
70. Paul Lewis, "Baghdad Hands UN a New List of Clandestine Atom Installation," *New York Times*, July 15, 1991, p. A1.
71. Leonard Spector of the Carnegie Institute indicated that Iraq's covert use of easily obtained technological information in its calutron program provided dark portents for the future. "It's cataclysmic. All this was being done in Iraq without anybody knowing it. So who else it doing it? Everybody in the community knew this kind of thing was a possibility. But to be confronted by an example is devastating." William J. Broad, "Iraqi Atom Effort Exposes Weakness in World Controls," *New York Times*, July 15, 1991, p. A6.
72. Michael Cross, "Japan Sidles Towards a Nuclear Future," *Washington Post*, May 31, 1991, p. A24. See also T. R. Reid, "S. Korean Leader Pledges Policy of No Nuclear Arms," *Washington Post*, November 8, 1991, p. A27; and David E. Sanger, "Bush Warns Seoul on Pace of Pacts With North Korea," *New York Times*, January 6, 1992, p. A12.

73. *Nuclear Power and Nuclear Weapons Proliferation*, vol. 2, p. 19. See also Albright and Hibbs, "Iraq and the Bomb," p. 21.
74. Paul Leventhal, "Is Iraq Evading the Nuclear Police?" *New York Times*, December 28, 1990, p. A35.
75. Relatively large margins of error in determining plutonium amounts at nuclear reactors suggest that there is a constant risk that a proliferator might divert the seventeen pounds of plutonium necessary for one nuclear bomb. Leventhal, "Is Iraq Evading the Nuclear Police?" p. A35. See also *Nuclear Power and Nuclear Weapons Proliferation*, vol. 1, p. 45; and David E. Sanger, "Japan Is Cautioned on Plan to Store Tons of Plutonium," *New York Times*, April 13, 1992, p. A2.
76. Despite its declared pledge never to build nuclear weapons, Japan's efforts to become energy-independent are noteworthy. Japan is currently amassing a stock of plutonium that will be larger than those existing in either the United States or the former Soviet Union, leading one Japanese nuclear physicist to suggest that, "Japan will become the world's number one plutonium country." Apart from monitoring shifts in the political winds, it will be necessary to keep tabs of possible third-nation diversion of this huge and burgeoning reserve. *Financial Times*, January 25–26, 1992, Section 1, p. 1. U.S. nuclear facilities were also deemed to have security gaps in protection of nuclear material. See Leventhal, "Is Iraq Evading the Nuclear Police?" p. A35. Japanese security of stores of U.S.-supplied enriched uranium was discovered in 1990 to have been so deficient that American officials were forced to devise a crash protection program. T. R. Reid, "Tokyo Official Criticizes Nuclear Power Program," *Washington Post*, April 22, 1992, p. A24.
77. "First Report on the Sixth IAEA On-Site Inspection in Iraq," p. 3.
78. "Report on the Seventh IAEA On-Site Inspection in Iraq," p. 6.
79. "Report on the Fourth IAEA On-Site Inspection in Iraq," pp. 13–14. See also "Iraq Tested Missile to Carry A-Bomb, a U.N. Report Says," p. A2.
80. Albright and Hibbs, "Iraq and the Bomb," p. 18.
81. "Inspectors Charge Iraq Has Ongoing Nuclear-Weapons Program," *UN Chronicle* (December 1991), pp. 12–14. See also *United Nations Press Release*, Department of Public Information, United Nations, December 18, 1991; and Spector and Smith, "North Korea: The Next Nuclear Nightmare?" p. 7. See also Patrick E. Tyler, "Israel Jets Spy Missions in Iraq, Prompting U.S. Protest," *New York Times*, October 9, 1991, p. A3.
82. Michael R. Gordon, "U.S. Fears Iraq Is Seeking a Long Range Missile Site," *New York Times*, April 24, 1990, p. A13.
83. Brooke, "Iraq's Nuclear Quest: Tentacles in Four Continents," p. 10. See also Lucia Mouat, "U.N. Plays Waiting Game With Iraq," *Christian Science Monitor*, February 10, 1992, p. 18.
84. Steven R. Weisman "North Korean Leader's Statement Renews Doubts on Nuclear Issue," *New York Times*, February 21, 1992, p. A9.
85. Steven Emerson, "The Postwar Scud Boom," *Wall Street Journal*, July 10, 1991, p. A12.
86. R. Jeffrey Smith, "U.S. Orders North Korea to Stop Scud Shipment," *Washington Post*, February 22, 1992, p. A15.

87. U.S. and Israeli officials note that the shipment might still be delivered to Syria by plane from Iran. Patrick E. Tyler, "North Korean Arms Ship Eludes U.S. For Iran Port," *New York Times*, March 11, 1992, p. A6. See also John Lancaster, "Suspected Scud Shipment Reaches Iran," *Washington Post*, March 11, 1992, p. A18.

88. The Aspen Strategy Group, *New Threats: Responding to the Proliferation of Nuclear, Chemical, and Delivery Capabilities in the Third World* (Lanham, Md.: Aspen Strategy Group and United Press of America, 1990), p. 115. See the discussion by Paul Doty and Steven Flank in chapter 3. The role of intelligence efforts in arms control verification provides a helpful model of how the intelligence community might also contribute to the Missile Technology Control Regime verification effort. For a discussion of this relationship see Herbert Scoville, Jr., "Intelligence and Arms Control: A Valuable Partnership," in *Intelligence: Policy and Process* (Boulder, Colo: Westview Press, 1985), pp. 318–23. See also Thomas J. Hirschfeld, ed., *Intelligence and Arms Control: A Marriage of Convenience* (Austin, Tex.: Lyndon B. Johnson School of Public Affairs, 1985); and Donald G. Boudreau, "On Advancing Non-Proliferation," *Strategic Requirements* (Summer 1992), p. 64.

89. Bruce W. Nelan, "Two Tales of Skullduggery," *Time*, October 22, 1990, p. 44.

90. For an excellent discussion of future developments in satellite technology, see William E. Burrows, *Deep Black: Space Espionage and National Security* (New York: Random House, 1986), particularly the chapters, "HALO, SPOT, Radar Farms, and other Exotic Assets," and "Arms Control Verification and National Security," which suggest that intelligence efforts will be considerably improved by continued satellite technology developments. See also Michael I. Handel, *War Strategy and Intelligence* (London: Frank Cass, 1989), pp. 18–19. Godson, ed., *Intelligence Requirements for the 1990s*, p. 14, similarly indicated that deception will become more difficult with technological improvements.

91. William Scott Malone, "Did the U.S. Teach Iraq to Hide Its Nuclear Arms?" *Washington Post*, November 3, 1991, pp. C1, 4.

92. The Aspen Strategy Group, *New Threats*, p. 119.

PART IV

Conclusions and Recommendations

Conclusions and Recommendations

ROBERT D. BLACKWILL and ALBERT CARNESALE

The question addressed in this book can be stated simply: What should the United States be doing about nuclear proliferation in addition to trying to stop it? Or, more specifically: How should the United States hedge against the acquisition of nuclear weapons by additional nations over the next ten to fifteen years? Each of the preceding chapters reflects the perspective of its author(s) on ways of preparing to cope with new nuclear threats to U.S. interests. This chapter presents our views on the approaches that appear to offer the most promise for U.S. policymakers.

NEW NUCLEAR THREATS

For more than four decades, U.S. planning for dealing with nuclear-armed adversaries focused sharply on the arsenals of the Soviet Union and, to a lesser extent, China. The United Kingdom and France, the only other declared nuclear weapons states, and Israel, with its undeclared nuclear status, have been and remain reliable U.S. allies.

India and Pakistan have more recently acquired the capabilities to produce nuclear weapons. It is, therefore, useful to treat both as

---

This chapter draws heavily on preceding chapters of this book. We are indebted to all of the other contributing authors for allowing us to borrow from their work so freely and without attribution.

among the "new" nuclear nations that might threaten U.S. interests. In light of the ambiguities presented by the nations of the former Soviet Union, these nations, too, should be considered as among the potential new nuclear states that might threaten U.S. interests.

"Russia" has replaced "the Soviet Union" in most U.S. strategic planning; however, Belarus, Kazakhstan, and Ukraine also have nuclear weapons deployed on their soil. All three have agreed to eliminate the weapons during the seven-year implementation period of the Strategic Arms Reduction Treaty, but uncertainties remain as to whether and when the commitments to eliminate them will be met.

Other countries that appear to be pursuing programs aimed at acquiring nuclear weapons within the next ten to fifteen years include: North Korea (which in 1993 announced and subsequently reversed its decision to withdraw from the Nonproliferation Treaty, and it remains unclear what the final outcome will be), Algeria, Egypt, Iran, Iraq, Libya, and Syria. Any industrialized country also has the technical capability to produce nuclear weapons.

Proliferation threatens both old and new U.S. security interests. Nuclear use anywhere in the world would violate a taboo that has grown in strength since World War II. In today's world of U.S. global superiority in conventional military forces, this taboo serves our interests more than ever. For at least the next decade, only China and the nuclear-armed nations of the former Soviet Union are likely to have strategic missiles or bombers capable of delivering nuclear weapons to the American homeland. But new nuclear threats to our friends, allies, forces, and bases overseas would reduce U.S. freedom of action and could embroil the United States in regional nuclear conflict.

DIPLOMATIC EFFORTS

The primary objective of postproliferation diplomacy should be to reverse, halt, or inhibit the spread and growth of nuclear arsenals. New nuclear nations should be persuaded to eliminate their weapons, to avoid transfers of the weapons and associated technologies, or, at a minimum, to declare policies of non-use or no-first-use, to forgo testing and deployment, and to accept quantitative and qualitative constraints.

Several bilateral diplomatic instruments could be used to achieve these goals, especially the promise of security guarantees and sanctions. It is easy to imagine a scenario in which a state threatens to "go nuclear" unless granted security guarantees. If the guarantees are not received, and proliferation occurs, hindsight could suggest that such guarantees could have prevented proliferation. And although hardly foolproof, security guarantees could well become even more attractive *after* a nation's acquisition of nuclear weapons, as a means of reversing proliferation. The proliferator could agree to destroy existing weapons and provide assurances to remain non-nuclear in the future as an exchange for the sought-after guarantee.

Security guarantees could also be extended to potential victims of new nuclear nations. Such guarantees might reduce the perceived benefit to the owner of the new arsenal, and might lower the incentives for neighboring states to acquire their own. Alternatively, postproliferation sanctions could be imposed unilaterally by the United States—for example, curtailing economic aid, blocking loans from international financial institutions, restricting trade, and withdrawing security guarantees.

Multilateral guarantees or sanctions may be more effective than unilateral actions, provided that the multinational coalition can agree on and adhere to the specific measures to be taken. For example, a security guarantee extended by NATO or by the United Nations could carry considerable weight. Similarly, sanctions imposed by the Group of Seven (G7) industrialized nations or by the UN would be more effective than comparable actions by the United States alone.

The international community could continue to strengthen the existing nuclear taboo by promoting the attitude that nuclear weapons are illegitimate. UN resolutions, support for extending and strengthening the Nonproliferation Treaty and associated International Atomic Energy Agency (IAEA) inspections, establishment of nuclear weapons free zones, and further restrictions on nuclear testing would all help.

The United States could assist new nuclear nations in making their arsenals safe, secure, and stable. Assistance to prevent nuclear accidents could include information about "one-point safety" designs that reduce the danger of unintended nuclear explosions; environmental sensing devices that prevent detonation in the absence of the physical phenomena associated with its means of delivery; and insensitive high explosives. To prevent unauthorized use the United States could share information on specialized transportation and storage facilities and permissive action links (PALs); to reduce the vulnerability of new arsenals it could convey information on warning systems, command and control equipment and procedures, techniques for weapons dispersal and hardening, and possibly on active defenses.

U.S. assistance on safety and security could engender the good will of the recipient nations and, more importantly, provide access to and influence over the proliferators' programs. On the other hand, it could be seen as a reward for proliferators, could reduce our own ability to take preemptive action against new nuclear forces and, by revealing U.S. technologies and procedures, could reduce the safety, security, and stability of our own arsenal. Overall, nuclear help should be considered as a serious but highly circumscribed and conditional policy option.

MILITARY MEANS

Nuclear proliferation would have profound implications for U.S. military strategy and planning. It would affect America's perceptions of its interests and commitments around the world. The primacy of deterrence as the military option of choice for dealing with nuclear threats would no longer be secure. Other options—such as preventive war, preemption, and defense—would merit serious consideration; they would also impose new requirements on the intelligence assessments of the capabilities, intentions, perceptions, and behavior of new nuclear nations.

American military forces, equipment, facilities, and communications are now and will remain for some time vulnerable to nuclear attack. In the event that U.S. forces must engage in military operations against new proliferators, they would be forced to operate from bases and naval platforms quite far removed from the adversary's forces. This could reduce the number of air attack sorties by U.S. forces, diminish the effectiveness of naval bombardment, and limit the ability to concentrate ground forces. As was the case in Cold War planning, airlifts will continue to be essential for rapid projections of power; specialized medical capabilities will still be required to deal with nuclear casualties; and troop reactions to nuclear attack will remain unpredictable.

Defenses, especially against shorter-range delivery vehicles, have a role to play against the new threats. Most new nuclear powers are unlikely to have access to bombers or missiles of intercontinental range within the next decade, so that current U.S. plans for defense of U.S. forces and interests overseas seem sufficient. New U.S. theater missile defense (TMD) systems should be consistent with the ABM Treaty which, unless and until it is revised or terminated, requires that they not be capable of countering long-range strategic ballistic missiles. Nonetheless, transfers of U.S. TMD systems to friends or allies should be scrutinized as carefully as proposed transfers of offensive weapons.

A "thin" national missile defense of the United States, of the kind called for in the National Missile Defense Act of 1991, might be able to mitigate the damage from an accidental, unauthorized, or deliberate attack involving tens of nuclear warheads, but it could not provide meaningful protection against a well-coordinated large attack of the kind that could be launched by a resurgent Russia. However, since long-range ballistic missiles are not likely to present a threat in the near term, expenditures for a thin nationwide defense do not appear to be warranted.

To hedge against the emergence of new nuclear-armed strategic missile threats, the United States should maintain a vigorous BMD research and development program, focusing primarily on technologies capable of providing defense against small- and large-scale attacks. In addition, designs of systems based on currently available BMD technologies (e.g., radars and interceptor missiles) should be upgraded regularly, enabling rapid mobilization to production and deployment of ground-based defenses.

Because every new nuclear nation will have access to unconventional means for delivering nuclear weapons, high priority should be assigned to hedging against this potential threat to the U.S. homeland and other vital areas. For example, attention should be given to improving the sensitivity of devices used in searching for nuclear weapons, to enhancing capabilities to monitor U.S. borders and points of entry, to reducing the response time of the Nuclear Emergency Search Team (NEST), and possibly to establishing an international NEST organization.

As a last resort, the United States retains the option of offensive military action to eliminate the adversary's nuclear capability. Even against a modestly armed nation, this would require a considerable exertion of political and military power. But if it were to succeed, forcible disarmament could help deter other would-be proliferators. On the other hand, the offensive operation could create its own escalatory momentum and pose substantial strategic risks. Preemption should be viewed as theoretically possible, but usually practically dubious.

Nuclear proliferation will create challenging new demands for intelligence collection and assessments. Information on the size, characteristics, and vulnerabilities of new nuclear arsenals will differ from the intelligence needed to prevent proliferation.

To achieve the penetrating changes needed to meet the new challenges, intelligence will require specific policy-oriented tasking from the highest levels of government; resources should be allocated primarily to serve U.S. national security interests, and only secondarily to satisfy the political demands for verifying arms control accords. Many of the traditional Cold War tasks are no longer central. In addition, decisionmakers will need to pose sharply those questions whose answers are most crucial to the successful selection and execution of promising policy actions for dealing with proliferation. Intelligence is in many ways the most demanding aspect of coping with new nuclear threats.

A POUND OF CURE

All of the various diplomatic and military measures for coping with new nuclear arsenals deserve serious consideration by U.S. policymakers. Most of them, however, appear to be either insufficient (e.g., extending the Nonproliferation Treaty or improving capabilities to detect transit of nuclear materials across U.S. borders) or difficult to implement (e.g., UN security guarantees to encourage nations to eliminate their nuclear weapons, or conducting a successful preemptive attack against a new nuclear arsenal). In our view, these measures would not by themselves assure adequate protections of vital U.S. security interests in a world of hostile new nuclear nations.

This book's exploration of what the United States should be doing about nuclear proliferation in addition to trying to stop it, reveals that: 1) the challenge of dealing with new nuclear threats is an extremely difficult one; 2) the measures identified thus far, while useful, would not fully meet that challenge; and 3) highest priority should be given to preventing nuclear proliferation and, where possible, to reversing it.

AN OUNCE OF PREVENTION

If a nuclear weapon were to be used against U.S. forces overseas or detonated in an American city with the expected disastrous effects, what would the United States and other nations around the world be willing to do to prevent recurrence of such a catastrophe? Would we insist on new and much tougher and intrusive norms to deal with new nuclear weapons states? In particular, would we be willing to impose unprecedented political and economic sanctions on other potential proliferators to convince them to abandon their nuclear plans? Would we be willing to insist upon on-site inspections in countries suspected of transgressing nonproliferation norms? Would we be willing to take military action to destroy the nuclear weapons–related facilities of nations which refused to do so themselves? Would we be willing to interfere in the internal affairs of would-be nuclear powers to alter their nuclear course, perhaps even to displace national leaders who aspire to having a finger on a nuclear trigger? Would we be willing to establish normative principles that would interpret pursuit of nuclear weapons as nuclear aggression, and pursuers of ambiguous nuclear programs as guilty until proven innocent? Would we be willing to commit in advance to join the world community in unprecedented political and economic sanctions and, if necessary, in military action, against *every* new nuclear nation?

Actions such as these are inconsistent with strict observance of the notion of national sovereignty traditionally valued so highly by the international community, including the United States. Yet, in recent years the world community has come to recognize that proliferation threatens all of its members, and may merit intervention to prevent or reverse it. Might we agree to compromise further the principle of national sovereignty in the wake of nuclear weapons use? Must we wait?

CONTRIBUTORS

Robert D. Blackwill is a lecturer in public policy at the John F. Kennedy School of Government, Harvard University. Previously, he was special assistant to President Bush for European and Soviet Affairs on the staff of the National Security Council. From 1985 to 1987 he was U.S. ambassador and chief negotiator at the negotiations with the Warsaw Pact on conventional forces in Europe. Formerly a career diplomat, he has served in Kenya, Britain, Israel, and the Department of State, and on the staff of the National Security Council. Ambassador Blackwill is the author of many articles on European security and East–West relations, and is coauthor of *Conventional Arms Control and East–West Security* and *A Primer for the Nuclear Age.*

Albert Carnesale is dean of Harvard University's John F. Kennedy School of Government, where he is Don K. Price Professor of Public Policy. His teaching and research focus on American foreign policy and international security, with emphases on the implications of technological change and on policies associated with nuclear weapons and arms control. He holds a Ph.D. in nuclear engineering, has consulted widely on foreign and defense policy matters, was a member of the U.S. delegation to the Strategic Arms Limitation Talks (SALT I, 1970–1972) and led the U.S. delegation to the International Nuclear Fuel Cycle Evaluation (1978–1980), a sixty-six-nation study of the relationship between civilian nuclear power and proliferation of nuclear weapons. Widely published, he is coauthor of *Living with Nuclear Weapons* (1983); *Hawks, Doves, and Owls: An Agenda for Avoiding Nuclear War* (1985); *Superpower Arms Control: Setting the Record Straight* (1987); and *Fateful Visions: Avoiding Nuclear Catastrophe* (1988).

Ashton B. Carter is on leave from Harvard University's John F. Kennedy School of Government, where he is Ford Foundation Professor of Science and International Affairs, and is serving as Assistant Secretary of Defense for Nuclear Security and Counterproliferation. He received his doctorate in theoretical physics from Oxford University, where he was a Rhodes Scholar. In addition to authoring numerous scientific publications and government studies, he has coedited and coauthored *Ballistic Missile Defense; Managing Nuclear Operations; Soviet Nuclear Fission: Control of the Nuclear Arsenal in a Disintegrating Soviet Union;* and *Beyond Spinoff: Military and Commercial Technologies in a Changing World.*

Paul Doty is founder and director emeritus of the Center for Science and International Affairs at Harvard University's John F. Kennedy School of Government, and is professor emeritus of public policy at the School. He has served on the president's Science Advisory Committee and on the General Advisory Committee on Arms Control. Professor Doty currently chairs the Dartmouth Conference Group on Cooperation in Security (with Russia) and is a member of the Committee on International Security and Arms Control of the National Academy of Sciences, the Defense Science Board Task Force on Proliferation, and the American Academy of Arts and Sciences Committee on International Security Studies. He is also on the boards of the Aspen Institute (Berlin), the Harriman Institute, and the MITRE Corporation.

Lewis A. Dunn is assistant vice president and manager of the Negotiations and Planning Division, Science Applications International Corporation. He is a former assistant director of the U.S. Arms Control and Disarmament Agency and served as ambassador to the 1985 Nuclear Nonproliferation Treaty Review Conference. His recent Adelphi Paper, *Containing Nuclear Proliferation*, was published by the International Institute for Strategic

Studies. He also is the author of an earlier book on proliferation, *Controlling the Bomb*, as well as co-editor of *Arms Control Verification and the New Role of On-Site Inspection*. He has a Ph.D. in political science from the University of Chicago.

Steven Flank is a dissertation fellow at the Center for Science and International Affairs at Harvard University's John F. Kennedy School of Government, and is a Ph.D. candidate in political science at the Massachusetts Institute of Technology's Defense and Arms Control Studies program. His dissertation examines the politics of ballistic missile development. Mr. Flank has worked at the Lawrence Livermore National Laboratory and the U.S. House of Representatives. He received his B.A. in physics from Cornell University and a master's degree in nuclear engineering from MIT.

Michèle A. Flournoy recently joined the U.S. Department of Defense, after having been a research fellow at the Center for Science and International Affairs at Harvard University's John F. Kennedy School of Government and coordinator of the Managing Proliferation and Avoiding Nuclear War Projects. She spent five years as a senior policy analyst in Washington, D.C., most recently at the Arms Control Association. Ms. Flournoy received her A.B. in social studies from Harvard–Radcliffe and master's degree in international relations and strategic studies from Balliol College, Oxford, where she was a Newton-Tatum Scholar. She has published numerous articles and book chapters on national security issues and, most recently, edited a volume on U.S. nuclear weapons policy after the Cold War.

Steven E. Miller is director of studies at the Center for Science and International Affairs at Harvard University's John F. Kennedy School of Government. He is also editor of the quarterly *International Security*. He has been a senior research fellow at the Stockholm International Peace Research Institute, and has taught defense and arms control studies at the Massachusetts Institute of Technology.

Joseph S. Nye, Jr., is on leave from Harvard University, where he is Clarence Dillon Professor of International Affairs. He currently serves in the Clinton administration as chairman of the National Intelligence Council. He is a fellow of the American Academy of Arts and Sciences; senior fellow of the Aspen Institute and director of the Aspen Strategy Group; and a member of the Trilateral Commission, the International Institute for Strategic Studies, and the Council on Foreign Relations. He has been deputy to the undersecretary of state for Security Assistance, Science and Technology, and chaired the National Security Council Group on Nonproliferation of Nuclear Weapons. His most recent book is *Bound to Lead: The Changing Nature of American Power*. His current research focuses on American foreign policy, nuclear deterrence and proliferation, and the changing nature of world politics.

Philip Zelikow is assistant professor of public policy at Harvard University's John F. Kennedy School of Government. From 1989 to 1991 he was director for European security affairs on the staff of the National Security Council, and earlier served as a foreign service officer with the Department of State. A former trial attorney and a member of the Council on Foreign Relations and the International Institute for Strategic Studies, he is the author of articles on European security, political-military issues, and criminal justice.

INDEX

ABM system 196–97. *See also* ABM Treaty
ABM Treaty, 55, 153, 154, 203–12 *passim*, 258. *See also* ABM system
Accidents, nuclear, 33, 34, 45; prevention of, overview of, 116–17, 255–58
Afghanistan, 78, 111
Agency for Accounting and Control of Nuclear Materials, 31
Agreement for Cooperation on the Uses of Atomic Energy for Mutual Defense Purposes, 106
Alberich (fictional country), 178–85, 186
ALCMs (air-launched cruise missiles), 108
Algeria, 24, 36–37, 71, 165
Angola, 63
Argentina, 31, 64, 68, 93, 114
ARROW system, 154, 202, 210
Aspin, Les, 141, 159*n*13, 206
Atomic Energy Act of 1946, 105–6
Atomic Energy Act of 1954, 106
Australia, 139

B-1B bombers, 173, 181, 186, 187
B-2 bombers, 173, 181, 186, 187
B-52H bombers, 173, 181, 186, 187
BCCI (Bank of Commerce and Credit International), 221
Belarus, 28, 29, 30, 199–200, 254; and the NPT, 84; and START, 72–73.

See also Soviet Union, former republics of
Biological weapons. *See* Chemical and biological weapons
Blackmail, "nuclear," 35, 40, 124
Blackwill, Robert D., 3–19, 216–50, 253–60, 261
BMD (ballistic missile defense), 196, 197, 200–213, 257; overview of, 201–3, 205–7
BMDO (Ballistic Missile Defense Organization), 206
Brazil, 31, 68, 88, 226–27, 229; and the NPT, 64, 93; and the U.S. nuclear help option, 114
Brilliant Eyes (space-based sensors), 202
Brilliant Pebbles (space-based interceptors), 202, 203, 207
Britain, 83, 99, 108, 136; and SDI, 211; sting operation of, at Heathrow Airport, 222; and the United States, collaboration between, 87, 97, 104–12 *passim*, 120, 121, 122; U.S. refusal to share information with, after World War II, 102
Bush, George, 29, 41, 111; and BMD systems, 202–3; letter to Saddam Hussein, prior to Desert Storm, 160*n*22, 193*n*8; and Pakistan's nuclear capability, 24; and U.S. nuclear weapons in South Korea, 27

Canada, 64, 203
Carnesale, Albert, 3–19, 196–215,
  253–60, 261–62
Carter, Ashton B., 216–50, 262
Castro, Fidel, 180, 189
CBO (Congressional Budget Office),
  207
Chemical and biological weapons, 174,
  178, 179, 184, 186; and the former
  Soviet republics, 73; and Iraq, 22,
  64, 67, 83, 107, 136–37, 171–72;
  and Israel, 22, 64, 67, 172; and
  Libya, 72; and Syria, 24; and threat
  assessment techniques, 234
Cheney, Richard, 85, 224
China, 21–32 passim, 199, 214, 253–
  54; and India, 25–26; and North
  Korea, 70, 71, 192n6; and no transfer, diplomatic objective of, 83; and
  the NPT, 108; nuclear tests by, 33,
  67; and the Pakistani proposal for
  talks (1991), 68–69; and the Soviet
  Union, 223; and the U.S. nuclear
  help option, 101, 108, 121–22, 123,
  124; weapons capability of, exagger-
  ations regarding, 169
CIA (Central Intelligence Agency), 5–6,
  68, 82, 245n27. See also Gates,
  Robert
Civilian deaths, 143
Civil wars, 6, 79, 117
Coalitions, 42, 156, 157, 186
Cold War, 32, 39, 61, 74, 78–79, 201,
  258; and BMD, 209; and Britain,
  collaboration with, 87; and confidence and security building measures, 62; and the CTB, 92, 93;
  Cuban Missile Crisis during, 40,
  180, 188–89; defense budget declines after, 139; deterrence during,
  overview of, 140–44; and intelligence techniques, overview of,
  230–32, 234; and NATO, 89, 153;
  and no-first-use pledges, 59; and the
  nonuse of nuclear weapons, 83; and
  primitive nuclear devices, defense
  against, 198; and rationales for providing nuclear assistance, 99; and
  U.S. military strategy, overview of,
  135–48 passim, 153–54, 157

Communist party, 29, 30
Concentration camps, 175
Confidence and security building measures (CSBMs), 26, 56, 62, 73; and
  India and Pakistan, 68–69; and the
  Middle East, 24, 72; and no-first-use
  pledges, 60; summary of, 74
Congress, 185, 190, 257; Atomic En-
  ergy Act of 1946 (McMahon Act),
  105–6; and the fictional depiction of
  a nuclear Iraq, 4, 9–10, 13, 14, 18;
  and the Gulf War, 41, 190; Missile
  Defense Act of 1991, 201–3, 212,
  257; Pressler Amendment, 111; and
  SDI, 206; Soviet Nuclear Threat Re-
  duction Act of 1991, 111; and the
  U.S. nuclear help option, 105–7,
  110–12, 122, 129n48
Cooper, Henry F., 207
Cost-benefit calculations, 143, 236
Coup d'états, 28, 79, 117
Covert programs, vs. open programs,
  84, 103–5, 109
Crimea, 87
CSBMs. See Confidence and security
  building measures (CSBMs)
CSS-2 missiles, 32
CTB (Comprehensive Test Ban), 92–93
CTBT (Comprehensive Test Ban
  Treaty), 59
Cuban Missile Crisis (1962), 40, 180,
  188–89

Defense budget, U.S., 139
Defense Department, 137, 141, 181,
  206
De Gaulle, Charles, 112
Demilitarized zones, 67, 170, 189
Desert Storm. See Gulf War
Deterrence, 39–43, 60, 79, 119, 135;
  and declaratory policy, 147–48; definition of, 140; and France, 122; immediate vs. general, 158n8; and
  India and Pakistan, 25; and Iran, 35;
  and Israel, 21–22; and the Korean
  peninsula, 35; logic of, and terrorism, 83; and U.S. military strategy,
  overview of, 135, 140–50, 157, 162,
  190, 191

Dictatorships, 39, 137, 143
Doty, Paul, 53–76, 262
Dunn, Lewis A., 20–50, 163, 262–63

Egypt, 24, 37, 66, 71, 200, 254. *See also* Middle East
Eisenhower, Dwight D., 66, 140
ENDS (Enhanced Nuclear Detonation Safety system), 116
Energy Department, 222
ESDs (environmental sensing devices), 116, 256–57
Evacuation measures, 118
Export controls, 34, 53, 57, 228; overview of, 60; and the Soviet Union, disintegration of, 30–31, 44, 49*n*37

F-15E Strike Eagle aircraft, 182
F-16 aircraft, 182
F-111F aircraft, 182
F-117A Stealth aircraft, 182
F/A-18 aircraft, 182
Fahd, king of Saudi Arabia, 42
Flank, Steven, 53–76, 263
Flournoy, Michèle A., 135–61, 263
France, 21, 136, 199, 200, 253; and Iraq, arms sales to, 225; and Israel, collaboration between, 54; and NATO, 100; and no transfer, diplomatic objective of, 83; and the NPT, 108; and SDI, 211; and the United States, collaboration between, 87, 97–112 *passim*, 120, 121, 122, 126*n*18
FRPs (fire resistant pits), 116

Gates, Mahlon E., 205
Gates, Robert, 3, 24, 26, 223–24, 231–32, 245*n*27, 245*n*31
Gelb, Leslie, 180
Germany, 32, 64, 88, 109, 175; and SDI, 211; U.S. intelligence installations in, 232
Golan Heights, 24, 66
GPALS (System for Global Protection Against Limited Strikes), 202, 203, 207, 211, 212
GPS (Global Positioning System), 240

Greenland, 203
Group of Seven, 90, 255
Gulf War, 38, 241; air campaign during, design of, 170, 176–78, 181, 184, 187; arms sales before, 221–22, 225; attitudes toward American intervention after, 41; authorization of, 41–42; bombing of Iraqi facilities during, 150, 170, 175, 176, 223, 240; Bush's letter to Saddam Hussein prior to, 160*n*22, 193*n*8; captured American airmen during, 190; cease-fire agreement, 62; civilian deaths during, 189; coalition, 42, 172; and Congress, 41, 190; decision not to use chemical weapons during, by Hussein, 83; as a demonstration of U.S. resolve, 145; deployment of U.S. forces to Saudi Arabia, 42; and the deterrence of other nuclear proliferators, 164; experience of preventative strikes, and U.S. military strategy, 150; and intelligence techniques, overview of, 216, 217, 218–30, 235; interest in nuclear free zones since, 58; and the Iraqi invasion of Kuwait, 3, 150, 155, 162, 235; monetary costs of, 190; the possibility of a nuclear Iraq during, hypothetical consideration of, 3, 4–19; public opinion polls prior to, 136–37, 138; revelations regarding Iraq's nuclear weapons program after, 20, 22–23, 34, 107, 227–28; Scud missile attacks during, 153, 154–55, 197, 206, 210, 241–42; SOF forces during, 181; ventilation-shaft bombings during, 240

Hiroshima bomb, 17, 20, 22, 238
Hitler, Adolf, 41, 175
Holocaust, 22
Human rights, 77, 137
Hussein, Saddam, 3–4, 6, 8–18, 23; Bush's letter to, prior to Desert Storm, 160*n*22, 193*n*8; comparison of, to Hitler, 41; and the use of chemical weapons, 83. *See also* Gulf War; Iraq

IAEA (International Atomic Energy Agency), 34, 54–75 passim, 80–89 passim, 219–26 passim, 256; American leadership as essential to, 46; Board of Governors, 58; expanded inspections by, 94–95; funding of, 58; general description of, 54–58; and the Korean peninsula, 26–28, 70, 71; and Latin America, 31, 64; and nuclear free zones, 58–59; and South Africa, 63; and uranium reactor fuel transfers, 164–65; and weapons-grade materials production cutoff, 60

ICBMs (intercontinental ballistic missiles), 30, 108, 195–97, 200, 203, 212

India, 21, 34–36, 38, 82, 84, 253–54; and Arab countries, 23; and China, 67, 68; efforts to develop nuclear capability by, general history of, 67–69; and the NPT, 65–66, 91–92, 101; and Pakistan, 24–25, 39, 68–69; and rationales for providing nuclear assistance, 99, 100–101; and sanctions, 88; Sikh separatists in, 41; and the Soviet Union, 25–26, 31; and U.S. military strategy, 199–200

INF Treaty, 57, 61

International Chetek Corp., 244n14

Iran, 35–45 passim, 71–72, 200, 254; efforts to match Israeli nuclear capability in, 24; and extremist subnational groups, 41; and Iraq, 35, 39, 71; nuclear reactors in, 165; and U.S. military strategy, 139, 143; and the U.S. nuclear help option, 112, 113, 123

Iraq, 3–22 passim, 37–38, 155–96 passim, 254; air defenses of, 165; and Alberich (fictional country), 178–79; Al-Tuweitha facilities in, 167; chemical and biological weapons stock of, 22, 64, 67, 83, 107, 136–37, 171–72; and Egypt, 40–41; and extremist subnational groups, 41; invasion of Kuwait by, 3, 150, 155, 162, 235; and Iran, 35, 39, 71; sanctions against, 88, 90; and Saudi Arabia, in the future, 32, 40–41; and the Soviet Union, 31, 164; and Turkey, 32. See also Gulf War; Iraq, nuclear weapons program of

Iraq, nuclear weapons program of, 23, 78, 107, 228; dismantling of, 62, 64–65, 69, 73; inspection of, 22–23, 34–35, 62, 65, 69, 73, 98, 219–20, 224, 226, 228; and intelligence techniques, overview of, 216, 218–30; and international banking, 223; Israeli bombing of, 23, 161n28, 165, 167–68, 169–70, 185; missile testing in Mauritania, 229; and the NPT, 54; and plutonium, 224–26, 228; and recruitment efforts, 222–24; successful weaponization of, hypothetical consideration of, 3, 4–19, 155–56, 162; as "undeterrable," 42, 45; as unsafe, 98; and uranium, 164, 165, 166, 219–20, 226–27, 228; and U.S. opinion polls, 136–37; Western companies involved in supplying, 220

Israel, 7–14 passim, 34–39 passim, 154, 206, 254; ARROW system of, 154, 202, 210; bombing of Iraq, 23, 165, 161n28, 167–68, 169–70, 185; and covert vs. open programs, 85; and the CTB, 92; Dimona reactor in, 60; efforts to develop nuclear capability by, general history of, 66–67; and Egypt, 66; and extremist subnational groups, 41; and France, 54; and the Golan Heights, 66; and Iran, 24; and Iraq's chemical and biological weapons, 22, 64, 67, 172; Mossad of, 225; and a "multinuclear Middle East," 21–24; and no transfer, diplomatic objective of, 83; and the NPT, 65–66, 91–92; and nuclear free zones, 93; possession of second-generation nuclear weapons by, speculation regarding, 34; proximity of, from hostile bases, and nuclear instability, 99; and sanctions, 87, 88; and SDI, 211; and U.S. military strategy, 136, 143, 154, 199–200; and the U.S. nuclear help option, 99, 100, 121, 124; and weapons-grade materials production cutoff, 60. See also Middle East

Italy, 213

Japan, 60–61, 109, 228; civilian nuclear power program of, 44; and the IAEA, 94; and the Korean peninsula, 27, 28, 31, 41, 70, 136, 173; and sanctions, 88; and SDI, 211
Johnson, Lyndon B., 196
Joint Argentina–Brazil Agency, 64
Joint Declaration for a Non-nuclear Korean Peninsula, 26
Joint Nuclear Control Commission, 26

Kalahari desert, 62–63
Kazakhstan, 28–30, 84, 199–200, 254; and START, 72–73, 109. *See also* Soviet Union, former republics of
Kemp, Geoffrey, 85
Kennedy, John F., 79, 112, 180, 189
KH-11 reconnaissance satellites, 121
Khaddafi, Muammar, 72
Kissinger, Henry, 110
Korean peninsula. *See also* North Korea; South Korea
Korean War, 192*n*6
Kuwait, invasion of, 3, 150, 155, 162, 235. *See also* Gulf War; Middle East

Latin America, 31–32; and the Treaty of Tlatelolco, 56, 58, 64, 80, 93. *See also* Argentina; Brazil
Legislation: Atomic Energy Act of 1946, 105–6; Atomic Energy Act of 1954, 106; Missile Defense Act of 1991, 202–3, 212; Pressler Amendment, 111
Libya, 37, 71–72, 139, 148, 200, 254; and former Soviet republics, 31, 41; and Israel, 22, 143; punitive U.S. raid against (1986), 170, 185; and sanctions, 88; and the U.S. nuclear help option, 112, 123. *See also* Middle East
Limited Test Ban Treaty, 56, 59
London Nuclear Suppliers Group, 60, 90

Manhattan Project, 22, 35
Mauritania, 229
Mello, Fernando Collor de, 31

Middle East: and confidence and security building measures (CSBMs), 24, 72; "multinuclear," Dunn on, 21–24; and the oil industry, 39, 40, 71–72, 177; peace process, 24, 58, 64, 72. *See also specific countries*
Miller, Steven E., 97–131, 263
Minsk agreement (1991), 29
Missile Defense Act of 1991, 202–3, 212
MTCR (Missile Technology Control Regime), 56, 109–10, 230

Nacht, Michael, 88
National Security Council, 137
NATO (North Atlantic Treaty Organization), 89, 256; and the nonuse of nuclear weapons, 83; and the Soviet Union, 153, 155; and the U.S. nuclear help option, 99–100, 106, 122
Nazarbayev, Nursultan, 29
Nazism, 175
NEST (Nuclear Emergency Search Team), 204–5, 213, 258
Nixon, Richard M., 110, 197
No-first-use pledges, 56, 59–60, 82–83, 87, 91, 254
Nordhausen concentration camp, 175
North Korea, 26–39 *passim*, 45, 78, 200; air defense system, 172; and Alberich (fictional country), 178–79; efforts to develop nuclear capability by, general history of, 69–71; fortified bunkers and caves in, 240; and the IAEA, 94; and intelligence techniques, overview of, 217, 218–30; and Japan, 27, 28, 31, 41, 70, 136, 173; and the NPT, 26, 27–28, 70, 147, 220; and the Soviet Union, 223–24; uranium ore in, 164; and U.S. military strategy, 136, 140, 147, 148, 163–79 *passim*, 189–90; and the U.S. nuclear help option, 99, 112, 113, 123
Norway, 175
NPT (Nonproliferation Treaty), 44, 53–66 *passim*, 73–80, 91–94, 225–26, 254; American leadership as es-

sential to, 46; Article 1 of, 107–8; Article 6 of, 92; Article 9 of, 108; extension of (1995), 32, 54, 57, 91–92, 259; and former Soviet republics, 29–30, 73; general description of, 20, 54–58; and India, 101; and Latin America, 64, 93; nontransfer provision of, 57, 60, 107–8; and North Korea, 26, 27–28, 70, 147, 220; and nuclear free zones, 93; and nuclear weapons states, legal status of, 20; and Pakistan, 65–66, 91–92; and South Africa, 31, 63, 84; and START, 32; and the U.S. nuclear help option, 101, 107–8, 110, 117

Nuclear Suppliers Group, 46

Nuclear weapons: "crude," 20, 81, 153; diversity of, range of, 34–38; estimated number of, by the year 2000, 34–35; first-strike, 142; locking devices, 103, 117–18; and the "one point safety" rule, 116; second-strike, 79; thermonuclear, 59, 81, 140; and the two-man rule, 118; unauthorized use of, 40, 41, 98, 117–18, 256, 257. See also Iraq, nuclear weapons program of; Nuclear weapons, dismantling of; Nuclear weapons free zones; Nuclear weapons states; Plutonium; Testing, of nuclear weapons; Uranium

Nuclear weapons, dismantling of, 55, 61–65; and the former Soviet republics, 30, 61–62, 73–74, 84; and Latin America, 31, 64; and South Africa, 31, 33, 62–63, 84. See also Iraq, nuclear weapons program of

Nuclear weapons free zones, 56, 89, 255; and the former Soviet republics, 28–30; and Latin America, 64, 93; and the Middle East, 66, 67, 93; overview of, 58–59; in southern Africa, 63

Nuclear weapons states: acknowledged and unacknowledged, 21, 32–33; definition of, 20–21; number of, Kennedy's prediction on, 79

Nye, Joseph S., Jr., 77–96, 263–64

Oil industry, 39, 40, 71–72, 177

Open Skies Treaty, 56, 67

Pakistan, 21–36 passim, 84, 199–200, 253–54; and the CTB, 92; efforts to develop nuclear capability by, general history of, 67–69; and India, 24–25, 39, 68–69; and no transfer, diplomatic objective of, 83; and the NPT, 65–66, 91–92; and sanctions, 87, 88; and START, 109; and the U.S. nuclear help option, 78, 99–101, 109, 111, 113, 114, 124

PAL (permissive action link) technology, 103, 117, 256

Palestinians, 67

Pan Am 103 bombing, 43

Patriot air defense system, 153, 154, 202–4, 206–7, 210; upgrading of, 207

Peacekeeping forces, 67

Pfaff, William, 79

Plutonium, 22, 34, 60–61, 164–65, 179; as a fuel for nuclear power generation, 44, 69; in India, 25, 67; in Iraq, 224–26, 228; in North Korea, 26, 27–28, 69–70

Poland, 32

Polaris submarines, 110

Powell, Colin, 180

Pressler Amendment, 111

Public opinion, 136–37, 138, 139

Pugwash meeting (1963), 104

Punitive raids, 43, 185

Reagan, Ronald, 111, 197, 205

Realignment, 86–87

Regime, concept of, use of, 80

Russia, 30, 60, 213, 255; arsenal of, capability of, 201, 208, 211, 212; and START, 29; and verified destruction of weapons, 61–62, 72–73. See also Soviet Union, former republics of

Safeguards. See IAEA (International Atomic Energy Agency)

"Safeguard" system, 197, 205, 208

SALT Agreements, 57, 108–9
SAMs (surface-to-air missiles), 196, 203
Sanctions, 72, 74, 260; ad-hoc, 90–91; and the Korean peninsula, 71; multilateral, effectiveness of, 88, 255; overview of, 87–88, 90–91; and South Africa, 78, 88
Saudi Arabia, 32, 42, 172, 206. *See also* Gulf War; Middle East
Schelling, Thomas, 174, 236
Scud missiles, 70, 72, 153–54, 197, 206, 210, 241–42
SDI (Strategic Defense Initiative), 197, 202, 203, 206–7
SDIO (Strategic Defense Initiative Organization), 202, 206, 207
Secrecy. *See* Covert programs, vs. open programs
Sentinel system, 196–97, 205
Shah of Iran (Mohammed Reza Pahlevi), 24
Sikh separatists, 41
SLBMs (sea-launched ballistic missiles), 108, 110, 195, 203, 212
SOF (special operations forces), 181
South Africa, 33, 60, 62–63, 124; and no transfer, diplomatic objective of, 83; and the NPT, 31, 63, 84; sanctions against, 78, 88
South Korea, 26–28, 31, 35, 39, 70, 189–90; and the IAEA, 94; and sanctions, 88; treaty relationship with, 43; U.S. intelligence installations in, 232; and U.S. military strategy, 27, 140, 147, 173; and the U.S. nuclear help option, 114, 123
South Pacific, test sites in, 120
Soviet Union, 7–21 *passim*, 101, 138, 169, 203, 253–54; and Afghanistan, 78, 111; August 1991 coup in, 28; and deterrence, 39–40, 140–44, 148, 154; dissemination of nuclear technology from, 23, 31, 35, 41, 44; and intelligence techniques, overview of, 216–17, 223–24; and NATO, 153, 155; and the nonuse of nuclear weapons, 83; and North Korea, 70;

and no transfer, diplomatic objective of, 83; and the NPT, 108; and Pakistan, 68–69; protection against unauthorized use in, 103–4; and SDI, 211; and START, 109; strategic personality of, 236; and the U.S. nuclear help option, 101, 103–4, 108, 111, 124. *See also* Cold War; Soviet Union, former republics of
Soviet Union, former republics of, 23, 25–26, 61, 65, 212; and intelligence techniques, 227, 228, 237–38; and NATO, 89; and the NPT, 29–30, 73; personnel and materials from, 28–29, 30–31, 35, 44, 49*n*37, 223–24, 225; and START, 29, 72–73, 109; and the U.S. nuclear help option, 97, 103, 111, 122, 123. *See also* Soviet Union; *specific republics*
START Treaty, 32, 57, 199, 254; and the former Soviet republics, 29, 72–73, 109; and the U.S. nuclear help option, 108–9, 118
Star Wars (SDI), 197, 202, 203, 206–7
State Department, 137, 222
Stockholm Conference, 62
"Strategic personalities," of proliferators, 217, 236–37
Sunderji, K., 84
Sung, Kim Il, 70
Survivability, 40, 98–99, 119, 121
Sweden, 139
Sweeney, Walter C., 180
Syria, 24, 37, 38, 143, 190, 200, 254; and extremist subnational groups, 41; and the Golan Heights, 66; and Israeli nuclear capability, 22; and resources from the former Soviet Union, 31; and Scud missiles, 229. *See also* Middle East

Taiwan, 70, 101, 124
Terrorism, 41, 72, 79, 189, 292; erosion of restraints on, 31, 43–44; and Libya, 170; and the logic of deterrence, 83; Pan Am 103 bombing, 43; "state-supported," 137, 170, 228; and unconventional means of deliv-

ery, defense against, 204, 208; World Trade Center bombing, 43, 208, 254

Testing, of nuclear weapons, 56, 59, 91–93, 254; atmospheric, 62, 87; by Britain, 120; by China, 67; exploding a fission device without, 81; by India, 67, 78; and nuclear help decisions, 114; and slowing vertical proliferation, 81–82; by South Africa, 62

THAAD (Theater High Altitude Area Defense) system, 202, 207, 210

Threat assessments, 217, 230–35, 237–38

Threshold Test Ban Treaty, 59, 230

Tiananmen Square massacre, 121

TLAM (Tomahawk missile), 182, 187

TMD (theater missile defenses), 199–200, 202–3, 207, 210, 212, 257

Treaties: ABM Treaty, 56, 153, 154, 203–12 *passim*, 258; CTB (Comprehensive Test Ban), 92–93; CTBT (Comprehensive Test Ban Treaty), 59; INF Treaty, 57, 61; Limited Test Ban Treaty, 56, 59; Open Skies Treaty, 56, 67; SALT Agreements, 57, 108–9; Threshold Test Ban Treaty, 59, 230; Treaty of Reconciliation and Nonaggression, 26; Treaty of Tlatelolco, 56, 58, 64, 80, 93. *See also* START Treaty

Trident submarines, 110

Tritium, 60, 68, 81

Truman, Harry S, 140

Turkey, 32, 172

Ukraine, 28, 30, 32, 139, 254; and the NPT, 84; and Russia, 86–87; and START, 29, 72–73; U.S. nuclear assistance to, 109. *See also* Soviet Union, former republics of

Unauthorized use, of nuclear weapons, 40, 41, 98, 117–18, 255, 256

United Kingdom, 21, 54, 199, 200, 211, 253. *See also* Britain

United Nations, 5, 7, 12–13, 42, 98, 255; Charter, 90, 91; and the IAEA, 94; and North Korea, 27; and the NPT, 55, 58; Security Council Resolutions, 22, 23, 62; and South Africa, 63; and U.S. nuclear help, 109

Uranium, 34, 60, 61, 67, 218; hexafluoride, 226–27; in Iraq, 164, 165, 166, 219–20, 226–27, 228; in North Korea, 26, 164; oxide (yellowcake), 226–27; in Pakistan, 68; in South Africa, 63

V-1 aircraft, 175

V-2 rocket, 175

Vanunu, Mordechai, 34, 85

Vietnam War, 9, 176, 190

Warsaw Pact, 89

Webster, William, 82

WMD (weapons of mass destruction) program, 170, 171, 173–75, 177–79, 184, 189

World Trade Center bombing, 43, 208, 255

World War II, 59, 102, 170; atomic bomb projects during, 112, 175; and targeting objectives, 175, 176

Yellowcake, 226–27. *See also* Uranium

Yeltsin, Boris, 30, 211

Zangger Committee, 60

Zelikow, Philip, 162–95, 264